NAPOLEON'S BRITISH VISITORS

NAPOLEON'S

BRITISH VISITORS AND CAPTIVES

1801–1815

BY JOHN GOLDWORTH ALGER

AUTHOR OF THE 'NEW PARIS SKETCH BOOK'
'ENGLISHMEN IN THE FRENCH REVOLUTION'
'GLIMPSES OF THE FRENCH REVOLUTION'
AND 'PARIS IN 1789-94'

Westminster
ARCHIBALD CONSTABLE
AND COMPANY, LTD.
1904

Edinburgh: T. and A. CONSTABLE, Printers to His Majesty

CONTENTS

CHAPTER I

CHAPTER II

THE VISITORS

CHAPTER III

AMUSEMENTS AND IMPRESSIONS

CHAPTER IV

CAPTIVITY

CONTENTS

CHAPTER V

TWO RESTORATIONS

APPENDIX

INTRODUCTORY

THE French Revolution, of which—philosophers regarding it as still unfinished—this book is really a
chapter, produced a greater dislocation of individuals
and classes than had been known in modern times.
It scattered thousands of Frenchmen over Europe,
some in fact as far as America and India, while, on
the other hand, it attracted men of all nationalities to
France. It was mainly a centrifugal, but it was partly
a centripetal force, especially during the Empire; never
before or since was France so much as then the
focus of political and social life. Men of all ranks
shared in both these movements. If princes and
nobles were driven from France there were some who
were attracted thither even in the early stages of the
Revolution, while Napoleon later on drew around him
a galaxy of foreign satellites.

To begin with the centrifugal action, history fur-
nishes no parallel to such an overturn of thrones and
flight of monarchs. With the exception of England,
protected by the sea, Scandinavia and Russia by
distance, and Turkey by Oriental lethargy, every
dynasty of Europe was shaken or shattered by the

volcano.   The Bourbons became wanderers on the
face of the earth.   Louis XVI.'s two brothers went
hither and thither before finding a secure resting-
place on British soil.   The elder, 'Monsieur,' Comte
de Provence (afterwards Louis XVIII.), fled from Paris
simultaneously with his crowned brother, but, more
fortunate than poor Louis, safely reached Belgium.
The younger, Comte d'Artois (afterwards Charles X.),
had preceded him by nine months.   Both re-entered
France in 1792 with the German and Royalist in-
vaders, but had soon to retreat with them.   Monsieur
betook himself first to Ham in Westphalia, and next
to Verona, but the Doge of Venice, fearful of displeas-
ing revolutionary France, 'invited' him to withdraw.
Russian hospitality likewise proved ephemeral, but in
England, first at Gosfield, then at Wanstead, and lastly
at Hartwell, he was able quietly to await the downfall
of the Corsican usurper.   D'Artois found halting-places
at Venice, Mantua, Brussels, and St. Petersburg, and
for a few days he was a second time on French soil
in the island of Yeu; but the failure of the expedition to western France soon obliged him to recross
the Channel, where Holyrood and eventually London
afforded him a refuge.   Of the jealousies of these two
exiled princes, and of the mortifications and dissensions of their retinues, it is needless to speak.   The
Duke of Orleans (the future Louis Philippe), deserting
the Republican army along with Dumouriez, after
teaching in a school in Switzerland, and after a visit
to America, where he spent a night in an Indian wig-
wam, also repaired to England.   There he was doomed

to long years of inactivity, though he would fain have joined the English forces in Spain, in which case, as having fought against France, he could scarcely have grasped the French crown. The Duc de Bourbon likewise settled in England, and it would have been well had his unfortunate son, the Duc d'Enghien, followed his example. The king's two aunts, one of them the reputed mother of the Comte de Narbonne, himself escorting them and destined to ten years of exile, found their way to Rome, but driven thence by the French, after many buffetings they ended their wanderings and their lives at Trieste.

These banished French princes had the doubtful consolation of seeing other regal or princely personages equally storm-tost. The Statthalter of Holland had to pass many years of banishment in England, and even stooped to soliciting a pecuniary indemnity from Napoleon. The Austrian and Prussian monarchs, though not actually driven out of their dominions, saw their capitals occupied by French armies, and had to bow to the stern dictates of the Conqueror. The rulers of German principalities were swept away by the hurricane. The Spanish royal family were consigned to the custody of Talleyrand at Valençay. The Portuguese princes took refuge in Brazil. Italian monarchs fared no better. The sovereigns of Piedmont had to retire to the island of Sardinia, the only possession remaining to them. The King of Naples was likewise driven from his continental dominions, British protection ensuring him a footing in Sicily. Italian dukes were rudely supplanted by Napoleon's relatives or other puppets.

Ferdinand III. of Tuscany was driven to Vienna, though subsequently assigned a duchy in Germany. Even the Papacy, which had long been unscathed by war or revolution, was overwhelmed by the current. Forced away from Rome, one Pope died in the French fortress of Valence, while another became a prisoner at Savona.

In France not merely the princes, but almost the entire nobility, were fugitives. England, Germany, Switzerland, and Russia were inundated with aristocrats, who at first, counting on a speedy and triumphant return, formed little colonies, in one of which Fanny Burney found a husband; but the exhaustion of their resources soon scattered them hither and thither. Some were descendants of Jacobite refugees, who found shelter in the very country whence their ancestors had fled. Adversity, in this as in other cases, brought out the best qualities of some and the worst of others. Frivolity and gravity, self - denial and selfishness, heroism and poltroonery, intrigue and probity, honour and unscrupulousness, existed side by side. Some formed royalist corps subsidised by foreign governments, or actually joined foreign armies, persuading themselves that they were thus fighting not against France but against a usurpation. The few who went to America, whether from choice, like the epicure Brillat Savarin, or from compulsion like Talleyrand, were spared this sad necessity of accepting foreign alms or serving foreign states. The Comte d'Estaing took office under an Indian rajah. Reduced to penury, those who remained in the Old World resorted to every

conceivable expedient.   The women were naturally the
greatest sufferers.   Delicate fingers which had never
done a stroke of work had to busy themselves in dressing dolls, in embroidery, in flower or portrait painting,
in nursing the sick, and even in milking cows and
making butter for sale.   Men brought up in luxury
deemed themselves fortunate if they could earn a
livelihood as journalists, translators, or teachers.   More
frequently they had to become book-keepers or tailors,
to keep wine shops, to sing at music-halls, to act as
prompters at theatres, and even to be water-carriers.
Some, alas! with the connivance at least for a time
of their princes, forged assignats.   Welcomed in some
quarters, mobbed or even expelled as vagabonds in
others, they had to exchange palaces for cottages,
sumptuous diet for the roughest fare, jewels and finery
for rags.   No wonder that humiliation and anguish
drove some to suicide, and the lives of many others
must have been shortened by privations.   Yet many,
with the traditional light-heartedness of Frenchmen,

'Laughed the sense of misery away.'

Besides the *noblesse*, which included the episcopate,
there were thousands of priests and hundreds of nuns,
who, fleeing from relentless persecution, found succour
from Protestant governments and Protestant philan-
thropy.   There were also ex-deputies and publicists,
whom the dungeon, and probably the guillotine, would
otherwise have claimed.   Lally Tollendal, the younger
Mirabeau, Mounier, and Montlosier, had sat in the
National or Constituent Assembly.   Mallet du Pan,

Etienne Dumont, Antraigues, driven to suicide, Lafayette, consigned to an Austrian fortress, and Dumouriez, offering military counsels to the English, may also be mentioned. It need hardly be said that wealthy foreigners like Quintin Craufurd, who had become numerous in Paris before the Revolution, were frightened away, leaving their property to be confiscated, for the Jacobins did not even recognise their right to quit France, which had become not merely inhospitable but dangerous. Not until the Consulate and the Empire did France again attract wealthy foreigners, or recover a portion of its then much impoverished nobility.

As for the immigration, though far less important in numbers and quality, it was not inconsiderable. Men of all nationalities hurried to Paris between 1789 and 1792 to see or serve the Revolution. There were English men and women like Paine (or shall we reckon him an American?), George Grieve, General Money, Thomas Christie, John Oswald, Helen Williams, and Mary Wollstonecraft. There were Americans like Barlow, Eustace, Paul Jones, and Joshua Barney; Germans like Cloots, Trenck, and George Forster; Belgians and Dutchmen like de Kock, father of the novelist, and Proly, a natural son of the Austrian statesman Kaunitz; Poles like Wittinghoff; Russians like Strogonoff; Italians like Rotondo, Cerutti, and Buonarotti; Spaniards like Olavide and Miranda. Most of these men embraced the cause of the Revolution as a religion, and were quite ready to fight in its behalf, in defence as they imagined of liberty and enlightenment, even against their native countries. Some of them paid the penalty of their enthusiasm by the dungeon or the guillotine. It is true that when Napoleon seized the reins such illusions could scarcely have remained, but even then there were numerous foreigners eager to serve him for the sake of lucre or adventure, not to speak of Irish refugees and Poles, whom he lured by the expectation of achieving their independence. Prince Leopold of Saxe-Coburg, little foreseeing his marriage with our Princess Charlotte or his elevation to the crown of Belgium, was anxious to become one of his aides-de-camp. Some men fought by turns for and against him. The Revolution indeed, though it ended by making Europe nationalist, made it for a time cosmopolitan. Napoleon did much, more-over, to eradicate patriotism, especially in the military class. Hence Bernadotte was not the only soldier who changed sides from personal pique or according to the prospects of victory, and he did not even imagine that by his appearance as an invader he would disqualify himself for supplanting Napoleon on the French throne. Jomini, a Swiss, after serving Napoleon in high rank, offered his sword to Russia, though Napoleon was com-pelled to acquit him of having treacherously revealed his military secrets. And Talleyrand, while accepting Napoleon's pay, intrigued with his foes, doubtless salv-ing his conscience, if indeed he had a conscience, with the notion that he was thus promoting the interests of France. Few men were so scrupulous as the Duc de Richelieu, a future French statesman, in stipulating that Russia should not send him to fight against his countrymen. As to the rank and file, they had of course no choice. Belgians, Dutchmen, Germans, Poles, Italians, had to join or combat French armies according to the political exigencies of the moment or the periphery of French rule. Napoleon's armies were thus a medley of nationalities, and the only wonder is that defections so rarely occurred.

Such was the France, such the Europe, to which this book relates. It is a chapter in the history both of England and of Napoleon. We first see Englishmen pouring over to Paris during the interlude or truce of Amiens, to make or renew acquaintance with it after ten years of hostilities, or to recover confiscated property. Peers, M.P.'s, soldiers and sailors, philosophers, scholars, merchants, were all eager to see the young Corsican who had already accomplished so much and was evidently marked out to accomplish much more. We next see hundreds of these non-combatants detained for eleven years on the paltry pretext of their being liable to militia service at home, and in defiance of all international courtesies. We see some of them not merely shifted from place to place, now permitted to reside in Paris, now relegated to provincial towns, but actually incarcerated in fortresses. We find the British Government standing on principle, and declining to exchange the thousands of French captives for these unfortunates, though there were not wanting men who urged on it the expediency of stooping to deal with Napoleon as with a mountain brigand or a barbarous chief, especially as he was arbitrarily imprisoning without trial Frenchmen whom he suspected or feared. We meet with cases of crying heartlessness among these detentions, relieved only by a very rare gleam of humanity or magnanimity. We then see the sudden collapse of this gigantic tyranny and the liberation, as from an immense aviary suddenly thrown opon, of grey-headed and despondent captives. This flight of caged birds is quickly followed by, we might almost say is coincident with, an influx of fresh visitors, mostly so unmindful of the past as to take for granted the stability of the restored monarchy. We see a few tourists repairing to Elba to get a glimpse of the dethroned Emperor, one or two of them sagacious enough to forebode that reappearance on French soil which was to scare away nearly all their countrymen. The curtain falls on the Hundred Days, but it is just raised to show us Napoleon pathetically trying with little success at St. Helena to master the language of his jailers.

The centenary of the Peace of Amiens seemed a suitable occasion for writing, not a political history of that truce, for on this there is nothing new to be said, but an account of its social aspects, of the visits paid to Paris by Englishmen, which had never before been so numerous, of the impression made on each other by guests and hosts, and of the experiences of those who on the resumption of hostilities found themselves detained as prisoners. French writers have shown how Napoleon treated his own subjects; it completes the picture of him to see how he treated Englishmen, who never, except his guardians at St. Helena when jailer had become prisoner, came into such close relations with him. I may fairly claim to have broken new ground. It is true that I gave two brief chapters on this subject in 1889 in my *Englishmen in the French Revolution*, but I have since met in the French National Archives and elsewhere with a mass of additional materials which enable me to go into much greater detail.   The starting-point of my researches was the discovery, for which and for other communications I am indebted to M. Léonce Grasilier, of a register of the principal foreign arrivals.[1]   I have also been favoured with information from three correspondents in reply to questions respecting their ancestors, and the *Dictionary of National Biography* has of course much assisted me, though in some instances the dates of birth given or left in doubt by it may be supplied or corrected by the register above mentioned, while visits to Paris have sometimes escaped the notice of its contributors.   I have likewise consulted at the Record Office the despatches of Anthony Merry, the predecessor of Lord Whitworth at the Paris Embassy, though these, like the Whitworth series edited by Mr. Oscar Browning, seldom stoop from political to social incidents.   But the most vivid picture of the life and treatment of the captives is gained from the police bulletin daily prepared for Napoleon and now preserved in the French Archives.[2]   They also throw a flood of light on the character of Napoleon's internal rule, yet, so far as I know, no French historian has as yet utilised them, and I have every reason to believe that I am the first English writer who has consulted them.   They have

[1] National Archives, F. 7, 2231.   See *English Historical Review*, October 1899.
[2] A. F. iv. 1490-1563.   References not otherwise indicated relate to the French Archives.

furnished me with most of the data respecting the captives.

As for printed sources, the reports of the Historical Manuscripts Commission have thus far brought to light but few letters written by visitors to their friends, yet many of these may still be in existence. The literature of the Verdun and other captives is disappointing. Sturt, Forbes, Pinkerton, Lawrence, and Blayney necessarily give individual experiences rather than a general history of the detentions. Not one of these writers, moreover, ventured on keeping a journal, which would have been obviously unsafe, and some of them, publishing their recollections while comrades were still in captivity, naturally omitted details which might have lessened the pity felt in England by revealing the failings of a small minority, or which might have goaded the jailers to increased rigour. The police bulletins, on the other hand, written for perusal by one man, a man whom it was dangerous to attempt to hoodwink, had no reason for reticence.

II

THE VISITORS

THE Peace of Amiens reopened France, and not merely France but central and southern Europe, to British travellers. Since the outbreak of hostilities in 1793 the 'grand tour' had been suspended. Maritime ascendency, indeed, had always ensured our communications with North Germany and Italy, but the risk of capture by privateers such as befell Richard (afterwards the Marquis) Wellesley, the Duke of Wellington's elder brother, on his return from Lisbon in 1794, coupled with intermittent campaigns and conquests by France, had virtually put a stop to foreign travel. Young noblemen in charge of tutors or 'bearwards' had ceased to traverse the Continent, and French schools had ceased to receive British students. The schools, moreover, had mostly been closed by the Revolution. An Arthur Wellesley, even if inclined, could not have studied horsemanship at Angers, nor could a Gilbert Elliot have been the comrade of a

Mirabeau at Fontainebleau.   So also as to girls.   Pente-
mont Abbey in Paris, where daughters of such aristocratic families as Annesley, Hobart, De Ros and De
Rathe had been educated between 1780 and 1789,
was shut, preparatory to conversion into a barrack,[1]
while the English Austin convent, where for 150
years Towneleys, Dormers, and Fermors had been
pupils, sometimes when adults returning as nuns,
though still in the possession of the community, had
not yet been reopened as a school.   London newspapers complacently calculated the money thus prevented from leaving the country.

It it true that a few of the Englishmen arrested as
hostages for Toulon in the autumn of 1793, though
released after the Terror, had been unable or unwilling to quit France.   Christopher Potter, ex-M.P.
for Colchester, in 1796 offered Lord Malmesbury, on
behalf of Barras, to secure peace for a bribe of half
a million.   Captain Henry Swinburne, commissioner
for exchanging prisoners, a collateral ancestor of the
poet, likewise found in Paris about that date Mrs. Grace
Dalrymple Elliott, ex-mistress of 'Egalité' Orleans,
who remained till 1801, Admiral Rodney's Portuguese
wife and her two daughters, Richard Chenevix, grand-
nephew of a Bishop of Waterford, Walter Smythe,
brother of the famous Mrs. Fitzherbert, two sons of the
Whitehall preacher Charles Este, and George Hamilton,
a Jamaica planter whose wife, a daughter of Lord Leven,
was afterwards, as we shall see, the companion of Sir
Herbert Croft; but of course there had been scarcely

[1] Jefferson also placed his daughter there.

any fresh arrivals.   Indeed it was illegal for British
subjects, unless with special permission, to cross over
to France.[1] They were liable at home to punishment
for the attempt, just as they were liable if they reached
the French shore to being prevented from landing or to
incarceration as spies.   Lord Camelford, Pitt's eccentric cousin, who threatened if Horne Tooke was refused
admission as a clergyman to the seat for Old Sarum,[2]
to nominate in his place his negro servant—a black
man in lieu of a black coat—was arrested in February
1799 when on the point of crossing the Channel; but
as his object was to examine the Mediterranean ports
he was liberated, being, however, deprived of his naval
post.   We shall hear of him again.   Boyd and Ker,
bankers of whom too we shall hear again, made their
way back to Paris in 1797 in the hope of recovering
confiscated property, but were promptly packed off.   A
London newspaper of that year mentions that two men
who had paid a Prussian captain eighty guineas for a
passage from Dover to Calais were also unceremoniously expelled.   Braham, however, and Miss Storace
got to Paris and gave concerts in 1797.   Thomas
Hardy, the radical shoemaker, managed to send
Thomas Paine a pair of shoes so good that Paine
lent them as a model to a Parisian craftsman, but
Hardy would not have found it easy to carry them over
himself.   Fishermen and smugglers, it is true, kept up
intermittent communications, conveying newspapers or

[1] This was granted in 1800 to John Cleaver Banks in order to
examine manuscripts in the National Library.

[2] Camelford, in 1802, sold the borough for £42,000 to Dupré
Porcher.

merchandise, but they seldom ran the risk of taking passengers. Even fishing-boats, moreover, which on both sides had been unmolested, were in January 1801 declared by the British Government liable to capture; but Bonaparte's threat of recalling Otto, the commissioner of exchanges, from a country where the laws and usages of war were disregarded and violated,[1] coincidentally with the resignation of Pitt on account of George III.'s objection to Catholic emancipation, led to this order being rescinded. Indeed the explanations given on this point by the new Addington Administration paved the way for peace negotiations.

There had been, it is true, isolated opportunities for Englishmen of forming or communicating impressions of France. Malmesbury[2] had not only been at Paris in 1796, but at Lille in 1797, on both occasions receiving an offer from Barras through a Bostonian named Melville—probably the son of Major Thomas Melville, one of the Boston tea-party, the last American to wear a cocked hat—to conclude peace for £450,000.[3] Malmesbury[4] and his staff on their return assuredly found

[1] *Times*, March 3, 1801.

[2] In January 1793, quitting his wife, he followed to Paris Aimé de Coigny, Duchess de Fleury, of whom he had become the paramour at Rome, and who had gone to London for her accouchement. Being arrested, he applied to her previous lover Lauzun to procure his release, but was liberated without any necessity of mediation and returned to London.

[3] Pitt was inclined in 1797 to entertain the overture, but the French *coup d'état* put an end to negotiations. See *Fortescue Papers*, iii. pp. 356-357. The French authorities ordered Melville's arrest, but he apparently fled in time, and coolly revisited Paris in 1802.

[4] The Jacobins were scandalised at the pomp with which he entered Paris, where the market-women waited on him to make and receive presents.

much avidity for information on the France trans-
formed by the Revolution. That staff consisted at
Paris of George Ellis, of the *Anti-Jacobin*, Lord Granville Leveson-Gower, of whom we shall hear again,
and James Talbot, afterwards Secretary of Legation
in Switzerland.[1] To avoid being mobbed they were
obliged to wear the republican cockade whenever they
appeared in the street. At Lille Malmesbury was
accompanied not only by Ellis and Talbot, but by
Henry Wellesley, afterwards Earl Cowley, and by
Lord Morpeth, afterwards Earl of Carlisle. Not
merely Swinburne but Captain James Cotes and
General Knox were also sent to Paris between 1796
and 1799 to effect an exchange of prisoners. They
must have been eagerly questioned on their return.
The notorious Governor Wall, who, living in the south
of France, had been refused service in the French
army,[2] went back to England in 1797, but clandestinely, and it would have been better for him had he
remained on the Continent. He had to conceal his
identity and his experiences.[3] But Sir Sidney Smith
had escaped from the Temple in 1798 after two years'
incarceration, and Napoleon in the following year

[1] Talbot, when acting at Berne in Wickham's absence in 1797,
advanced money to French conspirators for a scheme of massacring
the members of the Directory at the Luxembourg, and he applied to
his Government for further funds for that purpose; but Grenville
and Canning refused to countenance the scheme and directed him to
get back the money (Martel, *Historiens Fantaisistes*). Though thus
rebuked Talbot was not dismissed.

[2] J. F. Neville, *Leisure Moments*.

[3] Detected in 1802 he was hanged for the murder of Sergeant Armstrong at Goree in 1782.

released some English prisoners, sending them home with professions of a desire for peace. Sir Robert Barclay, a diplomatist captured at sea, was also, after half an hour's conversation, liberated by him. Lord Carysfort, whose mutinous crew had taken him to Brest, was likewise permitted, in November 1800, after nine months' detention, to visit his family on parole. Masquerier managed, moreover, in that year to visit Paris and to sketch Napoleon's portrait for exhibition in London. Tallien, on the other hand, captured by the English on his way back from Egypt, had been allowed in March 1800 to return to France, where he could give a glowing account of the attentions paid him by the Opposition leaders, and of his presence, the observed of all observers, at parliamentary debates. On re-entering Paris he found that his handsome wife, Thérése Cabarrus, had become the mistress of the army contractor Ouvrard, and she never rejoined him.

But, broadly speaking, Englishmen and Frenchmen had for nearly a decade been perfect strangers, so that a British cartoon entitled 'The First Kiss this Ten Years' depicted Monsieur François stooping to kiss Britannia with the words, 'Madam, permit me to pay my profound esteem to your engaging person and to seal on your divine lips my everlasting attachment.' To which Britannia replies, 'Monsieur, you are truly a well-bred gentleman, and though you make me blush, yet you kiss so delicately that I could not refuse you, though I was sure that you would deceive me again.'

The peace preliminaries were signed on the 1st October 1801. England, without waiting for the ratifications, released her 14,000 French prisoners,[1] and on the 23rd October Boulogne, for the first time for nearly nine years, saw the arrival of an English vessel bringing 160 of these captives.

It is not my purpose to enter into the details of the negotiations, nor need I dwell on the rejoicings for the peace. Cobbett in London had his windows smashed for refusing to illuminate, and the jury recommended to mercy three of the delinquents, but Cobbett, though invited by the judge to join in this recommendation, declined, stating that he expected justice. The London mob took the horses out of Otto's carriage and drew it, while Lauriston, grand-nephew of the famous speculator Law,[2] on coming over with the ratifications received ovations. On the 1st November Lord Cornwallis, ex-Governor of India, accompanied by his son, Lord Brome (afterwards the second and last marquis), by his illegitimate son, Colonel (eventually General Sir Miles) Nightingale,[3] his son-in-law, Captain Singleton, Colonel Littlehales (afterwards Sir E. Littlehales Baker), and Francis (brother of Sir John) Moore, started for Paris.[4]

[1] This was a saving of expense, for Napoleon had refused to pay the £2,000,000 demanded for their maintenance.

[2] It is pleasant to think that Lauriston, Macdonald, and Clarke, three men of British extraction, were among the few French generals who on Napoleon's return from Elba remained faithful to the Bourbons.

[3] M.P. for Eye in 1820.

[4] The suit of carriages for the use of Marquis Cornwallis in France consists of a town coach, the body yellow, with arms, supporters, crests, and the Order of the Garter, surrounded with mantles, all highly emblazoned. The lining morocco with rich silk lace, and reclining cushions of silk and morocco. The carriage crane-neck;

Amiens had been chosen for the negotiations, but Napoleon, evidently wishing Lord Cornwallis to see how firmly the Consulate was established, had invited him to come round by Paris on the plea of showing him the illuminations of the 9th November in celebration of the peace with Austria. The road from Calais to Paris, which had since 1793 been almost deserted, was hastily put in repair for him, and was soon to be dotted with mail-coaches and post-chaises. Cornwallis arrived on the 7th November; he alighted at the Hotel Grange Batelière, the finest in Paris, it being an old mansion with spacious grounds, and he was received by Napoleon on the 10th. Napoleon suggested to him a reciprocal expulsion of foreign conspirators, the Bourbon princes to be packed off by England, and the United Irishmen by France; but Cornwallis naturally evaded so delicate a question. Napoleon did not invite him to dinner, and did not rise to receive Lord Brome in his box at the Opera, an incivility much commented upon. Cornwallis gave a dinner on the 16th to Lord Minto, who was on his way home from the Vienna Embassy, and five other fellow-countrymen.

'After dinner,' says the *Times*, 'the company went to the Opera, where the performance was the *Mysteries of Isis*. Every part of the house was so crowded that numbers were

the hammer-cloth a bear-skin ornamented with silver paws. A town chariot painted to correspond, with arms, supporters, crests, and the Garter, but no mantles; crane-neck. A travelling coach, painted the same; crane-neck with imperials, etc. Harness has been made for twelve horses ornamented with silver in coronets, crests, and the Garter, with reins, tassels, and toppings, decorated with silk button-hangers.—*Times*.

unable to procure places.   Some couplets were sung in celebration of the union of the two nations, which excited an enthusiasm that displayed itself by universal and repeated bursts of applause.

'Lord Cornwallis was so extremely affected by the scene, that he shed tears !   On his rising to go away, the audience recommenced their testimonies of applause.   His Lordship showed how much he was flattered by the reception he had met with, by bowing to them in the most affecting manner. The following may be given as a specimen of the verses sung upon this occasion :—

> " Anglais, Français, restez unis,
>   Qu'à vos chants l'Univers réponde :
>   Quand de tels rivaux sont amis,
>   Qui peut troubler la paix du monde ? " '

Cornwallis also dined with Talleyrand, and Francis James Jackson, writing to Speaker Abbot (afterwards Lord Colchester), says :—

'What do you think of Lord Cornwallis, with all his dignity of decorum, dining the other day at a table of thirty covers with the kept mistresses, and being obliged to hand out the ugliest and frailest of them, because she was in keeping of the minister for Foreign Affairs ? '

On the 28th Cornwallis left for Amiens.   There Joseph Bonaparte conducted the negotiations, and he speaks highly of Cornwallis's straightforwardness. Cornwallis carried back with him to England cotton-velvet goods, to show his countrymen the superiority of Amiens looms, and the Calais municipality gave him a banquet before he embarked.[1]

---

[1] The termination of the Congress at Amiens was an object of the deepest regret to the Prefects and officers, civil as well as military.

Anthony Merry, who had been Consul in Spain, had
been sent to Paris in July 1801, succeeding Cotes as
Commissioner of Exchanges, but he assisted Cornwallis
at Amiens, and during his absence from Paris Francis
James Jackson, who had been Secretary of Legation
first at Madrid, then at Berlin, and afterwards at St.
Petersburg, and had been secretary to Pitt, acted as
chargé d'affaires.   Jackson was accompanied by his
brother George, to whom Parisian sights were a
novelty, and by Dawson Warren [1] and Hill as *attachés.*
Jackson, in reporting his arrival in November, stated
that he had been loaded with attentions such as 'the
most refined system of civility could suggest.'   On the
4th January 1802 he presented his credentials to
Napoleon, who said, 'I am very glad to see an English
minister here; it is essential to the civilisation of the
world.' [2]   Merry returning from Amiens, Jackson left
on the 18th April 1802,[3] and Merry remained at the
head of the embassy till December 1802.   He was

The establishment of each ambassador had its particular merit.   That
of Marquis Cornwallis was distinguished for the magnificence of his
liveries, and the splendour of his table and equipage.   On all his
grand dinners, his Lordship had twelve servants in rich liveries,
besides six *Valets-de-Chambre* also in a kind of scarlet uniform.

But in regard to the luxuries of the table, and the choice of his
wines, citizen Schimmelpenninck, the Batavian plenipotentiary, out-
did all other competition.   He had his turbot and eels from Holland,
pike and perch from the Rhine; and the heaths and woods of Provence supplied him with game.   No wonder that the absence of such
a man should be lamented by the *Mayor and Common Council* of that
city.—*Times,* April 2, 1802.

[1] The Warrens and the Jacksons were kinsmen, for in 1796 a Rev.
Dawson Warren had married Caroline Jackson.

[2] Despatches, Record Office.

[3] In 1809 he was appointed minister at Washington.

reproached with giving no dinner on George III.'s birthday on the 4th of June, but he was expecting to be superseded by Lord Whitworth, and his stipend probably did not allow of much display. The embassy was installed, as before the Revolution, in the Caraman mansion, faubourg du Roule.

Whitworth, formerly at St. Petersburg, had been appointed ambassador as early as April 1802, but on account of the delay in the nomination of the French Envoy to London his instructions were not drawn up till the 10th September, and he did not start till the 10th November. He went by Southampton and Havre, and was accompanied by his newly-married wife, the Duchess of Dorset, widow of the Ambassador to Paris of 1789, and by her two daughters. Her son, the young Duke of Dorset, remained at Harrow, where he was the schoolfellow and friend of Byron, but as we shall see he went over to Paris for the Easter holidays.[1] Whitworth's staff consisted of his brother, Colonel Whitworth, James Talbot, James Henry Mandeville,[2] Captain Edward Pierrepont,[3] and Benjafield, with the Rev. Thomas Hodgson as chaplain, and Dr. Maclaurin as physician. The Duchess of Dorset's retention of her first husband's title greatly puzzled the Parisians, many of whom actually believed that she was not married to Whitworth. According to Maria Edgeworth, the latter had at Paris the same house, the same wife, and the same horses as the Duke of Dorset had had

[1] He died from a hunting accident in 1815.
[2] Afterwards minister to the Argentine Republic.
[3] Son of Lord Pierrepont (created Earl Manvers in 1806).

in 1789, but the line should doubtless be drawn at the horses. He took with him six carriages, one of which had been the admiration of Londoners, though it was loss imposing than that taken over by a Dr Brodum, whose object was to promote the sale of his syrup for ensuring longevity. He presented his credentials on the 6th December 1802, and remained as we shall see till the 12th May 1803.[1]

The Dover and Calais mail packets did not recommence running till the 18th November 1801, but English visitors had begun to arrive as early as September or October, and Savary tells us that these pioneers facilitated the conclusion of peace, for they returned with assurances of the stability of the consular government. Napoleon on the 14th October instructed Fouché freely to admit English visitors, taking care, however, that they had Foreign Office passports, and were not French *émigrés*. One of them unfortunately lost his life. Charles John Clarke, of Hitchin Priory, had gone over with his wife. Their only child had died two years before, and they sought relief for their sorrow, intending to go on to Italy. Clarke was on a stand witnessing the fireworks of the 9th November in the Tuileries gardens when it gave way, and its eighty occupants were injured, Clarke so seriously, his spine being fractured, that after lingering nearly a month he expired. Napoleon sent his surgeon

---

[1] The embassy apparently required a Frenchman to translate or correct its letters to Talleyrand, for in 1804 François Soulès, who had lived twelve years in England and had translated English works, applied for the Legion of Honour on the ground that he had not only helped to capture the Bastille, but had been employed by Whitworth.

to make inquiries and offer his services, stating that he should himself call as soon as the patient was well enough to receive visitors.   Clarke, who had been six years married, was only thirty-one years of age.   His widow, several years his junior, carried his remains home.

Never before had there been such an influx of English visitors as during these eighteen months.   'All the idle captives of the land of fogs,' says M. Sorel, 'shook their damp wings and prepared to take their flight towards the regions of pleasure and brightness.'   Even the influenza or *grippe*, which prevailed in January and February 1803, did not deter them, and they mostly escaped the malady, an escape attributed to their being habituated to humidity.   'Ours,' says Samuel Rogers, who was one of the visitors, 'is a nation of travellers, and no wonder, when the elements, air, water, and fire attend at our bidding to transport us from shore to shore, when the ship rushes into the deep, her track the foam as of some mighty torrent, and in three hours or less we stand gazing and gazed at among a foreign people.   None want an excuse.   If rich, they go to enjoy; if poor, to retrench; if sick, to recover; if studious, to learn; if learned, to relax from their studies.'[1]   This, though written in 1839, is, with the exception of the reference to steam, applicable to the influx of 1801-1803.   A few went for health, taking Paris as a stage to Montpellier, then still in repute, Nice, or Italy, others to recover property or for business, a few for study, most for pleasure.   The current

[1] Rogers, *Italy*.

steadily swelled all the winter, spring, and summer.
One of the earliest packets brought sixty-three ladies,
and the Calais hotels were packed, seven hundred and
ninety-eight passengers landing in ten days. In the
last decade of Prairial (June 1802) there were ninety-
one arrivals, in the last decade of Thermidor (August)
ninety-seven, in the last decade of Fructidor (September) one hundred and fifty-six.[1] This last average of
fifteen a day seems small to us, but was surprising for
that time.   Merry states that there were once as many
as five thousand English in Paris, and that when he
left in December there were one thousand nine hundred.
In the autumn he sent home long lists of persons to
whom he had given return passports, and he had complained in May that he was so busy in issuing them
as to have no time to attend properly to diplomatic
business.

The cost of a trip to Paris was what in those days
seemed moderate.   For £4, 13s. you could get a through
ticket by Dover and Calais, starting either from the
City at 4.30 A.M. by the old and now revived line of
coaches connected with the rue Notre Dame des
Victoires establishment in Paris, or morning and night
by a new line from Charing Cross.[2] Probably a still
cheaper route, though there were no through tickets,
was by Brighton and Dieppe, the crossing taking 10 or
15 hours.   By Calais it seldom took more than 8 hours,
but passengers were advised to carry light refreshments

[1] A. F. 1539-1543.
[2] The return coach left Paris at 6 A.M., but from July 1802 there
was also a *berline* with six places which started at 4 P.M., travelled
all night, and arrived as soon as the morning coach.

with them. The diligence from Calais to Paris, going only four miles an hour, took 54 hours for the journey, but a handsome carriage drawn by three horses, in a style somewhat similar to the English post-chaise, could be hired by four or five fellow-travellers, and this made six miles an hour. £30 would cover the expense of a seven weeks' visit, including hotels, sight-seeing, and restaurants.[1] As for fashionable people, even if they went by coach to Dover, they posted from Calais to Paris, especially if they formed a family party and took servants with them. Some, like Lord Guilford, even shipped their own carriages, but he had to hire four sorry steeds at Calais, for horses were not allowed to land.[2]

Lord Elgin had four servants, Lord Yarmouth, with his wife and two children, had eight, Thomas Hope three, and Lady Maynard two. The journey occupied four days, if we may judge by the French General Hardy, who, captured in Ireland in 1798, had been exchanged—there being no English prisoner of equal rank—for four officers, four non-commissioned officers, and ten privates. It took him a day to get from London to Dover, another day for the crossing, and two days for the journey from Calais to Paris.

Passengers by Boulogne if arriving at low tide were landed in a singular fashion. Thomas Manning, of whom we shall hear presently, in a letter to his father communicated to me by his grand-nephew, Mr. E. B. Harris, says:—

[1] *Practical Guide . . . London to Paris.* R. Phillips, 1802.
[2] Mrs. F. E. King, *Tour in France.*

'The tide having ebbed, we were obliged to land without entering the inner harbour of Boulogne. It was night before the sluggish boat that the Boulogne mariners sent off could land us all, and a strange landing it seemed to me. The boat rowed towards the nearest shore till it ran aground, which happened in the midst of the breakers. In an instant the boathead was surrounded by a throng of women up to their middles and over, who were there to carry us on shore. Not being aware of this manœuvre, we did not throw ourselves into the arms of these sea-nymphs so instantly as we ought, whereby those who sat at the stern of the boat were deluged with sea spray. For myself I was in front, and very quickly understood the clamour of the mermaids. I flung myself upon the backs of two of them without reserve, and was safely and dryly borne on shore, but one poor gentleman slipped through their fingers and fell over head and ears into the sea.'

This primitive mode of landing had been noted in 1792 by William Hunter, who states that one of the 'mermaids,' unequal to the weight of a stout Englishman who had been reserved to the last, dropped him midway. Lanterns dimly lit up this curious scene.[1]

The return voyage had to be made on French bottoms, in order that the mercantile marine might be encouraged, and this regulation had its inconvenience, not to say dangers. The *Times* of 12th January, 1803, says :—

'A navy Officer, who recently returned from Calais, where

---

[1] In 1814, according to Kirwan, the fishwives no longer carried passengers on their backs, but wading through the water tugged or pushed small boats ashore. But Richard Bernard Boyle was carried ashore by three men, one holding each leg and the third pushing behind.

he had spent a few days, was actually under the necessity
of giving directions, and afterwards exerting himself with
alacrity, to preserve his own life and that of the other
passengers. The master of the vessel, who was very much
afraid of the violence of the wind, sat half-way down to the
cabin, with his head under the companion, and covered with
a huge night-cap, to prevent its reaching him, as he was (he
said) grievously afflicted with the rheumatism; and to the
repeated demands of the passengers, why he did not come
upon deck and give orders for the safety of the vessel, he
answered, deliberately, taking the pipe out of his mouth,
that there was no immediate danger, and if any should
arise, he had a good sea-boat, which would carry him and
all his crew safe to land.'

Let us now see who were the visitors, beginning not
with the earliest but by far the most eminent of them,
Fox. He had not seen France since 1788, when he
passed through with Mrs. Armistead on his way to
Switzerland and Italy. Waiting, like many other
M.P.'s, till his election was over, he started at Dover on
the 31st July 1802, again accompanied by the so-called
Mrs. Armistead (only now for the first time publicly
figuring as his wife, though they had been privately
married some years previously), by St. Andrew (afterwards Lord) St. John, M.P., and by John Bernard
Trotter, his secretary.[1] His nephew Lord Holland had
engaged rooms for him in the faubourg St. Germain,
but he seems to have removed to the hotel Grange
Batelière and eventually to the hotel Richelieu, the
mansion erected and formerly occupied by the

[1] Also his biographer. Trotter died in poverty in 1818, aged forty-
three.

notorious *roué*, Marshal (grand-nephew of Cardinal) Richelieu, who had entertained him in 1788. Fox's chief object was to consult French records for his life of James II., his ancestor, and he daily frequented the National Archives for that purpose, in company with St. John, Robert (afterwards Sir Robert) Adair, and Trotter. Talleyrand, after his return to England, sent him a complete copy of Barillon's despatches, which Fox had declared to be worth their weight in gold.

Many people in England fancied, however, that he was mainly bent on seeing Napoleon, and the caricaturists did not neglect so tempting a subject. Gillray, in a cartoon entitled 'Introduction of Citizen Volpone and his suite at Paris,' represented Bonaparte as seated on a chair surrounded by Mamelukes, while Fox and his wife,[1] both extremely corpulent, are bowing and curtseying, Erskine, in legal costume with his hand on his heart, and Lord and Lady Holland making up the group. Another caricaturist depicted the reception by the First Consul of Fox, Erskine, and Combe. To Fox he says, 'Fox, ha! How old are you?' To Combe, 'A brewer, Lord Mayor, ha! great pomp,' and to Erskine, 'Mr. Brief, ha! a great lawyer; can talk well. There, you may go.'[2] Trotter tells us what really occurred :—

'Bonaparte, of a small and by no means commanding figure, dressed plainly though richly in the embroidered

[1] Her age is given in the police register as sixty-three, but as she died in 1842 at the age of ninety-two, she was really only fifty-two. Fox's age, on the other hand, is given as fifty, whereas it was fifty-three. The ages in the register seem sometimes to be hotel-keepers' random guesses.

[2] Ashton, *English Caricature on Napoleon.*

consular coat, without powder in his hair, looked like a
private gentleman, indifferent as to dress, and devoid of all
haughtiness in his air. The English ambassador, after the
presentation of some English noblemen, announced to him
Mr. Fox. He was a good deal flurried, and after indicating
considerable emotion said—"Ah, Mr. Fox; I have heard with
pleasure of your arrival, I have desired much to see you.
I have long admired in you the orator and friend of his
country, who, in constantly raising his voice for peace, consulted that country's best interests, those of Europe, and of
the human race. The two great nations of Europe require
peace. They have nothing to fear [from each other]. They
ought to understand and value [esteem] one another. In
you, Mr. Fox, I see with much satisfaction that great statesman who recommended peace because there was no just
object of war, who saw Europe desolated to no purpose
and who struggled for its relief." '

Trotter adds that Fox, averse to compliments,
neither replied to nor reciprocated them, and that a
few questions and answers respecting his tour termi-
nated the interview.

Napoleon afterwards invited Fox to a dinner of two
hundred guests, to which he went unpowdered. John
King, of whom we shall presently hear, thought it
inconsistent of Fox to accept such attentions, which
acceptance he attributes to a desire to please his wife;
but Fox obviously could not decline an invitation from
the ruler of the land whose hospitality he was enjoying,
though he felt perfectly free to refuse to lunch with the
brewer Santerre, notorious for his part in the execution
of Louis XVI. According to the Rev. Stephen Weston,
Napoleon complimented Fox as the greatest man of a

great nation. Fox, as was to be expected, combated Napoleon's accusations against Pitt, and especially against Windham, of complicity in the infernal-machine plot of 1800. Thiers gives an account of Fox being taken by Napoleon to the Industrial Exhibition at the Louvre, when a courtier sarcastically pointed on a globe to the small space occupied by England, whereupon Fox, spreading his arms round the globe, said, ' Yes, but though we all spring from there we grasp the whole world.' The truth is that though Napoleon and Fox happened to be simultaneously at the Exhibition they did not come across each other.[1] It was Chaptal who conducted Fox over the Exhibition, and he tells us that Fox admired the specimens, but thought them too dear for common use, upon which Chaptal took him to the cutlery department, where Fox filled his pockets with cheap knives, and then to a watch stall, where he bought half a dozen watches at 13 f. a piece.[2] He frequented the theatres. Not only, however, was his French very imperfect, but he committed a great breach of decorum by not calling on the two minor consuls, Cambacérès and Lebrun. He had to apologise through Merry. Lebrun overlooked the blunder and received Fox on his reparatory visit, but Cambacérès was ruffled, and insisted that Fox should make an unceremonious call as though he had been before.

We learn this from a secret agent of the Bourbons,[3]

[1] Adair, *Mission to the Court of Vienna*, p. 505.
[2] Chaptal, *Industrie Française*, 1817.
[3] Remacle, *Bonaparte et les Bourbons*.

who also tells us that Fox, after his conversation with
Napoleon, said, 'It's all up with liberty.' He could
scarcely, however, have needed that conversation to
form this judgment, for Napoleon on the 2nd August
had been elected consul for life. Fox must have felt
much more at home with Lafayette, with whom he
spent a fortnight at La Grange, planting ivy round the
newly-erected towers as a memento. He dined in
Paris with Talleyrand and Junot, and went shooting
with General Berthier. Madame Junot thought he
looked with his dark grey coat like a Devonshire
farmer, but when talking his countenance was radiant
with intelligence, sagacity, and eloquence.[1] On the
16th September he attended a sitting of the Tribunat,
when the captain on guard, Boyer, thanked him for
having in 1795 obtained the unfettering, and all but
the liberation, of two hundred French officers at Por-
chester, a benefit which they would never forget. 'Our
chains were broken,' said Boyer : 'we were almost free.'[2]
At Versailles, on entering a room which he was told
had long been shut up, he found his own bust, along
with those of Algernon Sidney, Hampden, Chatham,
and Washington.[3] But was this a stratagem of
Napoleon to flatter him ? Curiously enough, Napoleon
on his dressing - table at the Tuileries had, as the
Edgeworths noticed, the bust not only of Fox but of
Nelson, for whom he also entertained great admiration.
He asked Mrs. Damer for a second bust of Fox,

[1] Duchesse d'Abrantès, *Mémoires*.
[2] *European Magazine*, 1802.
[3] Lascases speaks by mistake of a statue.

a commission which the lady could not execute till 1815.

Fox was criticised in England for taking tea with Helen Maria Williams, for it had been erroneously imagined, by Boswell among others, that she had marched exultantly over the bodies of the Swiss massacred in 1792. He was also twitted with meeting Arthur O'Connor, the United Irish exile. The fact was that he and Erskine went to dine with Madame Tallien without knowing that O'Connor would be there. Fox with great tact made the best of what he considered an unlucky incident by treating O'Connor exactly like the other guests, but Erskine was more embarrassed, for as counsel on his trial at Maidstone in 1798 he had vouched for O'Connor's loyalty, whereas the latter had since made a confession of conspiracy.

Fox remained till the 11th November. 'I have certainly,' he wrote, 'seldom spent a time pleasanter than at Paris, but I never in my life felt such delight in returning home.' In 1806 he reciprocated the civilities shown him by sending word to Talleyrand that a Frenchman called Guillet had called on him and offered to kidnap Napoleon. Guillet was consequently arrested in Paris, and consigned, not to prison, but to Bicêtre lunatic asylum, where he died twelve months afterwards. Canning was guilty of the bad taste, not to say ignominy, of censuring Fox in Parliament for giving this warning, the generosity of which was warmly appreciated by Napoleon, as he told Lord Ebrington at Elba in 1814.

The general election had come rather inopportunely

c

for visits to Paris, Parliament being dissolved on the
29th June, and the new House meeting on the 16th
November. Elections, moreover, were much less ex-
peditiously despatched than nowadays. Nevertheless
about eighty M.P.'s, mostly Foxites, as Liberals were
then called, but some Pittites or Ministerialists, went
over either before or after the elections. Some of
these M.P.'s are entitled to notice.[1]

Acheson, who in 1807 became Lord Gosford, revisited
Paris in 1814, and became Governor of Canada. Adair,
as we have seen, was the friend of Fox, and indeed was
destined to be his last surviving friend. When visiting St. Petersburg in 1791 his letters home were in
cipher, but forwarded through Whitworth, the ambassador, and he was absurdly suspected of having been
sent thither by Fox to thwart Pitt's policy.[2] Barclay,
as already mentioned, was a diplomatist, and had
been a prisoner in France. He had just married a
German lady at Hamburg. Baring was the famous
banker, and though deaf from his youth sat and voted
in Parliament. Benfield and Boyd not only come
together alphabetically, but had been partners in a
London bank which was wound up in 1799. Paul
Benfield went out to India in the Company's service,
and there made a fortune, partly by trade, partly by
fortification contracts and by loans. He advanced
money to the Nawab of the Carnatic, on conditions for
which Burke afterwards, with his customary vehe-
mence, branded him as 'a criminal who ought long

[1] For full list see Appendix A.
[2] *Dropmore Papers*, ii. 11.

since to have fattened the kites with his offal.' In 1777 he was ordered to quit India, but he was subsequently reinstated in his post, and returned to Madras. In 1780 he became M.P. for Cricklade, and in 1796 he exchanged that seat for Shaftesbury, another of his five pocket-boroughs. He was also recorder for Shaftesbury, such appointments being sometimes conferred on or sold by corporations to men not even lawyers. In 1796 he assigned the second seat to Walter Boyd, whose sleeping partner he had become in 1793. Boyd had had a bank in Paris, and had been an agent for the French Revolutionary Government in paying for corn from England; but threatened with arrest in October 1792 he had fled, with his partner Walter Ker. It was alleged in December 1794 that he had sold to the French Treasury drafts for ten million francs on London, boasting that they would be dishonoured; but the Finance Committee, on investigation, declared the charge unfounded. In 1795 Boyd contracted for an English loan, but in 1797 his bank fell into difficulties. Boyd had entered into imprudent speculations, and when he went to Paris, calculating on the restitution of his property, the change of government there frustrated his hopes, and he was expelled. In 1799 Pitt, apparently in order to extricate him from his embarrassments, concluded a second loan with him without inviting tenders from any other firm, on the plea that this had been promised him in 1793. A select committee of inquiry severely condemned this transaction, but an obsequious House of Commons condoned it. It did not, however, avert Boyd's bankruptcy.

The two partners were now among the earliest visitors to Paris. They went at the close of 1801, Boyd still hoping to recover property. They were on the point of losing their seats for Shaftesbury, Benfield having sold that borough for £40,000 to a Colonel Wood. We shall see by and by how they sped in France.

Best, who became successively Serjeant Best, Sir Thomas Best, and Lord Wynford, reached the judicial bench in 1818, and in 1824 was made Chief-Justice of the Common Pleas. Originally a Whig, he ended as a violent Tory. Brodrick was Secretary to the (India) Board of Control. Burdett speaks for himself, as when, on being greeted at Calais as the friend of Fox, he exclaimed, 'No, the friend of liberty.' In the summer of 1793 he had attended the clubs and the Convention. Father of Lady Burdett-Coutts, he began as a demagogue and ended as a reactionary. He boasted of his election for Middlesex having cost him £100,000. He, with his friend Bosville, called on Thomas Paine, giving him £240 to clear off his debts and return to America. He also called, with his old tutor Lechevalier, on La Réveillère Lepaux, the theophilanthropist, on whom he made no favourable impression.[1] Burdett, who had witnessed the early stage of the Revolution with more curiosity than sympathy, told Arthur Young, who had likewise seen something of that upheaval, that the Consulate was the completest military despotism that had ever existed.[2]

Lord George Cavendish became in 1831 Earl of

[1] La Réveillère Lepaux, *Mémoires.*
[2] A. Young, *Journal.*

Burlington, and succeeded his brother as Duke of Devonshire. Alderman Combe had been Sheriff of London in 1792 and Lord Mayor in 1799. Fox and Sheridan were godfathers to the son born to him during his mayoralty. Napoleon, according to Weston, said to him, 'You were Lord Mayor in a year of dearth. I know what it is to have to keep people quiet when bread is dear.' Unsuccessful at a by-election for the City in 1795, he had been elected in 1796. In 1800 he had convened a common hall to petition for peace. In 1805 he gave a dinner in his brewery to the Duke and Duchess of York, the Duke of Cambridge, Lady Anne Fitzroy, and other aristocratic guests. He ultimately resigned his aldermanic gown and seat in Parliament and confined himself to his business. He died in 1818.

Cowper was the son of Earl Cowper. Dallas, on returning home from the service of the East India Company, was the champion of Warren Hastings, and in 1793 and 1799 had written pamphlets against the French Government. The Marquis of Douglas, son of the Duke of Hamilton, was sent in 1807 as Ambassador to St. Petersburg. Ellis was afterwards Lord Seaford, taking his title from the little Sussex town for which he and his brother sat. Erskine, of whom we have already heard, became Lord Chancellor in the thirteen months' Administration of 'All the Talents.' His son David, who accompanied him, succeeded him in the peerage.

Fitzpatrick, the intimate friend of Fox and the uncle of Lord Holland, was, like Fox, fond both of the classics

and of gambling. He was an amateur actor and a wit.
He had made an impressive speech in 1796 in favour of
Lafayette, then a prisoner in Austria, and now visited
him at La Grange. In 1806 he became Secretary for
War. John Leslie Foster became an Irish Judge and
lived till 1842. Philip Francis, the Indian councillor
commonly regarded as the author of the *Letters of
Junius*, escorted three of his children, Philip, Elizabeth, and Harriet, who went on to Nice for the benefit
of Harriet's health. We have no letters from Francis
himself, but young Philip tells us that Bonaparte
renewed (?) acquaintance with his father and was very
civil. He likewise tells us that at Madame Bonaparte's reception he saw Bonaparte, after watching
her play for some time from behind her chair, drop a
purse into her lap as he moved away. Francis, with
his daughter Catherine, was again in Paris in January
1803, apparently from alarm at the miscarriage of
letters from Nice, and while there heard of Harriet's
death. The Miss Berrys had been very kind to her.
Francis had twice visited Paris in 1791, and his son
had learned French at Rouen in the summer of 1792.[1]
Lord Granville Leveson-Gower became the first Earl
Granville and Ambassador to France. His son we all
remember as Foreign Secretary. Graham, the Ripon
Graham, was the father of Sir James Graham the
statesman. Hare, who sat from 1781 to 1804 for the
Duke of Devonshire's borough of Knaresborough, was a
wit and a classical scholar who broke down in his
maiden speech and thenceforth remained silent. He

[1] *The Francis Letters*, 1901.

went to Paris for his health or fell ill when there, and
Fox called on the invalid, who died shortly after his
return. Jekyll, too, who had visited France in 1775,
was a famous wit and a great diner-out. He also
sat for a pocket-borough from 1787 to 1816, but his
wit did not come out in his frequent speeches. The
Prince Regent, fond of good talkers, made him in
1805 his Solicitor-General, and procured for him a
commissionership in lunacy and a mastership in
Chancery.

Johnston had been British Resident at Lucknow, and
was an authority on India.   Kinnaird, who in 1803 succeeded to the peerage, being intimately connected with
the Bonapartists, had information in 1817 of Cantillon's
intended attack on the Duke of Wellington, and sent
him an anonymous warning. He and his wife afterwards went to Paris to give information on the subject,
and the latter was arrested as an accomplice. Kinnaird
naturally complained of this as a violation of a virtual
safe-conduct. He had been expelled from France in
the previous year as a political intriguer. He eventually lived in Italy on an allowance from his creditors.[1]
Long, afterwards Lord Farnborough, had been Secretary to the Treasury, became a Commissioner of the
Treasury in 1804, and in 1806 was made Secretary for
Ireland. He had written pamphlets on the French
Revolution in 1795. Eventually he was known as an
art connoisseur, and George IV. sought his advice on
architecture. His father-in-law, Sir Abraham Hume,
accompanied him.

[1] Pasquier, *Mémoires*, vol. iv.

Lord Lovaine in 1830 succeeded his father as Earl of Beverley, and eventually in 1865, two years before his death, became Duke of Northumberland. He was the father of the Duke who adopted Irvingism and married Henry Drummond's daughter. He went on to Naples with his newly married wife, Louisa Wortley, and his father, and on their return they found themselves, as we shall see, prisoners. Macpherson had in 1785 been Governor-General of India. Sir C. Morgan became Judge-Advocate. Lord Morpeth became Earl of Carlisle and father of the distinguished statesman. Nicholl, a frequent speaker and a strenuous opponent of the war with France, had visited that country in 1788-1789 and had made the acquaintance of the Abbé Raynal and other economists. Paget, afterwards Sir Edward Paget, son of the Earl of Uxbridge, was destined, as we shall find, to pay a second and involuntary visit. He had already served in Flanders, Minorca, and Egypt. He had been one of the hostages given to the French at Cairo till they embarked in July 1801. He afterwards served in Sicily and the Peninsula and was Governor of Ceylon. Parnell was the great-uncle of the Home Rule leader. He became Secretary for War, Paymaster-General, and Treasurer of the Navy, and in 1841 was created Lord Congleton. Lord Henry Petty, Chancellor of the Exchequer at the age of twenty-five, and Pitt's successor in the representation of Cambridge University (where he defeated Lord Palmerston), became on his brother's death in 1809 Marquis of Lansdowne. After filling various high offices he survived till 1863 to the age of eighty, the Nestor of the House of Lords. Pollen, the accomplished son of a Surrey clergyman, had by one vote defeated the Duke of Norfolk's nominee at Leominster. He afterwards raised a corps of Fencibles, whom he accompanied to Nova Scotia. On his way home in 1808, after several years' travel in Russia and other countries, he was wrecked and drowned off Memel at the age of thirty-two. His wife applied for permission to return home through France, but the favourable answer being delayed, she embarked at Königsberg for England.[1] St. John, as we have seen, was the companion of Fox, and afterwards succeeded to a peerage. Scott was the elder son of Lord Chancellor Eldon, but predeceased his father, leaving a son to succeed to the title.

John Spencer Smith, page in his youth to Queen Charlotte, was a diplomatist. He was asked by Napoleon whether he was not Sidney Smith's brother, and Napoleon, on being answered in the affirmative, rejoined, 'He is a good fellow and a good officer.' Spencer Smith had been *chargé d'affaires* at Constantinople from 1796 to 1799, and there was a legend of his having married a rich Turkish widow. The truth is, his wife was daughter of the Austrian Baron Ratzbael. While staying at Venice for her health with her two sons in 1806, she was arrested as an alleged spy, and was to have been sent on to Valenciennes, but at Brescia, through the Marquis di Salvo, a friendly Sicilian, she escaped by a ladder from the window and made her way first to Austria and Russia,

[1] F. 7, 3759.

and ultimately to England.[1]   Napoleon had at the
same time tried to arrest her husband, then Ambassador at Würtemberg, but burning his papers he fled
in time.   Occupying himself with archæology, Smith
ultimately settled at Caen, where he died.

William Smith interests us as the grandfather of
Miss Florence Nightingale, and also of George Eliot's
friend, Barbara Smith, Madame Bodichon, whose husband introduced the eucalyptus into Algeria.   He is said
to have been the only English Nonconformist in the
Parliament of 1802, and his name was given to an
Act of 1819, which relieved Unitarians from speaking
of the Trinity in the marriage-service responses.   Lord
Hardwicke's Act of 1752, while repressing irregular
marriages, had inflicted a grievance on Dissenters by
requiring all marriages except those of Quakers and
Jews to be solemnised in churches.   Smith, in 1822,
tried to follow up his success of 1819 by introducing
civil marriage, but his bill, though passing through
the Commons, was shelved in the Lords, so that it
was not till 1836 that Lord John Russell revived and
carried it.   A London merchant, Smith had sat for
Sudbury and Camelford.   On his standing in 1802 for
Norwich, where Dissenters were and still are numerous,
Thomas Grenville, foreseeing that he would oust
Windham, directed his brother the Duke of Buckingham to return Windham for St. Mawes.   'Smith,'
said Grenville, 'was cooping up voters in barns and
houses, where they are kept drunk till the day of poll;
and in short, trying all the means of mischief that his

[1] Duchesse d'Abrantès, *Souvenirs*; di Salvo, *Travels in* 1806.

fertile talents can supply in the mysteries of election-
eering.'[1]   Smith, who was much respected, sat for
Norwich till his death in 1835, and was succeeded by
his son, Benjamin Smith.

Sturt, member for Bridport since 1784, was bred to
the sea, but came unexpectedly into possession of the
family estate in Dorsetshire. He retained, however,
his liking for the water, had a narrow escape in a
cutter race, and in 1800 was awarded the Humane
Society's medal for rescuing a man from drowning. He
now went to stay at Havre. In 1801 he had obtained
£100 damages from the Marquis of Blandford, son of
the Duke of Marlborough, for the seduction of his wife,
Lady Mary Anne Ashley, daughter of the Earl of Shaftesbury, whom he had married in 1788. The damages
were small because Sturt himself had had an intrigue
with Madame Krumholz, a famous harpist. Sturt's
sister, and he himself doubtless, had known Madame
Dubarry on her visit to London in search of her stolen
jewels. His nephew and namesake was an eminent
Australian explorer. His grandson was in 1876 created
Lord Alington.

The brothers Thellusson were sons of the Swiss
merchant Pierre Thellusson, who settled in England,
married in 1761 Anne Woodford of Southampton, and
died in 1797, leaving a strange will, by which two-
thirds of his property was to accumulate until the
death of his nine then living descendants for the
benefit of the eldest male descendant of his three
sons. The sons disputed the will, but it was pro-

[1] Buckingham, *Court and Cabinets of George III.*

nounced valid, though an Act of 1800 prevented any similar eccentricities. The testator's object, moreover, deservedly failed, for the litigation of 1856-1859 on the construction of the will devoured a large portion of the inheritance, which meanwhile had not inordinately increased. In visiting Paris the Thellussons may have hoped to recover money due to their father, for he had been French Consul in London, and was denounced by John Oswald at the Jacobin Club on the 30th September 1792, on the authority of Paine and Frost, as a vilifier of the Revolution and a friend of Pitt. Thellusson, Oswald alleged, had refused to forward consignments of arms to France. If we are to believe a scurrilous pamphlet by Rutledge, Necker, who was originally clerk to Thellusson's brother George in Paris, made the acquaintance of his future wife, Suzanne Curchod, through her being governess to the children of the Thellussons' sister, Madame de Vermeron. Fournier [1] suggests that the testator's object was not for the money to accumulate, but to meet the possible claims of descendants of guillotined Frenchmen who had intrusted funds to him; but this is obviously far-fetched. The eldest son, who did not visit Paris, was in 1806 created Lord Rendlesham.

Thompson, if, as seems probable, the same man as the M.P. for Midhurst 1807-1818, was the father of General Thomas Perronet Thompson, M.P., the free-trade orator. Tierney spent the summer and autumn of 1802 at Boulogne, but did not go on to Paris. One would have expected him, however, to search there

[1] *Les Rues de Paris.*

for traces of his father, who died during the Revolution after thirty years' residence in that capital. Tyrrwhitt was secretary to the Prince of Wales, and was afterwards Usher of the Black Rod. He was knighted in 1814. Villiers, eventually third Earl of Clarendon, was famous for telling long-winded stories. He was Envoy to Portugal from 1808 to 1810, and was uncle to the diplomatist of our own time. On his honeymoon in 1791, on his way to Rome, he saw the French king and queen dine in public at the Tuileries. Coulson Walhope, son of the Earl of Portsmouth, was on his honeymoon trip, from which, as we shall see, he never returned. Sir Thomas Wallace had previously visited Italy. He subsequently held various public posts, and in 1828 became Lord Wallace. Wyndham was brother of Lord Egremont; his other brother William, ambassador at Florence, had visited Paris in 1791. Lord Yarmouth, son and successor of the Marquis of Hertford, was destined to be depicted in *Vanity Fair* as Lord Steyne and in *Coningsby* as Lord Monmouth. He had in 1798 married Maria Fagniani, putative daughter of John Baptist Fagniani. Her paternity was claimed both by George Selwyn and the Marquis of Queensberry, commonly known as 'Old Q.' The latter bequeathed his property to Lord and Lady Yarmouth, a codicil which reduced the amount to £250,000 being declared invalid.

Eight of these M.P.'s, Erskine, Fitzpatrick, Francis, Jekyll, St. John, William Smith, Lord R. Spencer, and Thompson had voted with Fox in 1794 for peace with France.

Several ex-M.P.'s may be here mentioned. Passing
over Beckford, of whom we shall speak hereafter, there
was Philip Champion de Crespigny, King's Proctor,
who sat for Sudbury in 1796. Sir Harry Featherstonehaugh had sat in two Parliaments for Portsmouth. Sir
Abraham Hume, an F.R.S., had represented Petersfield
from 1774 to 1780. He collected old paintings, fossils,
and minerals, and ultimately published a biography of
Titian. Sir Elijah Impey, ex-Chief-Justice of Bengal,
had sat for New Romney in 1790. He was solicitous
of recovering money invested in the French funds, and
Madame Grand is said to have welcomed his arrival
as likely to facilitate proof of the divorce required for
her marriage to Talleyrand, for Impey had tried Grand's
suit against her. Sir John Ingilby was elected for East
Retford in 1781. Temple Luttrell, who sat for Mel-
bourne Port from 1774 to 1780, was son of Lord Irnham
and brother to the Earl of Carhampton. His sister
Anne, widow of Christopher Horton, had married the
Duke of Cumberland, so that when Luttrell was arrested
at Boulogne in 1793 he was styled George III.'s brother-
in-law. In 1789, as a member of the Jamaica Council,
he drew up a remonstrance to Parliament against the
suppression of the slave-trade. He had shown more enlightenment in the House of Commons in advocating
conciliation to the American colonies and in predicting
their indomitable resistance. Matthew Montagu, nephew
and heir of the great society leader Elizabeth Montagu
(née Robinson), to whose gatherings the term blue-stock-
ing was first applied, had sat in Parliament from 1786
to 1790 and was destined to re-enter it in 1806. In 1820

he succeeded his brother as Lord Rokeby. Richard
Oliver had in 1790 represented the County Limerick,
for which his son now sat; we shall hear of him again.
William Maule Ramsay, younger son of the Earl of
Dalhousie, regained his seat in Parliament in 1805.
In 1831 he was created Lord Panmure, and afterwards
succeeded his cousin in the title of Lord Dalhousie.
We shall hear of him, too, again. Henry Seymour,
a kinsman of the Duke of Somerset, had been the
penultimate lover of Madame Dubarry.[1] He arrived
with his daughter Georgina, widow of Comte de
Durfort, as early as the 1st November 1801, but did
not think it necessary or feasible, it seems, to claim
the restitution of his private papers, confiscated on
his flight in 1792. Even if he had claimed them he
would have missed a bundle of Madame Dubarry's
love-letters, which had somehow been abstracted, and
was discovered many years afterwards in a Paris book-
stall. Possibly having been registered as an *émigré*,
as though a foreigner could logically be so treated, he
feared that to claim his papers might have entailed
a denial of his right to revisit France. His French
wife, whom he had dismissed on good grounds, was
probably the 'Lady' Seymour who in 1806 was living
on a handsome income at Cleves. Sir Robert Smyth,
who had been unseated at Cardigan in 1775, but had
sat for Colchester in 1785-1790, had, like Luttrell,
suffered imprisonment in Paris during the Revolution,
but through Paine, with whom his wife corresponded

[1] See my *Englishmen in the French Revolution*, and *Westminster Review*, January 1897.

while he was in prison, had in 1796 obtained a passport for Hamburg. He now returned to Paris to open a bank, but making a journey back to London he suddenly died there in April 1802.

Prospective M.P.'s may here be mentioned. There was Lord Althorp, who, just of age, was sent by his father Earl Spencer, the great bibliophile, to France and Italy in order to cease running into debt and to acquire polish; but he refused to go into Continental society, was bored by pictures, and came home as unmannerly as ever, without having even learned French. He nevertheless developed into a prominent Whig statesman, and was Chancellor of the Exchequer in the Grey Cabinet. His accession to the Upper House in 1835 gave William IV. a pretext for dismissing the ministry. He then retired into private life. Alexander Baring, son of Sir Francis and afterwards Lord Ashburton, sat in the House of Commons from 1806 to 1835, was President of the Board of Trade in 1834, and in 1842 negotiated the Maine Boundary Treaty with America. A Mr. Benyon was probably Benjamin Benyon, M.P. for Stafford in 1819. Lord Blayney, who in 1806 was returned for Old Sarum, was shortly destined to revisit France against his will. Sir Charles Burrell, another visitor, was elected in the same year for Shoreham. Arthur Harrington Champernowne, elected for Saltash in 1806, was a friend of Samuel Rogers. Cæsar Colclough, who, imprisoned in 1793-1794,[1] had apparently remained in France, became in 1818 M.P. for Wexford. William Congreve, the inventor of the rocket bearing

[1] See my *Paris in* 1789-1794.

his name, became in 1812 member for Gatton, and in 1814 succeeded to his father's baronetcy. Sir Arthur Chichester sat for Carrickfergus in 1812. General Sir Charles Grogan Craufurd, son of Sir Alexander and nephew of Quintin Craufurd, translated Tieck's *History of the Seven Years' War*, and in 1800 had married the Dowager-Duchess of Newcastle. Sent as Commissioner to the Austrian army, he was wounded, and resigned his post in favour of his brother Robert, M.P. for East Retford in 1806. He died in 1821.

Lord Duncannon, who in 1844 succeeded his father as Earl of Bessborough, but in 1802 was only just of age, supported Catholic Emancipation, introduced O'Connell to the House of Commons when he refused to take the oath, and helped to frame the Reform Bill. In 1831 he was Commissioner of Woods and Forests; in 1834 he was called up to the Lords, and from 1846 till his death in 1848 he was Lord Lieutenant of Ireland. Robert Ferguson of Raith was a Scottish member in 1806-1807 and again in 1831-1841. Of him we shall hear, not to his credit. Hudson Gurney, a Norwich banker, of a famous Quaker family, had an uncle Bartlett Gurney, F.S.A., who in 1796 all but defeated Windham at Norwich. Bartlett had turned Unitarian, but in 1803 was buried with the Quakers. Hudson also renounced Quakerism, or rather Quakerism renounced him, on account of his contributing to the war patriotic fund of 1804, yet friendly relations were afterwards revived. He sat in six parliaments, and died in 1864 at the age of eighty-nine. I remember seeing him as a corpulent old man, who had to be lifted in and out of his carriage.

D

William Haldimand, son of a Swiss merchant settled
in London, was so precocious a financier that at twenty-
five years of age—seven years after his Paris visit—
he became a director of the Bank of England. His
brother, who accompanied him, apparently died young.
William represented Ipswich from 1820 to 1826. He
was munificent in his gifts to charities and to the Greek
war of liberation. In 1828 he retired to Lausanne, and
on his death in 1862 bequeathed most of his property
to a blind asylum there. His sister was Mrs. Marcet,
the friend of Sydney Smith, and well known as a
populariser of science and political economy. Hugh
Hamersley, M.P. for Helston in 1812, will come under
another category. Richard Heber, elder brother of
the bishop, and a great book-collector, was member
for Oxford University from 1821 to 1826. Sir Thomas
Liddell, elected for Durham in 1806, became Lord
Ravensworth and father of a Dean of Christchurch.
James Mackintosh, who in 1813, on his return from
Bombay, where he had been recorder, was elected for
Nairn, and retained the seat till his death in 1832, was
the author of the famous answer to Burke. Napoleon,
unaware that he had since 'abhorred, abjured, and
for ever renounced the French Revolution, the greatest
scourge of the world, and the chief stain upon human
annals,' complimented Mackintosh on his pamphlet,
—or rather intended to have done so—for the order of
presentations having been altered he addressed the
compliment to some other Englishman. Shortly after
his return Mackintosh defended Peltier, prosecuted for
libelling Napoleon. Viscount Maitland, afterwards

Earl of Lauderdale, was returned for Camelford in 1806. William (afterwards Sir William) Oglander sat for Bodmin. Viscount Ossulston sat for Berwick in 1820. Samuel Romilly, who in 1806 became Solicitor-General and M.P. for Queensborough, was the great advocate of the mitigation of the penal code, so as to limit capital punishment to cases of murder. He had seen Paris in August 1789. Sir William Rowley represented Suffolk in 1812, Sir Thomas Turton, Southwark in 1810-1820, and Sir Walter Stirling, St. Ives in 1807. William Young, whose father wrote a history of Athens, sat for St. Mawes and became Governor of Tobago.

There was a perfect swarm of peers and peers' sons;[1] the elderly or middle-aged anxious to see how Paris looked after the Revolution, the younger eager to make acquaintance with it. Some, moreover, were on their way to Italy, for Lemaitre found at Naples, in February 1803, Lords Aberdeen, Mount Cashell, Grantham, Althorp, Brooke, and Beverley, besides Sir Charles Douglas, Sir Thomas Tancred, and the Cheshire Egertons, with Lady Hester Stanhope in their charge. The Dowager-Duchess of Cumberland, whose marriage led to the Royal Marriage Act, a widow since 1790, was also on her way to Nice, but stayed a month in Paris for medical advice. According to the *Times* she paid a hundred guineas a month for second-rate apartments, and not having been presented at the Court of St. James's was not received by Madame Bonaparte, although previously to the Revolution she had been treated at Metz as a royal personage.

The Duke of Bedford interests us chiefly as the father

[1] See Appendix B.

of Lord John Russell, then a boy of eleven, who was
left behind with his two brothers at school.   The Duke
was not a stranger to France.   In March 1788 he and
his wife, the latter on the verge of her confinement,
were staying at Montpellier and waiting for that event.
Her father, Viscount Torrington, who was apparently
living in Paris, wrote to Louis XVI.'s Minister of the
Household to ask what should be done to certify the
expected birth.   This was of some importance, for the
traveller's elder brother was unlikely to marry.   The
Minister advised him to call in two local notaries,
adding that it might be well to get a certificate also
from the British Embassy at Paris.[1]   The child was born
on the 13th May, and became heir to the Duke of
Bedford, for his father had in March 1802 succeeded
his brother, who bequeathed £5000 to Fox.   He had
learned French when a youth at Orleans, together with
the Duke of Cleveland, and the Duke of Dorset then
took them both to Versailles, where Marie Antoinette
played billiards with them.   Both went on to Rome
where they went to Cardinal York's weekly receptions.
Sir Harry Featherstonehaugh was now his travelling
companion.   The Duke's arrival on the 20th April
1803 was considered a sign of the duration of peace,
but he apparently went over to fetch the Duchess
of Gordon and her daughter Lady Georgina, whom
he, a widower since October 1801, took for his second
wife five weeks after his return.   Georgina had been
engaged to his deceased brother, who left her a lock of
his hair, and her mother made her go into mourning

[1] O. 1, 486.

for him, saying, 'It is a feather in a girl's cap to have been intended for the Duke of Bedford.'[1] The Duchess was reported to have said that she hoped to see Napoleon breakfast in Ireland, dine in London, and sup at Gordon Castle, but this is a manifest invention. There may be more truth in the story that she obtained recruits in 1794 for her son's Highland regiment (now the 2nd Gordon Highlanders) by placing a shilling between her lips to be kissed by them, yet this seems a variation of the Duchess of Devonshire's kiss to a Westminster elector. She died in 1812. As for her daughter Georgina, who had an illness in Paris, she was a great dancer, and frequently danced, as Napoleon told Lord Ebrington at Elba in 1814, with his step-son Eugène Beauharnais. The *Times*, indeed, insinuated that she set her cap at the step-father himself. 'It is certain,' said that journal on the 12th January 1803,

'that some of our travelling Nudes of Fashion intended to conquer the Conqueror of the Continent. What glory would it have brought to this Country, if it could have boasted of giving a Mistress, or a Wife, to the First Consul. How pretty would sound Lady G—— (we mean Lady Godiva) Bonaparte?'

Wraxall's story that the Duchess wanted to wed her daughter to Eugène is confirmed by Maurice Dupin, George Sand's father, who met them at a dinner-party, and wrote to his mother that they were in love with each other, but that Napoleon would not listen to the

---

[1] *Life of Lord Minto.* Two other daughters married the Duke of Richmond and Marquis Cornwallis.

match. Georgina, he added, was reputed a beauty, but
like Eugène lacked a good mouth and teeth.[1]

The Duke of Newcastle, afterwards famous for justifying the eviction at Newark of forty tenants who refused
to vote for his nominee by saying, 'May I not do what I
will with my own?' was destined to give Gladstone his
first seat in the House of Commons; which Gladstone,
however, resigned in 1846 on joining Peel in free-
trade. The Duke was yet only a youth of seventeen, in
charge of his step-father Sir Charles Craufurd, who
has been already mentioned. The Duke of Somerset
deserves notice only as the father of the Duke of our
time, who was first Lord of the Admiralty and an
agnostic writer.

The Marchioness of Donegal was accompanied by her
sisters Mary and Philippa Godfrey, friends of Thomas
Moore. The Marquis and Marchioness of Tweeddale
(she was daughter of Lord Lauderdale) took with them
their young son, Lord James Hay.

Of the Earls, Aberdeen—Byron's 'travelled thane,
Athenian Aberdeen'—was the future Prime Minister of
1852. His six weeks in Paris were said to have cost him
£3000. Lady Bessborough had been at school at Versailles before the Revolution, and had been noticed by
Marie Antoinette. Beverley, a son of the Duke of Northumberland, had been created a peer in 1790. He had
distinguished himself by his courage during the riots
of 1780, and we have already heard of his son. Cadogan
had divorced his wife in 1796, so that she travelled by
herself. Camelford had refused to illuminate for the

[1] George Sand, *Mémoires.*

peace, and his house had consequently been sacked. He pretended in 1801 to be an American named Rushworth, but was arrested, and after some days expelled. In March 1803 he again landed at Calais, but was discovered and apprehended, for he was said to have boasted in London that he would kill Bonaparte. He wrote, however, from the Temple prison an abject letter to Napoleon, pleading that his mother would die if she heard of his arrest. He also threw out of the window a letter to Lord Grenville, which the picker-up was requested to forward, but it was intercepted. He was sent to Boulogne and shipped to England.[1] Jackson was afraid of his committing suicide, so that he must have shown symptoms of the mental derangement which led in 1804 to a fatal duel with Captain Best. He was reputed to be the best shot in England. Carhampton had in 1796 been commander-in-chief in Ireland. It was reported that incensed at having, in company with other English, to wait three hours in an anteroom without chairs, before being received by Talleyrand, he went next day to the Tuileries in colonel's uniform without epaulettes. Bonaparte asked him therefore whether he was a militia officer. ' No,' he proudly replied. 'Then what is your rank in the army ? ' ' I was Commander-in-Chief when the French army under General Hoche endeavoured to land in Ireland.'[2] It was scarcely fair of Carhampton thus to retaliate on Napoleon for Talleyrand's discourtesy.

---

[1] F. 7, 6307, 6339, 6534, 6481. He seems to have tried to conceal this adventure, alleging that he had been courteously received by Napoleon, which may have been true, but was not the whole truth.

[2] *Times*, December 21, 1802.

Cavan had just returned from Egypt, where he
had commanded a division under Abercromby. The
Cholmondeleys had been in Paris in 1791, their son
and heir being born there. We shall hear presently
of their equipages. The Countess (afterwards Marchioness) Conyngham is notorious for her *liaison*
with George IV. Egremont was long a prominent
figure in London society, but is more deserving of
notice as one of the earliest patrons of Turner the
artist. Elgin, of marble fame, was on his way home
from the Constantinople embassy. We shall have to
speak hereafter of his wife and her paramour Ferguson.
Fife, afterwards a distinguished general in the Penin-
sular War, wounded at Talavera and Cadiz, was great-
uncle of the present Duke of Fife. Fitzwilliam had
in 1794 been Lord Lieutenant of Ireland, where his
three months' rule was looked back to with regret.
Lady Granard, sister of the Earl of Moira, on her
honeymoon in 1780 had seen Cardinal York, and had
also witnessed a review by Frederic II. Guilford was
the son of the Lord North who lost us our American
colonies. He stayed seven months, and would have
remained longer but for the rupture.

Lady Kenmare (Mary, daughter of Michael Aylmer)
was known for her Sunday evening receptions in
London, and for a romantic story of her husband's
attachment to her before his first wife's death, or even
before his first marriage. A Gerald Aylmer, who also
visited Paris, was probably her kinsman. The Countess
of Kingston, who must not be confused with the
Duchess of Kingston, the notorious bigamist, was

accompanied by two unmarried daughters, probably
also by her other daughter, Lady Mount Cashell.   One
of these daughters had in 1798 been the occasion of a
duel in which her brother shot his adversary.   Lady
Lanesborough, daughter of the Earl of Belvedere, had,
as we shall see, found a second and plebeian husband.
Lauderdale had witnessed and sympathised with the
Revolution, Dr. (father of Sir John) Moore then accompanying him as physician.   His Whig opinions had
made him lose his seat as a Scottish representative peer
in the House of Lords, and his anxiety for the maintenance of peace made Whitworth shut his door to
him as one of ' our rascally countrymen.'[1]   His son,
moreover, a youth of eighteen, styled himself ' citizen '
Maitland.[2]   Minto, the Gilbert Elliot who, ward of
David Hume, was at school with Mirabeau, and was
consequently sent over in 1790 to bribe him into keeping France neutral in our threatened quarrel with
Spain over Nootka Sound, had been Governor of
Corsica.   He was one of the earliest visitors, was on
his way home from the Vienna Embassy, and was
destined to be Viceroy of India.   Mount Edgecumbe
was an amateur actor and musical composer.   His
wife,[3] with their young daughter Emma Sophia, afterwards Countess Brownlow and writer of *Reminiscences
of a Septuagenarian*, had previously been to Spa, where
she met the Duchess of Gordon, the Conynghams, the
Bradfords, Charles and Lady Charlotte Greville, and

[1] Cholmondeley and Guilford had also in 1794 voted for peace.
[2] *Notes and Queries*, February 6, 1892.
[3] Lady Sophia Hobart, daughter of the Earl of Buckinghamshire,
had been educated at the Bernardine convent at Paris.

Dudley and Lady Susan Ryder. She had a serious illness in Paris. Lord Oxford had a great admiration for Napoleon and also for Murat. His wife, who required change of climate, was very handsome, though not rivalling Madame Tallien. Pembroke was the father of Sidney Herbert, the statesman of our time, and in 1806 was Ambassador at Vienna. He stayed three months, and being an excellent observer and a patient listener, his account of Paris was eagerly sought for. Shaftesbury, uncle of the philanthropist of our day, took his wife, a daughter of Sir John Webb, and their daughter. Winchilsea was the father of the fanatical Orangeman who in 1829 fought a duel, on account of Catholic Emancipation, with Wellington, but happily without bloodshed. Viscount Falkland, less fortunate, was killed in a duel in 1809. Viscountess Maynard was the notorious Nancy Parsons whom Lord Maynard had married in 1766, in spite of her antecedents. She had been a widow since 1775, and had been the mistress of the late Duke of Bedford, who, by his will, continued his annuity to her of £2000. Lord Monck, who took over his wife and two daughters, was the grandfather of the Viceroy of Canada. He died shortly after his return, in June 1802. Viscount Strangford was afterwards Ambassador at Lisbon, Stockholm, Constantinople, and St. Petersburg, and translated Camoëns' *Lusiad*. Moore, Rogers, and Croker were among his friends.

We now come to the lowest grade of the peerage. Barrington, leaving a wife behind, but taking a mistress with him, probably went, from what we after-

wards hear, to escape his English creditors; but we
shall find that he got into debt in France.   Blayney
has been already mentioned among prospective M.P.'s,
for, being an Irish poor like Palmerston, he was eligible
for the Lower House.   Cahir, who crossed over as early
as June 1801, was afterwards created Earl of Glengall;
he remained till April 1802.   Invitations to Madame
Bonaparte's receptions were commonly obtained through
his wife's good offices.   Lady Carington was the wife
of one of Pitt's banker peers.   There was a rumour
that Pitt intended to marry her eldest daughter.   It
was her grandson who, in 1872, having horsewhipped
Grenville Murray on the steps of the Reform Club on
account of a scurrilous article on his family in *Broad
Arrow*, was convicted of assault at Clerkenwell sessions,
but was simply bound over to keep the peace.   Murray
shortly afterwards became an outlaw.   Cloncurry in
1859 published his reminiscences.   He was accompanied by his three sisters, of whom more anon.   He
dined with Napoleon, and made acquaintance with
Kosciusko, Helen Williams, and Madame Récamier.
He invited the two Emmets to dinner the day before
Robert's return to Ireland, from which he could not
be dissuaded.   Cloncurry in the winter of 1802 proceeded to Italy, where he presented a telescope to
Cardinal York, who gave him one of his medals, and
he returned home after the rupture by way of Germany.[1]   Lady Crofton, widow of Sir Thomas Crofton,
was a baroness in her own right.   Her daughter
Frances accompanied her.   Grantham, who was on

---

[1] Cloncurry, *Recollections*.

his way to Italy, in 1833 succeeded his aunt in the
De Grey earldom.   He was first Lord of the Admiralty
in 1834-1835, and Lord Lieutenant of Ireland in 1841-
1844, was a collector of sculptures, was President of the
Institution of British Architects, and published *Char-
acteristics of the Duke of Wellington.*   He was uncle
of the present Marquis of Ripon, ex-Viceroy of India.
Holland, who had seen Paris in 1791, protested in
1815 against Napoleon's captivity at St. Helena, and
Lady Holland, the divorced wife of Sir Godfrey Webster,
forwarded the prisoner books, in gratitude for which
kindness Napoleon sent her an antique diamond presented to him by the Pope.   Lady Holland's receptions
were afterwards famous.   Hutchinson had succeeded
Sir Ralph Abercromby in Egypt.   On his brother's
death he became Earl of Donoughmore.   In the
autumn of 1789 he had applied at Paris for an escort
to go and rejoin his family near Amiens, disturbances
having broken out there, but was told that order had
been restored.   He was Lafayette's aide-de-camp from
1789 to 1792.   Northwick was an art connoisseur.
Stawell was Surveyor of Customs for the Port of
London.

Of the eldest sons or other successors of peers,
Eardley deserves notice on account of the history of
his family.   Sampson Gideon, a Portuguese Jew, made
a fortune in London, and as a reward for financial
services obtained a baronetcy, not for himself, for a
Jew was then deemed ineligible, but for his son, then
at Eton, at the age of fifteen.   That son, Sampson the
second, was brought up a Christian by his English

mother, and was nicknamed 'Mr. Pitt's Jew.' In 1789 he was made an Irish peer as Lord Eardley, a title explained by his having married, in 1766, Maria, the daughter of Sir John Eardley Wilmot, Chief Justice of the Common Pleas. He was elected first for Coventry and afterwards for Wallingford, but retired in 1802. He had two sons, Sampson and William; the former was the visitor to Paris, but both died before their father, with whom the peerage expired in 1824. His three daughters married Lord Say and Sele, Sir Culling Smith, M.P., and Colonel Childers. Childers, the well-known member of the Gladstone Cabinet, was doubly descended from Pitt's Jew, for his father was an Eardley Childers, and his mother a Culling Smith. Colonel Molesworth was drowned with his wife on his way to the Cape in 1815.

The younger sons of peers comprised Arthur Annesley (son of Viscount Annesley), Lord William Bentinck, afterwards Viceroy of India (Duke of Portland), William Brodrick (Viscount Midleton), Lord John Campbell (Duke of Argyll), Lord George Cavendish (Duke of Devonshire), Robert Clifford (Lord Clifford), Colonel Robert Clive (Lord Clive), Edward Spencer Cowper (Earl Cowper), Keppel Craven (Lord Craven), Francis Cust (Earl Brownlow), Henry Dillon (Viscount Dillon), Lord Robert Stephen Fitzgerald (Duke of Leinster), Lord Archibald Hamilton (Duke of Hamilton), William Hill (Lord Berwick), John King (Lord King), George Knox (Lord Northland), Lord Frederic Montagu (Duke of Manchester), Augustus John Francis Moreton (Earl of Ducie), Arthur Paget (Lord Uxbridge), Henry

Pierrepont (Viscount Newark), Lord Arthur Somerset (Duke of Beaufort), John Talbot (Baroness Talbot de Malahide), and John Trevor (Viscount Hampden). Charles James Fox, Edward Paget, General Fitzpatrick Lord Robert Spencer, and Charles Wyndham, have been already mentioned as M.P.'s.

There were also several daughters of peers. Lady Elizabeth Foster, widow of John Thomas Foster, M.P., was daughter of the Earl of Bristol, and there were strange stories of her relations with the Duke of Devonshire. According to the generally accepted version [1] the Duchess, famous in election annals, was forced by her parents, at sixteen years of age, to marry the Duke, though she was in love with the Duke of Hamilton, who killed himself in despair. She refused, however, to allow him the rights of a husband, and Lady Elizabeth Foster, living harmoniously with them, had several children by the Duke, who were brought up under an assumed name. In 1789, however, the Duchess losing £100,000 at play at Spa, the Duke went over and paid her debts on condition of consummating the marriage. The result was the birth of a son and heir at Paris in January 1790. The Duchess died in 1806, and three years afterwards Lady Elizabeth agreed to marry the widower. Gainsborough painted her as Lady Foster in the picture mysteriously stolen in London in 1875 and recovered in America in 1900. She was now accompanied to Paris by her legitimate son, Augustus John Foster, who was just of age. In 1811 he was sent as Envoy to Washington, in 1814 to

[1] See article on Spa in *Nineteenth Century*, October 1902.

Copenhagen, and in 1824 to Turin.   In 1831 he received a baronetcy.   Lady Isabel Style, daughter of Lord Powerscourt, and widow since 1774 of Sir Charles Stylo, had been a prisoner in France in 1793, and now revisited France.   Lady Anne Saltmarsh was daughter of the Earl of Fingall.   Lady Hester Stanhope, daughter of Earl Stanhope, who was not yet her uncle Pitt's housekeeper, was, to avoid a stepmother, travelling with the Egertons, probably Sir Peter Warburton Egerton.

There was also Lady Mary Whaley, *née* Lawless, the widow since 1800 of an Irish M.P., nicknamed Jerusalem Whaley, for, having said in joke that he was going to Jerusalem, he won a bet (of £15,000 it is said) that he would really go thither.   At sixteen years of age this Thomas Whaley, inheriting £15,000 from his father, was sent to Paris with a ' bear-leader ' to learn French.   He there bought a town and country house, kept a pack of hounds, entertained company, and gambled, losing £14,000 at a sitting.   He returned to Ireland, compounded with his creditors, and squandered the Jerusalem bet money.   He revisited Paris in 1791, and witnessed the King's return from Varennes. He became a cripple for life by jumping from a drawing-room window on to the roof of a passing hackney-coach, or, as we should now say, cab.[1]   He gambled at Newmarket, Brighton, and London, and eventually settled in the Isle of Man, where he brought up an illegitimate family.[2]   He married, in January 1800,

[1] Cloncurry, *Recollections.*
[2] *Monthly Review*, December 1800.

Lady Mary Catherine Lawless, daughter of Lord Cloncurry, but died in the following November. His widow lived till 1831. She was accompanied by her sister, Lady Valentia Lawless, who afterwards married Sir Francis Burton, Lord Conyngham's half-brother, and by Lady Charlotte, who became Lady Dunsany. There was likewise a Lady Giffard, probably Lady Charlotte Courtenay, daughter of the Earl of Devon, who in 1788 had married Thomas Giffard of Chillington, Staffordshire. Lady Charlotte Greville, *née* Charlotte Bentinck, daughter of the Duke of Portland, was there with her husband Charles Greville, father of the diarist. Miss Caroline Vernon, maid of honour to the Queen, was a daughter of Lord Vernon and died in 1815. Lady Catherine Beauclerk was daughter of the Duke of St Albans.

The baronets included, besides several already mentioned, William Call, John Chichester, Simon Clark, John Coghill, William Cooper, James Craufurd, Herbert Croft, Thomas Clavering, Michael Cromie, George Dallas, James De Bathe, Beaumont Dixie, N. Dukinfield, Alexander Grant, John Honywood, John Hope, John Ingilby, William James, Richard Jodrell, Thomas Lavie, John Morshead, George Prescott, George Shipley, Charles Talbot, Thomas Tancred, Grenville Temple, Henry Tichborne, Thomas Webb, Robert John Wilmot, and Charles Wolseley.

Some of these will be mentioned hereafter. At present we need speak only of Sir Charles Wolseley, who, like Sir Francis Burdett, boxed the political compass. He witnessed, and apparently took part in, the capture of the Bastille. In 1819 the Birmingham Radicals nominated him their so-called 'legislatorial attorney,' and in the following year he was sentenced to eighteen months' imprisonment for a seditious speech at Stockport. He ultimately gave up political life, embraced Catholicism in 1837, and died in 1846.

Then there were also sons of baronets : William Abdy, who succeeded to the title in July 1803, Ashby Apreece, who predeceased his father in 1807, Alexander Don, Charles Jerningham, Raymond Pelly, John Wombwell, formerly a merchant at Alicante, Ralph Woodford, afterwards Governor of Bermuda, John Broughton, and William Oglander, who, already mentioned, succeeded to the title in 1806, while there were two future baronets, Thomas Hare and Charles Cockerell.

Next to legislators and aristocrats, military men were the most numerous class of visitors. Some passed through Paris on their way home from Egypt, which had just been evacuated, and others were actuated not so much by curiosity or love of dissipation as by professional duty, for they did not know how soon they might not have to encounter Bonaparte's legions. Of this swarm of visitors I can only mention a few. There were the two sons of Sir Ralph Abercromby, who had been killed at Alexandria. The elder was General George already mentioned, who, eventually succeeding his mother in the peerage, became Lord Abercromby. The younger, Colonel Sir John, served with distinction, but died at forty-four years of age without reaching the highest grade. Sir Charles Ashworth became a general.

E

Captain Benjamin Bathurst, son of the Bishop of Norwich, then eighteen years of age, was the diplomatist who in 1809 mysteriously disappeared on returning from a mission to Vienna. Napoleon was accused of having him murdered, but the probability is that he was killed for the sake of his valuables by the ostler of a German inn who was afterwards unaccountably affluent. His daughter Rose, at the age of seventeen, was drowned at Rome in 1824 by her horse slipping backwards into the Tiber, and his brother in a race at Rome was killed by a fall from his horse. Three disasters in one family.

William Bosville, commonly styled Colonel, though he had only been a lieutenant in the Guards, must be ranked with soldiers for want of any other suitable category, though he was more wit than soldier. He had, however, served in the American War. He dined every Sunday with Horne Tooke, and, as we have seen, accompanied Sir F. Burdett, whose election he had zealously promoted. He dressed like a courtier of George II.'s time. He visited Cobbett in prison and presented him with £1000. Paine, on reaching the United States, sent a message to 'my good friend Bosville.' Francis Burke, who had been in the Franco-Irish brigade, became a British general.

General James Callender had served in the Seven Years' War and had been Secretary to the Paris Embassy under the Duke of Dorset, who, on his recall in October 1789, deputed him to wind up his accounts. He had more recently been Inspector-General at Naples, and had been sent by Nelson to the Ionian

NAPOLEON'S BRITISH VISITORS 67

Islands, where he remained till the peace. While in
Paris he made the acquaintance of a Madame Sassen,
a German, and on being detained he sent her to Scotland with a power of attorney, styling her his beloved
wife, to see after his affairs. When released, however,
he denied having married her, and the Court of Session
declared the marriage not proven, but awarded the lady
£300 damages. This latter decision was annulled by
the House of Lords, and the lady passed the rest of her
life in fruitless litigation. Callender, who married three
times, died in 1832 at the age of eighty-seven. The
French Police Register describes him, the reason why
is not obvious, as a swindler. On succeeding in 1810 to
the estates of his cousin, Sir Alexander Campbell, he
assumed the baronetcy also, but without right to it.[1]
General John Francis Cradock had served in India and
in Egypt, was destined to serve in Spain, and in 1819
became Lord Howden. He altered the spelling of his
name to Caradoc. His son, aide-de-camp to Wellington
in Paris in 1814, and afterwards military *attaché* at the
Paris Embassy, there married in 1830 the widow of the
Russian General Bagration, an ex-mistress of Metternich. In July 1830 he was deputed by the Duke of
Orleans to follow the fugitive Charles x. and ask him
to confide to him his grandson that he might be proclaimed king. Charles was inclined to consent, but the
child's mother, the Duchess of Berri, dissuaded him, not
thinking that her boy would be in safe keeping. On
Caradoc reporting his failure Louis Philippe accepted
the crown.

[1] *Notes and Queries*, May 4, 1901.

James Ferrier, brother of Susan the novelist, had figured in the siege of Seringapatam, and was questioned about it by Napoleon, always interested in India, which he thought he should have conquered but for Sir Sidney Smith and Acre. 'When he speaks,' Ferrier wrote home to his sister, 'he has one of the finest expressions possible.' General Dalrymple had visited Paris in 1791. General Henry Edward Fox was a brother of the great statesman. He was on his way home from Egypt, where he had refused to allow Lord Cavan to ship Cleopatra's needle.[1] Cavan had dug it out of the sand of centuries and set it upright, but Fox seems to have thought Cavan's love of antiquities an absurd craze, and the needle consequently had to wait seventy years for transport to England. Afterwards Commander - in - Chief in Ireland, Ambassador at Palermo, and Governor of Portsmouth, Fox was accompanied by his son Stephen, also destined for diplomacy. General George Higginson, who married in 1825 a daughter of Lord Kilmorey, lived till 1866, and his widow reached the age of ninety-eight, surviving till 1890. General Baron Charles Hompesch was a Hanoverian in the English service. Very shortsighted, in 1806 he brushed against a man named Richardson and two ladies in a London street, and a duel ensued, in which his antagonist was wounded. On his death in 1822, at the age of sixty-six, he could boast of having taken part in three sieges, seven pitched battles, and thirteen minor engagements. Robert Lovelace, probably a son of Robert Lovelace of Clapham,

1 *Courrier de Londres*, July 1802.

was reminded by Napoleon that he bore the name of Richardson's hero. Napoleon at eighteen had devoured *Clarissa Harlowe*, but at St. Helena he found it un-readable.

General John Money served in America under Burgoyne, and not finding employment at home had fought for the Belgian insurgents in 1788, had joined the French army in 1792, and had witnessed the capture of the Tuileries. The German Œlsner, who met him at Verdun in October 1792, describes him as a thoroughly English Hotspur (*degenkopf*).[1] In 1761, aide-de-camp to General Townshend, he was famed for standing on a horse's back without a saddle and then leaping with it at full speed over a five-barred gate. Hyde Park was the scene of his feats of horsemanship. He had a perilous balloon ascent in 1785, being nearly drowned in the North Sea. George Monro, probably a son of Sir Harry Monro, M.P., was apparently the Captain George Monro who was sent to Paris in September 1792 to send reports after the suspension of diplomatic rela-tions.[2] He had to pretend to fraternise with the British Jacobins in Paris, but he became suspected and left in January 1793. In 1796 he complained that though promised a handsome provision no fresh post had been conferred on him.[3] General George Morgan, who went on to Nice, had been Commander-in-Chief in India, Sir Hildebrand Oakes, afterwards

---

[1] *Minerva*, January 1793.
[2] See my *Englishmen in the French Revolution*.
[3] *Dropmore Papers*, iii. 286, 472.

Governor of Malta, had served in America and Egypt. Captain Charles John O'Hara was doubtless one of the illegitimate sons of the general who should have married Mary Berry, and who was captured by the French at Toulon in 1793. Captain Samuel Owens was an equerry to George III. Major William Norman Ramsay had served in Egypt, was afterwards in the Peninsula, and was killed at Waterloo. Colonel John Rowley, of the Engineers, was an F.R.S. and inspector-general of fortifications. He became a general in 1821, and died in 1824. General Sir Charles Shipley, a distinguished military engineer, became in 1813 Governor of Granada. Colonel Edward Stack, a native of Kerry, had served in the Franco-Irish brigade before the Revolution, had been aide-de-camp to Louis XV., and had accompanied Lafayette to America. He was on board Paul Jones's *Bonhomme Richard* when it captured the *Serapis*. He belonged to the orders of St. Louis and Cincinnatus. He joined the *émigrés* at Coblentz, but afterwards entered the English army, in which he rose during his detention in France to be major-general. He was arrested as a spy in May 1803, but was liberated on parole. If his age is correctly registered as forty-five in 1802, he was seventy-six at his death at Calais in 1833.

Captain Francis Tulloch, of the Artillery, had in singular circumstances made the acquaintance of Chateaubriand. Converted to Catholicism in London in 1790 by the Abbé Nagot, he had been induced to resign his commission and to sail with Nagot and

three other priests from St. Malo for Baltimore, in order
to become a priest and settle in America. Chateaubriand, a fellow-passenger, remonstrated with him,
urging that, however ardent a Catholic, he ought not
to abandon his family and his profession. The young
man seemed to listen to him, but the priests recovered their ascendency, and on reaching port he
left with them, not even bidding Chateaubriand fare-
well. He must, nevertheless, have changed his purpose, for in 1802 he was still in the army, and he
eventually married and had seven children, two of
whom wedded French noblemen. In 1822 Tulloch
renewed acquaintance with Chateaubriand, then Ambassador at London. In 1827 there were family
differences among his children, which gave rise to
recriminatory pamphlets. Lastly, there was John
Alexander Woodford, son of Sir Ralph Woodford
(afterwards Governor of Trinidad, Envoy to the Hanse
towns, and to Denmark). He was apparently the
Colonel Woodford who in 1815 began digging up the
bones of the killed at the battle of Agincourt, exciting
such a commotion in the district that the French
Government asked the Duke of Wellington to stop
him.

Naval officers had less inducement to visit Paris,
yet a number of them figure on the register. One
of them, moreover, was a claimant to a French dukedom. Philippe d'Auvergne, a Jersey man, son of a
navy lieutenant, had been adopted in 1788 by the
last Duc de Bouillon, a descendant of Turenne, as
a remote kinsman and heir (his only son being an

idiot), in preference to nearer relations whom he disliked.[1] The fascinating young sailor, whose elder brother
had declined the heirship, lived with the old duke
till the Revolution, when he rejoined the English
navy, and from his station at Montorgueil in Jersey
superintended the despatch of men and money to
assist the Chouans. The duke having died in 1802,
d'Auvergne now went over to try and recover his confiscated estates, but the French Government arrested
him in September 1802 on the ground of his co-
operation in the civil war. If a French duke he was
of course liable to punishment, but if still or again
a British subject he could not be prosecuted for
the performance of professional duties. Merry, his
letter to whom was at first suppressed, claimed him
as a British subject, and he was released after about
a week from the Temple but expelled. Major Du-
maresq, a fellow Jersey man, had been arrested with
him. D'Auvergne rose to be an admiral, but the
Congress of Vienna rejected his pretensions to the
dukedom. His romantic career ended in 1816 at the
age of seventy-one. Admiral Tollemache (afterwards
Lord Huntingtower) had an adventure at Paris. He
was playing billiards when a French bully nudged
his arm and spoilt his stroke. On the man doing
this a second time Tollemache pitched him out of
the window and then, warned by the landlord, ran
for his life.[2] Other actual or prospective admirals
included Sir Eliab Harvey, who fought at Trafalgar,

---

[1] Lord Sheffield and his daughter visited Bouillon in 1791.
[2] *Fortnightly Review*, July 1892.

Francis Ommaney, William Hoste, Robert Dudley Oliver, John (afterwards Sir John) Talbot, John Temple, Sir John West, Sir James Hawkins Whitshed, and Sir Edward Berry. Nelson, on being condoled with by George III. on the loss of his right arm, presented Berry as his right hand, and it was Berry who caught him in his arms when wounded at the battle of the Nile.

But the most interesting and tragic naval visitor was Captain John Wesley Wright, an Irishman and secretary to Sir Sidney Smith. He had in 1796 been captured and imprisoned with Smith, and had escaped with him by means of a forged order. He was sent in March 1803 as an *attaché* to the Paris Embassy, albeit Whitworth pointed out to his Government that this was a very injudicious selection. Whether he remained at the embassy till Whitworth's departure is not clear, but in May 1804 he was again captured off the coast, where he had been landing royalist insurgents. He was consequently regarded as an accomplice of Georges in the conspiracy to assassinate Napoleon, and was again confined in the Temple. Gravina, the Spanish Ambassador, interceded for his being treated as a prisoner of war, but Napoleon replied that as a criminal he could not be exchanged for an honest French officer, though he might be given up to the British Government to be dealt with as it chose, he being convinced that Lord Hawkesbury (afterwards Lord Liverpool) was alone responsible for having thrice landed conspirators against his life. This overture, if indeed it was an overture, came to

nothing, and at Georges' trial Wright was brought up
as a witness. He was threatened with sentence of
death by court-martial if he refused to give testimony,
but he insisted on the status of a prisoner of war,
responsible solely to his own Government for his acts.
In October 1805 he attempted to escape, whereupon
Napoleon ordered the 'wretched assassin' to be im-
mured in a cell in lieu of having the run of the
building. On the 25th October he was found dead
in his cell. He seems to have been a religious man,
and a few days before, on his mathematical instruments being taken from him, he had emphatically
repudiated resort to suicide. Moreover he had on the
previous day ordered three shirts and a French conversation book. The French Government, however,
maintained that he had killed himself on hearing of
the defeat and surrender of the Austrian army at Ulm.
Sidney Smith, on revisiting France after Waterloo,
made minute inquiries, and all the documents were
shown him, but he could come to no positive result.
Lewis Goldsmith says he was told by Réal and Des-
marets that Wright had been tortured like Pichegru
in order to extract evidence from him, and consequently could not have been released without this
infamy committed by Fouché being exposed; but he
was certainly not tortured prior to Georges' trial, and
why should he have been tortured afterwards, or, if
tortured, why should he have been allowed to live till
October 1805? Sidney Smith erected a monument
over his tomb in Père Lachaise. It had a long Latin
inscription which, without directly accusing the Napo-

leonic authorities, insinuated foul play, for it described Smith as 'confined in the Temple, a prison infamous for its midnight murders.' Strange to say this monument is now undiscoverable, and the cemetery keepers deny that Wright is on their registers, yet the record of his interment was found and duly copied in 1814.[1] Mystery is thus added to mystery.

William Sidney Smith, nephew of Sir Sidney, was captured along with Wright and was sent to Verdun. His knowledge of French proved useful in 1814, when on board the vessel which conveyed Napoleon to Elba.

Diplomatists and other public functionaries took the opportunity of making acquaintance with France or French statesmen. Francis Drake, bearing the name of the Elizabethan hero, but claiming descent from an older family, had been at the Copenhagen legation, and was in 1794 Minister at Genoa, whence he sent Grenville letters from Paris furnished to him by the royalist agent d'Antraigues, who was then at Venice, and at first in the service of Spain; but the agency was transferred to 'Monsieur' (afterwards Louis XVIII.), who was living at Verona.[2] D'Antraigues employed correspondents or spies in Paris who, whether from credulity or knavery, sent him the most fabulous stories written in sympathetic ink or in cipher. The letters of which Drake thus received copies were published in the second volume of the *Dropmore Papers*

---

[1] *Naval Chronicle*, 1816, p. 98.

[2] Drake does not give the source of the letters, but this may be inferred from Pingaud, *Un Agent Secret sous la Révolution*.

of the Historical Manuscripts Commission, where they were heralded with a flourish, but their worthlessness has been exposed by M. Aulard, the most competent French critic. This royalist agency in Paris was discovered in 1797, and on Napoleon's advance into Italy Drake fled to Udine. Temporarily unemployed by the Foreign Office, Drake in 1802 seems to have visited not only France but Italy. In 1803 he was Minister at Munich, and was enticed by Napoleon into dealings with Méhée de la Touche, a spy who sold himself to all parties and betrayed all. Méhée was for a time a secretary to the Paris Commune and had a long career of trickery. Napoleon, always anxious to bring British diplomacy into ridicule, gave orders that a suitable man should be found to entrap Drake, and Méhée answered his purpose admirably. He pretended to give information of political feeling in France and to concert a royalist rising for the overthrow, if not for the kidnapping (a euphemism for assassination), of Napoleon. Drake advanced money to this pretended spy, who took all the letters to Paris, where they were forthwith published, bringing odium and derision on the English Foreign Office. An attempt was also made to capture Drake, as well as Spencer Smith, who was slightly implicated; but he fled precipitately, and the Elector of Bavaria at the instance of Napoleon refused any longer to recognise him as envoy. He had obviously broken the eleventh commandment, so vital in diplomacy, 'thou shalt not be found out,' and neither he nor Spencer Smith was again sent abroad. Wickham, however, who had equally com-

mitted himself, became in 1802 Chief Secretary for
Ireland, and would have been sent as Envoy to Austria
and Prussia, but that those powers, afraid of offending
Napoleon, declined to receive him. He consequently
retired on a pension of £1800. English diplomacy
was no match for Napoleon with his flagrant violation
of traditions and courtesies. Retiring to his Somerset
home, Drake was highly esteemed by his neighbours;
for his tombstone at St. Cuthbert's, Wells, speaks of
his integrity and firmness as a magistrate and as
recorder of that city.[1] He married a daughter of Sir
Herbert Mackworth, an ancestor of the poet Mackworth Praed.

Alexander Cockburn, consul at Hamburg, took the
opportunity of visiting Paris with his Creole wife,
Yolande de Vignier, and his son, the future Lord Chief-
Justice, was born in France during this visit. Cockburn was in 1825 appointed Minister to the Central
American Republics. Sir John Craufurd, another
nephew of Quintin Craufurd, was Minister to Lower
Saxony from 1795 to 1803. He had visited Paris in
1791, and he now repeated his visit. We shall see that
he stayed longer than he liked and took French leave.
Charles Richard Vaughan, afterwards knighted, made
a tour in France and Germany, and then accompanied
Sir Charles Stuart (ultimately Lord Stuart de Rothesay)
to Spain, where he wrote an account of the siege of
Saragossa. He rejoined Stuart as Secretary at the
Paris Embassy at the Restoration, and was eventually

---

[1] I am indebted for this and other data to Miss Evelyn Drake of
Grampound, a great-granddaughter.

Envoy to Washington.   Arthur Paget, son of Lord
Uxbridge, was one of the earliest visitors, being allowed
a passport through France in September 1801 on
his way to succeed Minto at Vienna.   He reported
to Lord Hawkesbury that he found the roads much
better than he expected and the land well cultivated,
but the towns manufacturing silk and velvet complained of bad trade, and peace with England was
universally desired.   Bonaparte, he said, was generally
liked, for people dreaded a revolution, yet Sieyès, he
was told at Vienna, had declared that the Consulate
would not last through the winter.[1] George Stuart,
his chief subordinate at Vienna, also visited Paris.
Sir Robert Liston, originally tutor to Gilbert and Hugh
Elliot at Paris, and afterwards secretary to the latter,
was Ambassador in America from 1796 to 1802, was
afterwards sent to Holland and Turkey, and lived to
the age of ninety-three.   Colonel Neil was Consul at
Lisbon.   We may also mention a future diplomatist,
Charles (afterwards Sir Charles) Oakley, son of the
ex-Governor of Madras, who, when at the Washington
legation, offered to marry Madame Patterson, and she
was not then disinclined to accept a suitable successor
to Jerome Bonaparte.   Those who were or had been
in other departments of the public service included
Thomas Steele, Paymaster-General, John King, Under-
Secretary at the Home Office, Henry William Bentinck,
Governor of St. Vincent, Perkins Magra, Consul at
Malta and naturally interested in the fate of that
island, Donkin, secretary to George III., and Brook,

[1] *Paget Papers*, 1896.

head of the London detective force, who was sent
to report on the Paris system, while Napoleon sent a
French detective to see what was done in London.
There were also Sir Charles Warre Malet, ex-acting
Governor of Bombay, and Sir Robert Chambers, late
Chief-Justice of Calcutta, who before going out to India
had been intimate with Dr. Johnson.   This, as we shall
see, proved to be his last journey.

Law, physic, and divinity were not numerously represented.   Besides Erskine and other barristers sitting
or destined to sit in the House of Commons, there was
John Campbell, a future Lord Chief-Justice and Lord
Chancellor, and the biographer of his class.   He saw
the 'little Corsican,' and visited Tallien.   Thomas
Wilde, afterwards Lord Chancellor Truro, was registered, doubtless in joke by himself or his companions,
as M.P., though he was as yet only twenty years of age.
Curran, who had been before in 1787, dined with Fox.
Deploring the failure of the Revolution, he disliked
Napoleon.   He little foresaw that he was about meanly
to disown his daughter Sarah on account of her
attachment to Emmet.[1]   Stewart Kyd, a friend of Horne
Tooke, prosecuted with other Radicals in 1794, had
passed four months in the Tower, but had now sobered
down and become a legal writer.   The French police
suspected him of being a spy.   He had, in 1796, assisted
Erskine in defending Thomas Williams, the publisher
of Paine's *Age of Reason.*   A native of Arbroath, he
died in London in 1811.   William Duppa is best
known as brother of the artist and as the biographer

[1] See *Cornhill Magazine*, September 1903.

of Michael Angelo.   Charles Henry Okey ultimately
settled in Paris.

The physicians included Charles Maclean, who had
been with Lord Elgin at Constantinople, and had also
been in the East India Company's service, but had
been sent home by Wellesley on account of his quarrel-
some disposition.   Landing at Hamburg in 1801, he
proceeded through Holland to Paris, in order to advocate the establishment at Constantinople of an international institute for the study of the plague.   He was
anxious for information on French suicides, and Holcroft
had recommended him to apply not to a specialist but
to Fauriel, the Sanscrit scholar.   He denied the con-
tagiousness of epidemics, and his medical crotchets,
coupled with his controversial temper, prevented his
being employed by the Government, wherefore he considered himself an ill-used man.   George Birkbeck,
the future founder of mechanics' institutes, must be
reckoned among the doctors: he accompanied Curran.
Peter Mark Roget, a nephew of Romilly and a friend
of Bentham, as yet Swiss rather than English, went
as travelling tutor to the two sons of John Philips, a
Manchester merchant, Edgeworth's son accompanying
them.   His *Treasury of English Synonyms* is well
known.   William Woodville, the disciple of Jenner, and
physician to the Smallpox Hospital, had been with
Nowel to Boulogne in the summer of 1801, at the
solicitation of Dr. Antoine Ambert, to introduce vaccination during a smallpox epidemic.   He was an accomplished botanist.   Dr. Wickham, another visitor, was
likewise a friend of Jenner.   On the other hand there

were two strong opponents of vaccination. William Rowley, physician to the Marylebone Infirmary and an accoucheur of repute, and Benjamin Moseley, of Chelsea Hospital, who had been trained in Paris, and who had a strange theory that the changes of the moon influenced hemorrhage of the lungs. Tuthill (afterwards Sir George Tuthill) took over his handsome wife, of whom we shall hear again. James Carrick Moore, brother of Sir John, became director of Jenner's vaccine institute. Benjamin Travers, as yet articled pupil to Sir Paston Cooper, was the first hospital surgeon to make of ophthalmia a special study. Thomas Young was inspector-general of hospitals. Of his distinguished homonym, although also a doctor, we shall speak among scientists. Of John Bunnell Davis and Farrell Mulvey we shall hear later on. James Carmichael Smyth, physician to George III., was destined to be the step-grandfather of Thackeray, for his son Major Henry Carmichael Smyth married Thackeray's mother in India, and 'sat' for the character of Colonel Newcome. The physician received £5000 from Parliament for curing a jail distemper at Winchester in 1796 by nitrous acid; albeit a Dr. Johnston and a Frenchman also claimed the discovery. James Chichester Maclaurin, physician to the Paris Embassy 1790-1792, returned in the same capacity in 1802. He died in 1804 at the age of thirty-nine. His predecessor Macdonnal also revisited Paris. Michael O'Ryan had practised at Lyons, where Louis Badger, a silk-spinner of English descent, one of the victims of the Revolution—mistaken for his brother Pierre, he refused to undeceive his executioners,

F

but Pierre was shot a week later—had married his wife's sister. Fleeing from the Revolution back to Ireland, O'Ryan now went and settled in Paris. He was a great advocate of quinine.

Cardinal Charles Erskine, by virtue of his rank, claims priority among the clerical visitors. His father, Colin Erskine, son of Sir Charles, a Fifeshire baronet, was an artist at Rome, where he married a Roman lady. A letter to the French Government of 1808 giving an account of the College of Cardinals says :—

'Erskine, 65 years of age, affects the greatest indifference to the present state of things (Napoleon's rule), speaking of the Emperor with apparent moderation, but a dangerous man, perhaps the most dangerous of all; educated at the English college.' [1]

He was on his way back to Rome, after having been a kind of legate in England, where in 1801 he had had the invidious task of requiring the resignations of the French *émigré* bishops on account of the Concordat. Fourteen, however, out of the eighteen, headed by Arthur Dillon, Archbishop of Narbonne, refused to comply, and seven colleagues on the Continent followed their example. A good scholar, excellent company, and a loyal Briton, Erskine died in 1811 in Paris, having been interned there by Napoleon, and was buried in the Pantheon.[2] Dr. Gregory Stapleton, Bishop of the English midland district, went to St. Omer to try and recover the property of the English college of

[1] A. F. iv. 1503.
[2] *Notes and Queries*, November 30, 1901.

which he had been the head until the Revolution, but he died there, without having continued his journey to Paris, on the 5th April 1802. A fellow prelate was Dr. Troy, President of Maynooth, and ultimately Catholic Archbishop of Dublin, who was anxious to obtain fuller restitution of the confiscated property of the Irish colleges in France and to re-open them, for Maynooth with its two hundred seminarists was insufficient. He went to Lord Cornwallis, who, however, was unable to help him. A staunch loyalist, he had assisted in carrying the Union, and was consequently in receipt of a State pension. William Walsh until the Revolution had been the head of the Irish college in Paris. Driven away by that event, he eventually recovered his post. Father Peter Flood, who had narrowly escaped the massacre of September 1792,[1] was sent over by the Irish Catholic bishops to effect the fusion of all the Franco-Irish colleges. Tuite, who till the Revolution had been head of the English college at Paris, found that building converted to secular uses. John Chetwode Eustace, formerly chaplain to the Jerninghams, a Maynooth professor and a very liberal Catholic, had visited Paris in 1790, and was destined to pay a third visit in company with Lord Brownlow, Robert Rushbrooke, and Philip Roche.

Edward Stanley, the future Bishop of Norwich, and father of Dean Stanley, represented the Church of England, for he had just been ordained. He was on his way to Switzerland, and was disappointed at not seeing Napoleon. He was over again in 1816, when

[1] See my *Englishman in the French Revolution*, p. 130.

he heard drunken English soldiers singing on the boulevards:

> 'Louis Dix-huit, Louis Dix-huit,
> We 've licked all your armies
> and sunk all your fleet.'

And the French royalists imagined the song to be complimentary.[1]

Anglicanism was also represented by Stephen Weston, grandson of a bishop, who had been to Paris in 1791, and published rather flippant accounts of both trips. Then there was John Glasse, rector of Hanwell, a good classical scholar, whose sermon in 1793 on behalf of the French *émigré* priests made light of the differences between Catholicism and Protestantism. Hanwell is associated with lunacy, and Glasse in 1810, in a fit of mental derangement, hung himself at the Bull and Mouth Inn, London. John Sanford was a witness of the scene between Napoleon and Lord Whitworth on the 13th March 1803, and in *Notes and Queries* of the 3rd April 1852, as the only surviving witness—for the Duchess of Gordon, her daughters, and Mrs. Greatheed were then dead—he gave an account of it. W. Hughes, landing at Dieppe in June 1802, visited Rouen, Caen, Blois, and other provincial towns before proceeding to Paris. Of John Maude, fellow of Queen's College, Oxford, we shall hear hereafter, as also of Churchill.

The Church of Scotland may be credited with John Paterson, for he was probably the future missionary to Russia and Scandinavia. Alexander and Joseph Paterson may have been his brothers.

[1] *Early Married Life of Lord Stanley of Alderley.*

Nonconformity was represented by William Shepherd of Gatacre, Lancashire, an intimate friend of Brougham, author of a life of Poggio, and also of a history of the American Revolution.   The latter work Lord John Russell read in manuscript before publication.   Shepherd had educated one of Roscoe's sons, and was now escorting members of the Roscoe family.   He took with him a letter of introduction to Miss Williams, at whose house he met Carnot and Kosciusko, spending a most agreeable evening.   On repeating his visit in 1814, however, he apparently, judging by the silence of his *Paris in* 1802 *and* 1814, neglected to renew the lady's acquaintance.

Turning to philosophers, scholars, and scientists, priority is due to Jeremy Bentham and Malthus.   Bentham exercised the French citizenship conferred on him in 1792 by voting for Bonaparte's life-consulate, an act not very consistent with his radical doctrines.[1] His father had taken him over to France in 1764. Malthus, who, though a clergyman, should be classed as a philosopher or economist, little imagined how Frenchmen, mostly without having heard of him, would practise his principle.   He revisited the Continent in 1825.   Richard Chenevix, the mineralogist, who had witnessed and been imprisoned during the Revolution, had taken Brussels and Jena on his way to Paris.

The Institute had in December 1801 elected as foreign associates Banks, Priestley, Herschel, Neville Maske-

---

[1] Again in 1831, at the request of Lafayette, he addressed to 'my fellow-citizens of all places and times' a pamphlet on a Second or Upper Chamber.

lyne, James Rennell, the geographer, and Henry
Cavendish in the class of physics and mathematics;
Fox in that of history and classics, and Sir Benjamin
West in that of art. There had apparently been an
idea of also electing Arthur Young, Horne Tooke,
Sheridan, Watt, and Sir John Sinclair. Herschel, Fox,
and West were the only three of the eight nominees
who acknowledged the compliment in person. Herschel had the more reason for doing so as he had in
1790 been elected an associate of the old Academy of
Sciences before it was swept away by the Revolution.
Sir Charles Blagden, Secretary of the Royal Society,
whose name is attached to the law of congelation, was
presented to Napoleon, who told him that Banks
was much esteemed in France, and indeed Banks had
repeatedly obtained the restitution of consignments
to the Jardin des Plantes captured at sea by the
English.[1] Blagden seems, though a scientist, to have
had a mission from the English Government, for
Andreossi, the French Ambassador at London, writing
to Regnier on the 8th April 1803, reported a statement
of General Miranda, who was intimate with Blagden:
'He is in the pay of the Government; they were not
at first satisfied with his reports, but he has changed
his tone, and they are now better pleased.' Andreossi
added: 'I am certain that he has spread it about
here (in London) that I was in treaty on behalf of the
Minister of the Interior for the purchase of a machine

---

[1] Bonaparte, with similar courtesy, had in 1800 sent the Royal
Society Marchand's *Voyage autour du Monde,* and in 1802 he presented
copies to George III. and all the European sovereigns.

for "dividing" mathematical instruments, an object of great advantage to French industry, and requiring some precautions in order to be carried out.' Blagden doubtless renewed his acquaintance with Desgenettes, the army doctor, who since his visit as a young man to London in 1784 had accompanied Napoleon to Egypt, and was destined to accompany him to Moscow. Blagden, pronounced by Dr. Johnson 'a delightful fellow,' was also acquainted with Count Rumford, for whose daughter's hand he was an unsuccessful suitor.[1] After Waterloo he spent half the year in France and died there. Bonnycastle, Professor of Mathematics at Woolwich Academy, described by Leigh Hunt as rather vain of his acquirements, but a good fellow, fond of quoting Shakespeare and of telling stories, was another visitor, probably in the company of his friend Fuseli. Dr. John Fleming, Professor of Natural Philosophy at Aberdeen, published in 1842 a *History of British Animals.* Osborn, an F.R.S., was living in 1806 at Weimar, where he explained to Goethe the battle of Trafalgar. Edward Pigott, the discoverer of the variable star in Sobieski's belt or sword, had observed the transit of Venus at Caen in 1769, and that of Mercury at Louvain in 1786. He dated an astronomical paper from Fontainebleau in 1803, and in 1807 he observed the great comet, but the date and place of his death are uncertain.[2]

Perhaps the most eminent man of this category, scarcely less eminent than Herschel (though the latter

[1] *Atlantic Monthly*, February 1893.
[2] A Mrs. Pigott, living at Geneva 1807-1815, may have been his widow.

discovered the planet now named after him, but originally styled by him the Georgium Sidus and by Frenchmen, Napoleon), was Thomas Young. He was the author of the undulatory theory of light, ridiculed at the time in the *Edinburgh Review* by that shallow scientist Brougham, yet now almost universally accepted, and he was the first to decipher Egyptian hieroglyphics. His uncle, Richard Brocklesby, the physician and friend of Johnson, Burke, Reynolds, and Wilkes, bequeathed him £10,000, besides his house, library, and pictures. In 1801 Young, originally tutor to Hudson Gurney — both being then Quakers, but both destined to renounce Quakerism— and a medical practitioner, had found his true vocation as Professor of Natural Philosophy at the Royal Institution and editor of the *Nautical Almanac*. He has a nephew, a rent-collector at Bristol, who, however tells me that he was not born till after his illustrious uncle's death.

It is difficult to draw an exact line between scholars, connoisseurs, and savants. Charles Towneley was famous, like Elgin, for his marbles, the fruits of his Italian travels from 1765 to 1772, and purchased after his death in 1805 by the British Museum. Turberville Needham, the scientist, had been his tutor in Paris in 1752, when his uncle John, translator of *Hudibras* into French verse, seems to have looked after him. Sir Abraham Hume, who has been already mentioned, was a famous collector of minerals and precious stones, and had purchased pictures by the old masters at Vienna and Bologna. He was one of the founders of the

Geological Society, and lived to be at eighty-eight the senior F.R.S. Joseph Ritson, the antiquary, had been in Paris in 1791, when he was enthusiastic for the Revolution, and he actually adopted the Jacobin calendar. A strict vegetarian and an avowed materialist, he was latterly insane. Stephen Martin-Leake, herald and numismatist, sent over three of his sons, William, Stephen, and John, the two last likewise heralds. William Taylor, the friend of Southey, son of a Norwich manufacturer, and educated by Mrs. Barbauld, at Palgrave, Suffolk, had been sent on the Continent by his father in 1779, went again in 1788, and now repeated his visit. He was one of the first to introduce German literature to English readers. He met Paine at a dinner given by Holcroft, and had an introduction to Lafayette from his uncle Dyson, a Norfolk man whose son had taught Lafayette farming.[1] Taylor went back an anti-Bonapartist. Paine had probably opened his eyes to Napoleon's tyranny. Alexander Hamilton, a future F.R.S., had been in the East India Company's service in Bengal, and on returning to England, after accompanying Lord Elgin to Constantinople, had continued his Sanscrit studies. He took with him his Creole wife and a promising son. Few as were then the students of Sanscrit, fewer still were the students of Chinese. Thomas Manning was one of them. Son of the rector of Diss, Norfolk, in whose church Wesley preached a few weeks before his death, though all other church pulpits had long been closed to him, Manning was also at Holcroft's dinner, and we

---

[1] An E. Dyson died at Palgrave in 1812, aged eighty-seven.

may imagine his being questioned about Diss by Paine, who had been a journeyman staymaker there. In his letters to his father—all beginning 'Honoured sir,' and subscribed 'your dutiful son'—he mentions the Abbé Sicard, the teacher of the deaf and dumb, Carnot, Madame de Staël, Chateaubriand, and Laharpe. Manning, who suggested to Charles Lamb his roast pig essay, and was also intimate with Coleridge, is buried, like Malthus, in Bath Abbey.

Artists flocked to Paris to see the spoils from Italy collected at the Louvre. There was West (not yet Sir Benjamin West), with his son Raphael, who was expected to prove himself worthy of his Christian name, but failed to do so. It was this visit, perhaps, which left West no time to send a new picture to the Royal Academy exhibition in 1803; but he should not have attempted to palm off as new a 'Hagar and Ishmael' which he had exhibited in 1776. President though he was, the Academy insisted on its withdrawal. Opie was there with his wife, Amelia Alderson, who years afterwards gave an account of her visit in *Tait's Magazine*. Seated on the boulevards, the future Quakeress sang 'Fall, tyrants, fall,' a pæan on the Revolution singularly out of place under the iron rule of Napoleon; but she had not yet discovered him to be a tyrant. Opie was so dazzled the first day by the white glare of Paris houses that he talked of leaving at once to avoid blindness, but the alarm soon passed off. Bertie Greatheed, the dramatist, was accompanied by his son, who copied assiduously at the Louvre, besides sketching a capital likeness of Napoleon. His copies

were said to be so good that Napoleon refused at first
to let them leave France, but relented on the young
man's death.[1] Erskine also induced Napoleon to sit for
his portrait to Philips, R.A., who finished it through
the courtesy of Josephine while her husband was at
supper. The portrait was sold at Erskine's death and
was apparently purchased by Lord Howden. Howden,
who latterly lived at Bayonne, bequeathed it to the
sub-prefecture of that town, where it still hangs, but
not in a prominent place, so that it escaped notice
till 1895, when, in a controversy on the colour of
Napoleon's eyes, attention was called to it.[2] Richard
Cosway, the miniaturist, and his wife, the musician and
historical painter, repeated their visit of 1786, when
Richard was trying to sell to Louis XVI. some Raphael
cartoons which he had bought of Bonfield. André
Chénier, the poet destined to the guillotine, was then
passionately in love with Mrs. Cosway. He addressed
verses to her, some in her name in full, others inscribed 'd. r.,' a contraction for d'Arno, on the banks
of which river she was born. A Polish poet, Niem-
cewics, likewise enamoured of her, went to see her in
London in 1787. She now studied at the Louvre,
next went to Lyons, and then to Lodi.[3] She subsequently started a school in Paris, which did not
succeed, went again to Lyons, and eventually became
head of a convent near that city. Daughter of an
English hotelkeeper at Leghorn, she thus played many

[1] *Monthly Review*, 1826.
[2] *Revue Hebdomadaire*, October 19, 1895.
[3] Paris *Temps*, December 13 and 25, 1878.

parts.   Another female artist, Mrs. Damer, had been captured by a French privateer in 1779, but gallantly allowed to proceed to Jersey, where her father, Field-Marshal Conway, was governor.   Josephine, whom she had known before her marriage, introduced her to Napoleon, who, as previously stated, bespoke a bust of Fox.   Strawberry House had been bequeathed to her by Horace Walpole.   John Claude Nattes, one of the earliest of water-colourists and a topographical draftsman, took views of Paris, Versailles, and St. Denis.   For unaccountably exhibiting drawings not his own, he was in 1807 expelled from the Water Colour Society, but he then resumed sending to the Royal Academy.   Masquerier, of whom we have already heard, was again in Paris.   Let it suffice to name Sir Martin Shee, President of the Royal Academy; Fuseli; Flaxman, who with his wife accompanied West; Duppa, who had witnessed French spoliation at Rome in 1798; Farrington, who accompanied Rogers; Bowyer, the fashionable portrait painter and illustrator of Hume's *History*; Edward Hayes, the miniaturist, and his father, the more distinguished painter, Michael Angelo Hayes; George Bryant, engaged by the sportsman Thornton; William Dickinson, with his son, of whom we shall hear later on; Boddington; Hoppner, the naturalised German;[1] Thomas Daniell; William Turner; Andrew Wilson; John Wright; Robert Flin; William Sherlock, who forty years before had studied in Paris, the

---

[1] His 'Countess of Dysart' was sold in June 1901 for 14,050 guineas, the highest price ever given at an auction in England for a picture.

illustrator of Smollett's *History*; B. D. Wyatt, the architect; Abraham Raimbach, the engraver; Charles and James Heath and Jervis, also engravers; and Thomas Richard Underwood. Likewise an artist in her way was Mary Linwood, who in 1798 had opened an exhibition of art needlework, viz. copies of a hundred pictures of old masters and modern painters, and who went on working till the age of seventy-five, when eyesight failed her. Her Napoleon in woolwork is now in the South Kensington Museum.

But few actors had time—they can scarcely have lacked inclination—to visit Paris. John Philip Kemble, however, described in the register as *rentier*, went to see his old college at Douai, which he found so dilapidated that he had not the heart to inspect his old room. Arriving in Paris in July 1802, he made the acquaintance of Talma, who showed him, with his companions Lords Hollands and Cloncurry, over the Louvre. He then proceeded to Madrid to study Spanish acting. His brother Charles likewise went to Paris on his way to Vienna and St. Petersburg, not reappearing in London till September 1803. Their father Roger, a less accomplished actor, who never played but once in London, and then for the benefit of his son Stephen, is said to have spent from May 1799 to October 1802 in Italy and France; but this seems unlikely at his age, for at his death in December 1802 he was over eighty. Edmond John Eyre, the son of a clergyman, had left Cambridge without a degree in order to take to the stage. He was, however, an indifferent actor at Bath and Bristol. He published his *Observations made at Paris*.

We may couple with the Kembles and Eyre Mrs. Charlotte Atkyns, though she had long left Drury Lane where she was known as 'the pretty Miss Walpole.' She married in 1779, at the age of twenty-five, Edward Atkyns of Ketteringham Hall, Norfolk, who died in 1794. She was in Paris during the Revolution, and was one of those who endeavoured to effect the escape of Marie Antoinette. In 1809 she celebrated George III.'s Jubilee by a feast to the villagers of Ketteringham, at which she herself proposed the loyal toasts. The death of her only son in 1804 had then left her sole mistress of Ketteringham, but she seems ultimately to have lost her property. She was an ardent believer in the sham Dauphin Bruneau, but was nevertheless pensioned after 1815 by Louis XVIII. and died in Paris about 1829.

Let us turn to inventors. Congreve has been already named. James Watt had not seen France since 1786, when his advice was called for on the Marly aqueduct. This time he does not appear to have had any professional purpose, albeit that aqueduct was again out of repair. Thomas Wedgwood, one of the three sons of the great potter, was the future inventor of photography. An invalid in search of health, he required change of scene. He deserves mention for settling an annuity on Coleridge, and as the friend of Sydney Smith. He first went to Brussels, joined Poole in Paris, went on with him to Switzerland, and returned home in August 1803. Greathead, another inventor, doubtless wished

to introduce his lifeboat. Robert Salmon, steward to
the Duke of Norfolk and clerk of the works at the re-
building of Carlton House, had invented a chaff-cutting
machine, and probably wished to make it known in
France, while William Story took out a patent for a
blue dye.

There were also men of business and men who went
over on business. Sir Elijah Impey, who has been
named among the ex-M.P's, had been chosen as delegate
by a meeting in London of claimants for compensation
for confiscated property, an article in the treaty having
stipulated that such claims should be promptly settled
by the tribunals. The article was nominally applicable
to both countries, but England, of course, had had no
revolution and had confiscated little, if any, French property. No such claims were settled before the renewal
of hostilities, for Whitworth, reporting a conversation
with Napoleon on the 23rd February 1803, says :—

' I alleged as a cause of mistrust and jealousy the impossibility of obtaining justice or any kind of redress for any of
His Majesty's subjects. He asked me in what respect.
I told him that since the signing of the treaty not one
British claimant had been satisfied, though every Frenchman
of that description had been so within one month after that
period.'

The claims, as we shall see, were revived in 1815,
when France gave a lump sum of sixty millions, leaving
the English authorities to adjudicate on the separate
claims. The claims certainly presented difficulties, for
Merry, on the 12th May 1802, speaks of ' clamorous
demands,' and on the 23rd June of ' incessant and some-

times intemperate applications'; while on taking his
departure in December he expressed mortification at
having the claims unredressed.[1] Even private papers
were not restored, perhaps because being mostly tradesmen's bills they were not thought worth reclaiming,
but possibly because troublesome formalities were necessary. Merry had been directed to back the claim of
the Duke of Richmond to the Aubigny estates conferred by Louis XIV. on his ancestress, Charles II.'s
mistress, but in January 1803 Napoleon decreed that
no British subject could possess landed property in
France, and in 1807 Aubigny was definitely confiscated.

Among the business men, bankers may be allowed
precedence. I do not reckon Rogers among them, for
his visit had no more to do with banking than that of
his brother-in-law Sutton Sharpe with brewing. But
there were Boyd and Benfield, of whom I have already
spoken. I have also mentioned Sir Francis Baring
and his son Alexander. Hugh Hamersley, son of an
Oxfordshire clergyman, and named Hugh on account
of descent from Sir Hugh Hamersley, Lord Mayor of
London in 1627, was one of the earliest lovers of
Théroigne de Méricourt. According to her confessions
or interrogatories when a prisoner in Austria, he promised her marriage, and she remained with him till
1785; but on coming into possession of his patrimony
he took her to Paris, there indulged in dissipation, and
returned without her, but settled 200,000 f. on her.
Such a statement of course requires verification, but
the tradition at her birthplace is that she eloped with

[1] Despatches, Record Office.

an Englishman in the hope of becoming a public singer in London, for she had a fine voice. Œlsner states, however, that after bearing a son to Persan de Doublet, who dismissed her with an annuity of 12,000 f., she went to London and lived with the Italian singer Carducci, a eunuch whom she induced to take with him to Italy, but they quarrelled and parted at Genoa.[1] Œlsner is likely to have ascertained the true version of her antecedents. Did Hamersley inquire for the poor lunatic in 1802?[2] He had been agent for the French Government in the maintenance of French prisoners in England until it changed its system and left England to support them. Madame Dubarry, on recovering her stolen jewels in London, deposited them with Hamersley. He subscribed £315 to the patriotic fund of 1803, and in 1812 was M.P. for Helston. On his death in 1840 his bank was wound up and yielded only 10s. in the pound. He had married in 1810 Margaret, daughter of John Bevan, a Quaker banker, and I remember his nephew or cousin as Chairman of Oxfordshire Quarter Sessions. Herries, brother of Sir Charles Herries, probably went to fetch his wife, who had been an eye-witness of the Revolution. Thornton and Power, English bankers at Hamburg and other Continental towns, opened a branch at Paris in 1802, and in 1805 John Power applied for French citizenship; but the police reported unfavourably on the application, alleging that the Hamburg bank acted for the English

[1] *Revue Historique* (Paris), Jan. 1903.
[2] The visitor of 1802 may, however, have been not Théroigne's lover, but her lover's son.

G

Government and that the Paris branch had furnished money to the conspirator Georges, though pleading ignorance of his criminal purpose. Thornton, they added, was an illegitimate son of the well-known M.P. and writer on finance.[1] Thornton and Power seem to have amalgamated with Perregaux, who had dealings with London banks. Kensington was another London banker. William Dawes, assistant secretary to the Bank of England, was probably commissioned to report on the newly established Bank of France, and Mollien relates how Napoleon, on being shown an intercepted letter from a Paris to an English banker advising him to subscribe for its shares, exclaimed, 'Such are merchants! Disputes between governments do not disturb their alliances.'

Speaking of merchants, William Ewart was the eminent Liverpool merchant after whom Gladstone was named on account of his father's intimacy with him, while Judah, Henry, and Abraham Salomons were doubtless the uncles of Sir David Salomons, the first Jew returned to Parliament. There were also Joseph,[2] Leon, and Moses Montefiore, of Bologna origin, the first of them already the father of Sir Moses Montefiore the philanthropist, then a youth of eighteen. This Moses Montefiore was on his way to Leghorn. James and Thomas Payne, eminent booksellers of the second generation, were doubtless bent on picking

[1] A. F. iv. 1494.

[2] Joseph Montefiore, arrested in 1803 on returning from a visit to London, is described as having been born there and as residing at Marseilles.

up rare volumes. James, succeeding to the business of Elmsley, had already profited by the dispersion of such treasures in the Revolution—the Lamoignon collection for instance. He had secured many prizes for Lord Spencer to enrich the famous Althorp collection, which in 1899 was purchased by Mrs. Rylands and presented to Manchester. He also had dealings with the British Museum and the Bodleian; and had supplied some rare English books to the Paris National Library, and helped in its catalogue.

William Hayes was another bookselling tourist, and there was John Nichols, the printer and publisher, the biographer of Hogarth and for nearly half a century editor of the *Gentleman's Magazine*. He had just retired from business, and with his two daughters went to the south of France. Then there was Thomas Poole, the friend of Paine, the friend also of Coleridge and Sir Humphry Davy. He went to hear the Abbé Sicard lecture to the deaf and dumb.

From books to horses is a long jump. Edward Tattersall had been sent over in 1775 on an invitation from M. de Mezières, equerry to Louis XVI., and had much enjoyed himself. His father Richard, who supplied horses for the French royal stud, told the French host not to spoil the boy, but to make him keep his place, as he would have to earn his own livelihood.[1] The mention of Tattersall naturally suggests Philip Astley, who hoped to recover ten years' rent for his old circus, which had been converted into barracks; but

[1] Many of Richard's letters to Mezières, in indifferent spelling, are in the French Archives, T. 132.

while engaged in securing this, his London circus, in which he had introduced French performances, was burnt down. William Boffin Kennedy was a well-known florist who had Josephine as a customer, for in 1801, in a letter to Otto at London, she sent a list of flowers to be ordered of him. Lastly there was Dorant, proprietor of the York Hotel, Albemarle Street, London, who went over to cash £2000 in assignats, but found them worth just 12 f. He acted as cicerone, familiar as he was with Paris, to young George Jackson of the Embassy.

We now come to authors, whom we have reserved till nearly the last, not because they were the least important, rather the reverse, but because they are the most numerous. They may be conveniently divided into writers on Paris—chiels taking notes—and writers on other subjects. As to the former, it must be confessed that few of these accounts of Paris possess much merit or interest. There are, however, some notable exceptions. Thomas Holcroft, as 'dogmatic, virulent, and splenetic as ever' says King, had been prosecuted in 1794; but on the acquittal of Horne Tooke and others the case against him was abandoned. He had been to Paris in 1783, and again in 1785 to fetch his son back from school, when along with Bonneville, Paine's future host, he wrote down Beaumarchais's *Figaro* from hearing it at the theatre, being unable otherwise to procure a copy in order to have it performed in London. He had paid a third visit in 1799-1801, and he was now accompanied by his second wife Louise Mercier, who was born in France but brought up in Eng-

land.[1] He also took his daughter Fanny, the future
novelist and translator, who married first Dr. Badams
and secondly Danton's nephew Merget.   Holcroft in his
Travels from Hamburg to Paris (1804) gives a good
picture of Parisian society.   J. G. Lemaistre, who went
to claim a legacy, was one of the earliest visitors, for he
started in October or November 1801, remaining till May
1802.   In the latter year he published a *Rough Sketch of
Paris.*   He went on to Switzerland, Italy, and Germany,
and in his *Travels after the Peace of Amiens* (1806) he
gave a curious account of his dining with Cardinal York,
then already getting into his dotage.   Lemaistre was the
son of an Indian judge, was described by Erskine as 'a
most agreeable, good-natured, sensible man,' and was
obviously of French or Channel Isle descent.   Sir John
Carr, a Rugby scholar, wrote numerous books of travel,
his *Stranger in France* (1803) being his first attempt.
In 1898 it was translated into French by M. Albert
Babeau.   No other visitor of 1802 has had a similar
honour, but *Paris as it was and as it is* by Francis
William Blagdon, a teacher of languages, was translated
at the time into German.

John King, the author of *Letters from France*, reprinted I think from the *True Briton*, had a singular
career.   He was the son of poor Jewish parents, was
apparently named (not of course christened) Isaac, and
was brought up at a Jewish charity school.   Thomas
Paine, with whom he was afterwards to break lances,

---

[1] She was the daughter of Sebastian Mercier, and after Holcroft's
death married James Kenney, the dramatist.   She died in 1853.
Her brother accompanied Holcroft back to England, but the printing-
office started by them did not succeed.

knew him young, penniless, and friendless, a flaming
Radical. Clerk in a Jewish counting-house, he made
use of his good abilities and started as a money-lender
and bill-discounter, advancing money on post-obits to
spendthrift heirs. He was also a frequent speaker at a
debating club in Carlisle Street. In 1783 he published,
dedicating it to Fox, *Thoughts on the Difficulties and
Distresses in which the Peace of* 1783 *has involved the
People of England.* He lived in style, and is described as a banker at Egham, but seems to have been
simply a broker. As such, nicknamed 'Jew King' or
'King of the Jews,' he became notorious for litigation,
figuring frequently in the courts as plaintiff, defendant,
or witness, and he was roughly handled by cross-
examining counsel. He was, moreover, twice imprisoned for debt. He had previously visited France,
and in December 1792 he had denounced the Revolution. Twitted by Paine with his change of opinions, he
replied that the Revolution, not he himself, had
changed. At Paris he was accompanied or joined by
his wife the Dowager-Countess of Lanesborough, a
widow since 1779, and is said to have procured her son
a rich wife.[1] In any case he himself had obtained a
potentially rich wife, for the Countess in 1814 came
into possession for life of the estates of her brother, the
Earl of Belvedere. A police note by Desmarest of the
2nd October 1802 gives no flattering account of King:—

'This Englishman, a branded swindler, has just incurred another disgrace. His daughter, daughter of Lady

[1] The son, who married Elizabeth Latouche, died in 1806, leaving a
son who became a lunatic in 1826 and died unmarried in 1847.

Lanesborough his wife, last night quitted King's house to rejoin her husband M. de Marescote (Marquis Luigi Marescotti) of Bologna.   King for nine years had detained this young woman from her husband, and had always refused to give her up.   He required Marescote to fetch her in England, because he would then have presented heavy bills, which he would have forced him to pay even by litigation.   Madame M. took advantage of her stay in Paris to rejoin her husband.   All this happened under the eyes and with the approval of the Italian Minister, Marescalchi, who beforehand informed the Minister of Justice.   Mr. King has confined himself to preferring a charge of robbery against Miss Oliver, Madame M.'s lady's-maid.   King pretends to have had promises from two ministers for starting a rival English paper in Paris.   He wrote some days ago to General Moreau, Santerre, Tallien, and a fourth person to invite them to dine with him, which they refused.   It is presumed that his object was simply to obtain answers from them which he hoped to produce in London and thus make fresh dupes.   He is always careful to write his letters in his own name and that of Lady Lanesborough, the latter name procuring him deference and answers.   Senator Perregaux (a banker) who has been consulted respecting this foreigner, regards him as a swindler and as a dangerous man.'

This report must be a mixture of fact and fiction, for even if King, on Lady Lanesborough's departure from Paris in October 1802, was left in charge of her daughter, he could not have been sequestrating her for nine years.   Marescotti, moreover, when arrested at Cassel in 1807 and incarcerated at Bouillon, is described in another police report as a needy adventurer employed by the English Government.   A German translation of Goldsmith's book on Napoleon was in his possession, and he was charged with circulating pamphlets of the same kind. He was released in the following year, on the understanding that his brother at Bologna would keep him out of mischief.[1] No mention is made of his wife, who had probably quitted him. Thomas Moore met her at Bologna in 1819 (her mother also he saw in Paris in 1821), and she lived till 1840. King's banking partner Lathrop Murray, who pretended to be a baronet, became bankrupt in the summer of 1802, pleading in excuse that he had fallen a prey in Paris to King's wiles, backed by French wines and by Lady Lanesborough's attractions. Returning to England, King was arrested for debt in 1802, but published his book in 1803, and in the following year he issued a pamphlet entitled *Oppressions deemed no Injustice toward Some Individuals*. This was a protest against his rough handling in the Law Courts. He also published a *Universal System of Arithmetic*, but after his wife's accession to her brother's property, he lived abroad with her in good style. He died at Florence in 1823, and his wife, aged eighty-seven, in 1828.[2] His *Letters from France* are not without interest. He mentions that Santerre, when lunching with him, justified his beating the drums at Louis XVI.'s execution, his object being to prevent royalist cries which would have led to bloodshed.

King naturally brings us to his fellow Hebrew, Lewis Goldsmith. Born at Richmond, Surrey, about 1773, he seems to have been in 1792 at Frankfort and

[1] F. 7, 3755 and 3759.
[2] *Monthly Review*, Nov. 1823, and *Gentleman's Magazine*, Feb. 1824.

in 1794 in Poland, whence he wrote to Lord Stanhope,
urging him to bring the Polish cause before Parliament.
Stanhope, however, though sympathising with Kosciusko, stated that the Anglo-Prussian alliance debarred
him from doing so.   In 1795 Goldsmith, as a friend of
Joel Barlow, wrote a preface to the second part of
Barlow's *Advice to the Privileged Orders*, an exhorta-
tion to kings and aristocrats to renounce their doomed
prerogatives.   According to Lord Campbell, Goldsmith
had been an emissary of all the great European powers,
yet in 1801 he published a pamphlet entitled *The
Crimes of Cabinets*, in which he denounced the British
and Continental Governments as bent on dismembering
France.   It was to escape prosecution for this tirade
that he went to Paris, his wife Rebecca with their
daughter joining him.   He alleges, but it is difficult
to believe him, that he was taken to Dieppe in order
to be given up to England as a conspirator in exchange
for Peltier, and that no such exchange being feasible
he was sent back to Paris.   There, it is clear, he offered
his services to Napoleon, who conceived the idea of
starting an English newspaper in Paris to circulate
his ideas in England and its colonies.   Curiously
enough Napoleon was an unconscious plagiary of the
Commonwealth, which in 1650 founded or supported
a French weekly newspaper, *Nouvelles Ordinaires de
Londres*, for circulation on the Continent.[1]   That

---

[1] It was published by William Dugard, a Worcestershire man, but
to judge by his name, of French extraction.   He was master of
Merchant Taylors' School, London, printer to the Council of State,
and a friend of Milton.   See *Dictionary of National Biography*, which
does not, however, mention his newspaper.

newspaper lasted only eight years, and the Paris *Argus* lasted about as long. There must have been a staff of English compositors to bring it out. It gave copious extracts from the London journals, but was violently anti-English or at least anti-ministerial in its tone. Goldsmith afterwards disclaimed responsibility for its diatribes, insisting that he simply inserted the articles sent him. In November 1802 Napoleon ordered five hundred copies to be regularly sent to the French West Indies in order thence to reach the neighbouring British colonies. The paper was described by Merry as a ' despicable publication.' But in February 1803 Goldsmith was dismissed, which Whitworth notified as a sign of peace, the paper having changed its tone. His successor was Thomas Dutton, ex-editor of the *Dramatic Censor*, who soon incurred disgrace and imprisonment. Goldsmith, pleading penury, asked for 7000 f. compensation. He had, he said, been promised the proprietorship, and had been put to great expense by his wife bringing over her furniture from England. He had also paid in advance for his daughter's schooling,[1] and being threatened with assassination by the English in Paris he was anxious to leave.[2] He remained, however, for in 1804-1805 he published with Barère the *Memorial Anti-Britannique*. He also translated Blackstone into French, and he advertised in the *Petites Affiches* in 1805-1806 as a pupil of Scott and Schabracq, London notaries, and as a sworn interpreter ready to undertake translations and other business.

[1] This daughter apparently died in childhood.
[2] *Souvenirs et Mémoires*, Oct. 1899.

Returning in 1809 to England with a passport from
Dunkirk for America, he was imprisoned for a short
time in Tuthill Fields, but on his release began to
write violently against Napoleon. Goldsmith published
in 1811 the *Secret History of the Cabinet of Bonaparte,*
and he proposed in 1815 that a price should be set
on Bonaparte's head. In spite of these provocative,
not to say scurrilous, publications, he after Waterloo
settled down quietly in Paris till his death in 1846 as
solicitor to the British Embassy. One of his duties
was to hand over the letters or parcels which in those
days of dear postage and carriage were franked by
the Foreign Office, and a friend of mine, sent as a young
man to Paris to get a French polish, remembers how
Goldsmith used to quiz or banter him on the supposed
feminine source of such consignments. But the most
romantic event in Goldsmith's career, a kind of parallel to King's marriage, was the marriage in 1837 of
his handsome daughter Georgiana, born in Paris in
1807, to Lord Lyndhurst, ex-Lord Chancellor. 'I lived
in Paris,' she told Augustus Hare in 1881, 'with my
father, and I was nobody. I never expected to marry.
Why should I ? I had no fortune and no attractions.'
Lyndhurst first saw her when visiting Paris with his
first wife. He went over again, a widower, in 1837 and
made her an offer. Hare speaks of her 'clever vivacity
acquired by her early life in France.' 'I had,' she
told him, 'twenty-six years of the most perfect happi-
ness ever allotted to woman.' Both husband and wife
were curious links with the past, for the former, son
of the artist Copley, was born at Boston, U.S., in 1772,

four years before the Declaration of Independence, while the widow survived till 1891.

Another man who boxed the political compass was James Redhead Yorke. Visiting Paris in 1792, full of enthusiasm for the Revolution,[1] and imprisoned for sedition at Dorchester, he not only fell in love with his jailer's daughter, whom he married on his release, but turned anti-Gallican. He nevertheless in 1802 renewed acquaintance with Paine, who said to him, 'Do you call this a republic? Why, they are worse off than the slaves in Constantinople.' Yet Paine had originally, like many intelligent Frenchmen, admired Napoleon. Yorke's *Letters from France* were reprinted, like King's, from a newspaper.

A fourth erratic journalist was William Playfair, brother of the Edinburgh geologist. He had helped to capture the Bastille, but was so disillusioned with the Revolution that on returning to London in 1792 he advocated flooding France with forged assignats as the surest means of overturning the Republic. For this Louis Blanc has pilloried him, but reprehensible as the scheme was, Playfair—what an irony in his name!—was not even entitled to originality, for forged Congressional notes had been circulated during the American War of Independence. Although the English Government did not act on Playfair's suggestion the royalist *émigrés* did so, and Napoleon, as we shall see, followed the evil example by counterfeiting English, Austrian, and Russian notes. Playfair on this second visit to Paris had no literary purpose, but

[1] See my *Paris in* 1789-1794.

in 1820 he published a criticism on Lady Morgan's book on France. His editorship of *Galignani's Messenger*, his inventions, never lucrative, and his pecuniary troubles need not be detailed. Like King and Goldsmith he must be pronounced an adventurer and a weathercock.

Another journalist, James Parry, had just disposed of the *Courier*, and settled in France. If, as Lord Malmesbury and Goldsmith allege, he had been in the pay of the Directory he deserved, if contempt, forbearance, yet as we shall find he did not obtain any.

Colonel Thomas Thornton had visited France before the Revolution, and had shown hospitality in England to *émigrés*. He was the only visitor whose object was sport, and he took fourteen hounds with him, albeit game was scarce, as for twelve years the peasants had had it all their own way. Wolves, however, still existed. He published in 1806 *A Sporting Tour through France*, and going again after Waterloo he purchased Pont-sur-Seine. The mansion, indeed, had been destroyed by the Cossacks, but the outbuildings were capable of habitation. He sold the property, however, in 1821 to Casimir Périer, the grandfather of the future President of the Republic, and died in Paris seven years later, leaving a will in favour of an illegitimate daughter which was annulled by the English tribunals.

We now come to two lady writers. One was Frances Elizabeth, daughter of Sir Francis Bernard, Governor of Massachusetts, and wife of the Rev. Richard King, a Cambridgeshire clergyman. She was intimate with Hannah More, and founded district visiting societies and schools. She published a *Tour in France* in which she mentions that Boulogne was full of English who had remained there during the Revolution, and that you could scarcely enter a shop there without being addressed in English. She spent seven months in Paris. The other was Anne Plumptree, novelist and translator, daughter of a Huntingdonshire clergyman, and granddaughter of a Cambridge don. She accompanied the Opies. Though a democrat, she admired Napoleon and actually wished him to invade England. Her *Narrative of a Three Years' Residence in France* (1810) relates chiefly to provincial life, which is an agreeable change after so many books on Paris. I have already mentioned Francis William Blagdon, a prolific author, who, having previously visited France in 1784, published *Paris as it was and as it is*. I may also mention William Thomas Williams, author in 1807 of *The State of France*; David Morrice, a schoolmaster, with his *View of Modern France* and *Practical Guide from London to Paris*; Stewarton who wrote anonymously or otherwise against Napoleon and Talleyrand; and Israel Worsley, with his *State of France* (1806). Worsley went back to Dunkirk after Waterloo to re-open a school. In 1828 he undertook to prove the descent of the American Indians from the lost tribes. George Tappen, who was interested in painting and architecture, published a *Tour through France and Italy*.

John Dean Paul, a banker and future baronet, went

over in August 1802 as one of a party of five, accompanied by two servants and a courier.   He tells us
in his anonymous book, *Journal of a Party of Pleasure to Paris*, that a young friend of his in the uniform
of the Wiltshire Militia was tapped on the shoulder
in the Louvre and asked to what regiment he belonged.
The inquirer was Bonaparte, who frequently thus
accosted British officers.   Paul's son and heir, then
an infant, became unpleasantly notorious fifty years
later.   His daughter married in 1827 Edward Fox
Fitzgerald, son of Lord Edward.   She lived till 1891.
William Beckford, the author of *Vathek*, had paid
several visits to Paris.   In October 1782 he passed
through it on his way home from Naples.   'A little
impertinent, purse-proud puppy,' Samuel Meek styled
him in his diary, for though staying at the same hotel
he had refused to answer an inquiry respecting a
nephew of Meek at Naples.   He was again in Paris
from April 1791 to June 1792, when he ordered a
tapestry for his London house, and went on to
Lausanne, where he purchased Gibbon's library.   He
paid a third visit in February 1793, and left in May
with a passport from the municipality viséd by Lebrun,
the Foreign Minister; but the Calais authorities detained him until the Convention had been consulted.
He left behind him his two riding-horses, which were
seized for military baggage trains.   The General Safety
Committee, declaring them unfit for such work, ordered
them to be restored,[1] on the ground that Beckford had
offered to present two cart-horses which would be

[1] A. F. ii. 288.

much more serviceable, and that from love of liberty
he had lived much in France. We hear no particulars
of his visit of May 1802.

As for authors on non-French subjects, their name
is legion. Let us begin with poets. Wordsworth, it
is true, did not go further than Calais, but I have
already named Rogers, who had also seen Paris during
the Revolution, and now paid it a second visit. He
described Napoleon as having a very strong profile,
a sallow but not disagreeable complexion, light grey
eyes, and scarcely perceptible eyebrows. Fox commissioned Rogers to buy andirons for him in the Palais
Royal Arcades. Then there was Walter Savage Landor,
who started with admiration for Napoleon, but found
' not an atom of liberty left.' He witnessed the festival
in the Tuileries gardens in honour of the life-consulate,
and he wrote to his brother: 'I expected that the sky
would have been rent with acclamations. On the contrary, he (Bonaparte) experienced such a reception as
was given to Richard III. He was sensibly mortified.
All bowed, but he waved to and fro, and often wiped
his face with his handkerchief. He retired in about
ten minutes.' On returning home and reprinting his
Gebir, Landor appended a qualifying note to his line:

' A mortal man above all mortal praise.'

He called on Paine, and in his *Imaginary Conversations* (fifth series, XI.) introduced a minute description
of him. He represents him as uncombed, unshaven,
and unwashed, and as solacing his misfortunes by
brandy, yet he makes him foresee Napoleon's inor-

dinate ambition and fall.   Landor revisited Paris in 1814 and 1840.   Paine, by the way, was escorted to Havre at the end of August 1802 on his way to America by Thomas, or 'Clio,' Rickman, a versifier if not exactly a poet, who named his six sons Paine, Washington, Franklin, Rousseau, Petrarch, and Volney. They were surely to be pitied.   Another versifier was William Parsons, who in 1785 had published a magazine at Florence and had associated there with Madame Piozzi, Robert Merry, and Bertie Greatheed.   Greatheed, as we have seen, was also now in Paris.

Amongst other writers of works of imagination were Thomas Hope, the author of *Anastasia*, art connoisseur, and father of Beresford Hope;[1] William Combe, who had married Mrs. Cosway's sister, author of *Dr. Syntax*, a book widely read in its day; and Edgeworth, who was arrested and but for Whitworth's remonstrance would have been expelled.   He fancied that he had been taken for a brother of the Abbé Edgeworth, Louis XVI.'s confessor, a distant kinsman whom he had never even seen; but the police register[2] states that he had indulged in 'indiscreet talk.'   His eldest son Lovell, as we shall find, did not come off so lightly. Edgeworth was accompanied by his fourth wife, his distinguished daughter Maria, and her younger half-sister Charlotte.   He had intended to stay two years, but happily left in time.   Maria revisited Paris in 1820.

[1] His age is registered as thirty, which, if correct, settles the date of his birth.
[2] F. 7, 2232.

H

More matter-of-fact writers included Anthony Aufrere, an art connoisseur, a contributor to the *Gentleman's Magazine*, a translator from the German and Italian, and editor of *Lockhart's Letters*. Hazlitt, the critic and essayist, who was introduced to Prosper Merimée's father, the artist, copied at the Louvre, and paid a second visit in 1824. Filon fancifully suggests that the unborn Prosper was influenced by his mother's impression of Hazlitt. There was also John Allen, the Edinburgh Reviewer, a 'man of vast information and great conversational powers,' says Macaulay, but who, living with Lord Holland from 1801 till his death in 1843, wrote little. John Gifford, the Tory pamphleteer, editor of the *Anti-Jacobin Review*, a continuation of the famous *Anti-Jacobin*, had been the author, concocter, or arranger of *Letters from France in* 1792. His visits to France did not lessen his insular prejudices. In contrast to him there was David Williams, Nonconformist minister and schoolmaster, but now best known as founder and secretary of the Royal Literary Fund. He had been in Paris in the winter of 1792, but seemingly did not attend the British dinner at which an address to the Convention was adopted. Madame Roland regretted that he had not been elected a member of that body in lieu of Paine, but he had reason to congratulate himself on this. Lebrun, Minister of Foreign Affairs, entrusted him with a letter to Grenville regretting the imminence of hostilities and suggesting that, as in the previous war, a few packets might continue to ply between Dover and Calais;[1]

[1] *Révolution Française*, February 1890.

but the letter received no answer. James Anderson, whose extensive view ranged from chimneys to cattle-breeding and political economy, had corresponded with Washington on 'moral philosophy and agricultural topics.' Last, but far from least, was Henry Hallam, as yet a young man of twenty-five.

We now come to four men who made France their home. Quintin Craufurd, a nabob from Manila, acting on his maxim, 'Make your fortune where you like, but enjoy it at Paris,' settled there in 1780. He provided the carriage in which the royal family in 1791 attempted to escape. He himself had gone to Brussels, perhaps expecting to meet them, and not venturing to return, his furniture was confiscated. He was now able to resume life in Paris, and frequently played whist with Talleyrand, for cards were his passion. Herbert Croft, nominally a clergyman as well as a baronet, though he had little of the reverend about him, and was dependent on a Government pension of £200, had been the friend of Johnson, whom he furnished with a life of Chatterton. He, like Boswell, was duped by the Ireland forgeries. Just too late to succour Chatterton, he was also just too late to succour a French poet, Grainville, a cousin of Bernardin de St. Pierre; but he happily did not foresee a more direct connection with a third suicide, that of his brother and successor in the title, Princess Charlotte's surgeon. He wrote in the *Argus* in 1805 in favour of peace. Becoming the companion of Lady Mary Hamilton, daughter of Lord Leven, another state pensioner (but only to the amount of £80), Croft in

1809 engaged Charles Nodier as his secretary, and Nodier for two years turned into French his and the lady's productions. Both these amateur authors died in 1816.

The third Anglo-Frenchman was John Fraser Frisell, a Glasgow student who in 1792, at the age of sixteen, went to France to complete his education. Enthusiastic for the Revolution, he was imprisoned for fifteen months at Dijon during the Terror. That imprisonment, however, procured him the lifelong friendship of fellow-captives, Guitant and his wife, who offered him a home from 1794 to 1802, and he thus became intimate with Chateaubriand and Joubert. Chateaubriand styled him the Greek Englishman. Marrying a Frenchwoman, he indulged his passion for Greek authors, for the chase, and for travelling. On the death of a daughter in 1832, Chateaubriand, then himself a political prisoner, wrote an elegy on her. Frisell published in French a treatise on the British constitution, and presented a copy of it to Louis Napoleon in Switzerland, who promised him in return his own sketch of a French constitution. Frisell also contributed to the *Journal des Débats*.[1] He turned Catholic just before his death, which took place at Torquay in 1846.

The fourth Anglo-Frenchman was Henry Grey MacNab, a scion of a Scotch-Irish family who had studied under Reid at Glasgow University. When detained in 1803 he went to Montpellier for eleven years, there studying medicine, political economy, and pedagogy. Before quitting England he had published

[1] *Fraser's Mag.* 1860 : *le Correspondant*, 1897-1898.

a pamphlet against a proposed tax on coal, and in Paris in 1808 he wrote on education, on Robert Owen, of whom he was an enthusiastic admirer, and on the state of the world at the beginning of the 19th century. He was honorary physician to the Duke of Kent, to whom he dedicated his book on Owen and whose portrait he prefixed to the French translation. He died in Paris in 1823, leaving an unfinished work on premature burial.

Some visitors deserve notice on account of kinsmen or friends. There are Mary and Agnes Berry, for instance, the 'sister-wives' of Horace Walpole, one of whom, born in 1743, survived till 1852. They accompanied their father. Mrs. Damer introduced them to Napoleon, his mother, Josephine, and Madame de Staël. This last lady thought Mary by far the cleverest English-woman she had met. The Berrys had seen Paris in 1791. They must have been pleased with their visit in the spring of 1802, for they went again in October with Mrs. Damer on their way to Nice and Geneva, passing through Germany and embarking at Hamburg for England in May. We may dispose more summarily of Francis (brother of Sir John) Moore; William Monsell, whose son, successively Paymaster-General, Postmaster-General, and Vice-President of the Board of Trade, became Lord Emly; and Sir Herbert Pakington, grand-father of the Secretary for War of 1867-1868. Henry Bickersteth, surgeon, was the father of the hymnologist and of Lord Langdale, Master of the Rolls, while Sir Henry Tichborne and his brother James were respec-tively great-uncle and grandfather of the Roger

Tichborne personated by Arthur Orton. Henry Herbert
Southey, a youth of nineteen studying medicine at
Norwich, had there made the acquaintance of William
Taylor, whom he now accompanied. His brother, the
poet, had, on a visit to Norwich in 1798, formed a
friendship with Taylor, in spite of their political and religious differences. Young Southey became physician to
George IV. and Queen Adelaide.[1] Timothy Priestley
must have been the son of Timothy, brother of the
famous Priestley. The two brothers, both Nonconformist ministers, differed in doctrine. James Wollstonecraft was probably one of the three brothers of
Mary. He was a London merchant, and in 1798 had
been expelled from Paris, apparently as a suspected spy.
A Mr. Adderley was probably Charles Bowyer Adderley,
great-uncle of the present Lord Norton, but he may
have been Thomas Adderley, an Irish M.P. in 1790.
Mrs. Peploe of Herefordshire, who accompanied her
husband, was the aunt of Sir George Cornewall Lewis.
Anthony Storer, Secretary of the Paris Embassy in
1783, was apparently the nephew and heir of Anthony
Morris Storer of Purley, a man of fashion and a
bibliophile, an M.P. in 1772. General Scott was
probably the father-in-law of Canning and of the Duke
of Portland; he was reputed to have made money at
previous visits by gambling, and Canning's wife had a
bequest of £100,000. Shuckburgh Ashby Apreece had
a fascinating wife, the widow of a John Kerr. Her
literary receptions at Edinburgh were famous, and

---

[1] Another brother was captured at sea during the war and incarcerated at Brest.

people fancied she was the original of Madame de
Staël's *Corinne*. Again a widow, she married in 1812
Sir Humphry Davy. A Mr. Tilt was probably the
father of John Tilt, a Brighton physician who introduced into England the speculum, with which he had
become acquainted through Récamier. Denis Disney
Ffytche was doubtless the nephew of Dr. John Disney, a
Lincolnshire vicar related I think to the Tennysons,
who became a noted Unitarian minister in London, and
also of Lewis Disney of Swinderby, who added his wife's
name of Ffytche. If so, he must have been bent on
recovering his uncle's property at Chambourcy, near
Paris, for Lewis Disney, leaving for Switzerland with
his two daughters and their governess in March 1793,
had been classed as an *émigré* and had vainly pleaded
for restitution. James Forbes, a nabob of whom we
shall hear again, was the grandfather of Montalembert,
the French historian. Of Richard Trench, a barrister,
father of Archbishop Trench, we shall also hear later
on. John Sympson Jessopp, a landowner and barrister,
was destined to be the father of Dr. Augustus Jessopp.
He was accompanied by his younger brother, and we
shall hear of them too again.

Should we reckon among Englishmen George Francis
Grand, Madame Talleyrand's first husband? He was
a native of Lausanne, but entered the East India
Company's service, started an English factory, and
married in India Catherine Noel Judde, daughter of
Peter John Worle, a Dane, harbour-master of Chander-
nagor. He divorced her in India, and in 1798, having returned to Europe in straitened circumstances,

obtained a French divorce likewise. He now repaired to Paris, to solicit through his ex-wife's influence a Government appointment; but he was unjustly suspected of seeking to extort money from Talleyrand. It was alleged, indeed, that he exacted 80,000 f. by a threat of disputing the validity of the divorce, and that on returning to London he demanded an additional £10,000. 'Never did a husband,' writes a Bourbon agent, 'make so much profit out of his wife's infidelity, and never did a man play so pitiful a role as M. de Talleyrand.'[1]   What is certain is that Grand was assigned a post at the Cape under the so-called Batavian republic, really a French dependency. When England seized the Cape he remained there till his death in 1821.[2] He is said to have married again.

There were fugitives from law or justice, and other black sheep. William Ward, yeoman and land-agent of Benenden, Kent, who had been enthusiastic for the French Revolution, got into difficulties—'through slovenly book-keeping' says Mr. C. F. Hardy, editor of the *Benenden Letters*,—and took refuge in France, where he died in 1821, aged ninety-three. He had settled at Valenciennes, and under the Berlin decree of 1807 was for five years, in spite of his age, treated as a prisoner of war. His honesty seems unimpeachable, but as much cannot be said for another land-agent, Thomas Stone, who had acted for the Duke of Bedford and for Lord Digby. They had every apparent reason to trust him, for he was an Enclosure Commissioner and was employed by the Board of Agriculture in writing

---

[1] Remacle.   [2] *Gentleman's Magazine.*

county reports. His love of style and conviviality, however, led him astray, and he now absconded to Paris with his wife and five children, leaving a large sum due to Lord Digby. He for a time lived in luxury, affected to be bent on improving French agriculture, and talked of buying and stocking a large farm. In reality he had no money, and in 1804 ho was charged with forging a cheque, but was acquitted. He more than once applied for permission to visit Normandy to buy sheep, but was refused.[1] Latterly dependent on the earnings of his wife and daughter, he died in Paris in 1815, at the age of eighty-three. Speaking of land-agents reminds me that some small English land-owners, as the Marquis of Buckingham was informed, sold their property, invested part of the proceeds in the funds, so as to ensure the same income as before, and had settled in France on land purchased at ten and a half years' rental. Such cases, however, must have been very rare, and Napoleon, as we have seen, debarred foreigners from holding real property; but Thomas Talbot, brother of an admiral, may have had the idea of colonisation in France, though he ultimately obtained a grant of 5000 acres on the shore of Lake Erie, where he founded Port Talbot. As for artisans who went over, enticed by reports of high wages and cheap living, they were speedily disillusioned and were glad to return.

We may include among the outlaws, though he was not of English birth, Bodini, who had been editor of *Bell's Messenger* and had been expelled under the Alien Act. He joined the staff of the *Argus* in Paris. A

[1] A. F. iv. 1503.

note of the French police describes him as a man of caustic speech, turning everything into ridicule, and consequently having no friends. He pretended, it says, to have made important revelations to Napoleon, for whom, according to another account, he dissected, so to speak, the London newspapers.

We come lastly to *émigrés* who took the opportunity of returning to France, for several of them were Britons by birth, while others, having resided in England, possess some interest for us. There was Charles Jerningham, who had served in the French army, and now, reclaiming confiscated papers, pleaded that he had never in exile fought against France.[1] Lady Jerningham, his mother, however, was so patriotic an Englishwoman that on the renewal of the war she proposed to raise and head a body of six hundred men, who, in case of invasion, should drive all the cattle from the East Anglian coast into the interior of the country. Daniel Charles O'Connell, of Darrynane, styled in France Count O'Connell, uncle of the Liberator, was one of the earliest arrivals. Entering the French army in 1762 at the age of seventeen, he had taken part in the siege of Gibraltar in 1766, and in 1788 had drawn up articles of war by which the French army is still governed. On the fall of the monarchy he went to England, where in 1796 he married the Countess Bellevue, an exile like himself. In February 1802 he repaired to Paris with his wife and two step-daughters, in the hope of recovering her property in St. Domingo. He calculated on returning in August,

_____
[1] F. 7, 5735 ; T. 1112 ; *Jerningham Letters.*

but he stayed, as we shall see, too long.   He was
naturalised in 1818, and was made a French peer; he
died in 1835.   Another *émigré* was Arthur Dillon, a
connection of the guillotined general of that name,
who had with difficulty escaped from France during
the Terror.   Curiously enough Réné de Montalembert,
though an *émigré*, visited Paris as an English officer,
for in 1799 he had entered the British army, and had
served in the West Indies and Egypt.   He afterwards
served in India and Spain, rising to the rank of lieu-
tenant-colonel, but after Waterloo returned to France
and was appointed to an embassy at Stuttgart.   He
had married in 1808 James Forbes's daughter, Eliza
Rose, and their son, mostly brought up by Forbes, was
the historian of whom Pasquier aptly said, 'he is an
Anglo-Saxon Frenchman.'   Fagan, ex-captain in Dillon's
regiment, who also re-entered France, was despatched
in 1810 by Fouché, without Napoleon's knowledge, to
discuss peace with Lord Wellesley.   This occasioned
Fouché's dismissal.   Alexander d'Arblay preceded his
English wife, the famous Fanny Burney.   His friend
Lauriston had arranged that, after serving a year in
St. Domingo, he should retire from the French army
on a pension; but on his writing an indiscreet letter to
Napoleon to say that he could never bear arms against
England he was struck off the roll.   Hoping, however,
that Napoleon's irritation would evaporate, he sent
for his wife and child in April 1802, and on war breaking out they were unable, being French subjects, to
return to England till 1812, when, during the Emperor's
absence, d'Arblay managed to procure a passport for

them. He himself had meanwhile obtained a post in
the Ministry of the Interior.   Lally Tollendal, who went
over to obtain restitution of his property, had also
married an Englishwoman, Amelia Hardcastle, and in
April 1802 she rejoined her husband and his daughter
by his first wife.

The most prominent of the returning exiles was
Calonne, Louis XVI.'s Minister of Finance. He was
the man who, when asked by Marie Antoinette to do
something which she acknowledged to be difficult,
replied, 'If it is merely difficult, madam, you may
consider it already done: if it is impossible it shall
be done.' Shortly after his dismissal from office he
had married Madame Haveley, widow of a rich Paris
financier. She is described as English, but I am unable to ascertain her maiden name. Taking refuge
in England in 1788, and there assisting Madame La
Motte in her scurrilous pamphlet on the diamond neck-
lace, Calonne was at first very bountiful to his fellow-
exiles, but he soon quarrelled with them. He went
to Paris in May 1802, but must have intended returning to England, for he had applied to Merry for a
passport when he was taken ill, and expired on the
30th September. Another prominent politician was
Montlosier, the member of the National Assembly who,
in opposing the confiscation of the bishops' revenues,
exclaimed, 'You deprive them of their gold crosses,
but they will take the wooden cross which has saved
the world.' He had edited the *Courrier de Londres*,
which was so favourable to Napoleon that he was
allowed to return from exile and have his paper partly

NAPOLEON'S BRITISH VISITORS 125

printed in Paris. It was, however, suppressed after a few weeks, and Montlosier was appointed editor of the *Bulletin de Paris,* in which he requited British hospitality by vilifying the English. In all other respects his political career down to his death in 1838 was highly creditable. Cazalès, who before emigrating had deprecated violent measures in the National Assembly, also re-entered France, and was offered, but declined, office under the Consulate.

The Duke and Duchess de Fitz-James—he was a descendant of James II. with the bend sinister—were *émigrés* of a different stamp, being staunch royalists. So also, I believe, was Colonel O'Mahony. Patrick Wall, who at eighteen had in 1745 been with the Young Pretender, had been wounded at Culloden, and had then entered the French army, in like manner returned to France. An uncle, also a Jacobite refugee, had bequeathed him a handsome property. He died at Chatillon-sur-Seine in 1809.

The returning exiles included a multitude of priests. Sir John Carr crossed over from Southampton to Havre with some of them, one being, he says, ninety-five years of age, who was scarcely expected to land alive. There were also wives and daughters of Toulon refugees. It is unpleasant to read in Henri Martin's history that some of these clerical passengers afterwards repaid the hospitality they had enjoyed, by vilifying England in episcopal pastorals, in order to curry favour with Napoleon.

III

AMUSEMENTS AND IMPRESSIONS

Parisian Attractions—Napoleon—Foreign Notabilities—Mutual
Impressions—Marriages and Deaths—Return Visits.

IT is now time to ask what was seen and done by the
visitors. The rue de Rivoli did not yet exist, and
a labyrinth of dingy streets separated the Tuileries
from the Louvre, but the Champs Elysées were an
agreeable promenade, though of course not yet ter-
minated by the Arc de Triomphe, and the Bois de
Boulogne had recovered from the vandalism of the
Revolution, while on Sundays, when Napoleon held
receptions at St. Cloud, the road thither was as
crowded with carriages as that to Versailles before
1789. Lovers of art had the opportunity of inspect-
ing the spoils of Italy, a portion of which had to be
restored in 1815, though but for Napoleon's escape
from Elba restitution would not have been demanded.
He told Lord Ebrington who, as will be seen, visited
him in that island that he felt some remorse at having
thus despoiled Italy, but he had then thought only
of France. Not only was the Louvre thus enriched
with paintings and sculptures,[1] but the bronze lion

---

[1] Weston tells us that some of the pictures, much damaged in
transit, had had to be repaired. Shepherd noticed many soldiers at
the Louvre gazing triumphantly at the pictures conquered by them.

and horses of Venice had been placed on pedestals outside the Tuileries.   The biennial Salon also opened at the Louvre in September 1802, and in another part of the building was the Industrial Exhibition visited, as we have seen, by Fox.   This, according to a police report, particularly interested the English.   'Among them,' it says, 'have been noticed artisans, who were never tired of examining and admiring, while others tried to understand the mechanism of the objects exhibited.   Some observers conclude that this study may lead to imitation of these productions in England.' But the visitors might be proud of seeing several of their countrymen among the medallists, viz., Hall, who had a pottery at Montereau, near Fontainebleau, and Christopher Potter, of whom more anon.   Engraving on glass, too, had been carried to perfection by Robert May O'Reilly, an Irishman whose factory attracted visitors.   He published in 1803 a monthly magazine on arts and manufactures.   A member of the British Club at Paris in 1792-1793, he had since served in the French army.   He audaciously visited London during the peace, thus risking arrest for high treason.[1]   There was also the opportunity of witnessing Fulton's steamboat experiments on the Seine.   Fulton mostly lived in Paris from 1799 to 1804, vainly trying to interest the Government first in torpedoes and then, with a view to the invasion of England, in steam navigation. He lived with Joel Barlow, with whom he speculated in panoramas, then a popular novelty.   Both, however, went over to England in the summer of 1802.

[1] Redhead Yorke, *Letters from France.*

Merry granted a passport to Barlow, but did so by mistake in ignorance of his relations with English agitators, and he suggested that a list of obnoxious foreigners should be sent him, so that he might in future refuse such applications. Yet Barlow after all used an American passport. In notifying a passport to Fulton, Merry, mindful of his proposal for blowing up English vessels, added the warning, 'verbum sap.' Fulton was back in Paris in August in 1803, for in that month his steamboat, in the presence of Carnot and Volney, went up and down the Seine for an hour and a half. Another, but much less important, improvement in locomotion was the first attempt, at the instance of Dillon, a Hiberno-Neapolitan engineer, to introduce foot pavements. Guizot married his daughter as his second wife. Professor Charles, whose future young wife was Lamartine's *innamorata*, lectured on chemistry, moreover, to fashionable audiences. His electrifying machine and scientific apparatus at the Louvre were inspected by Carr. Dupuis, who had sat in the Convention, could be heard expounding his cosmical explanation of myths, which had been enthusiastically adopted by his friend Lalande and by the Abbé Barthélémi. Dupuis also claimed to have in 1778 invented semaphore signals.

The Abbé Morellet, last survivor of the Encyclopedists, might be met in society, full of revolutionary and pre-revolutionary experiences; and Roget de l'Isle, the author of the Marseillaise, frequented Frascati gardens. Henri Beyle was also in Paris, having just quitted the army, and was taking lessons in English

from Dawtram and an Irish Franciscan whom he calls
'Jeki,' but nobody could foresee in him the future
Stendhal, who was to illumine French literature; nor
did Sutton Sharpe, junior, till long afterwards make his
acquaintance.   Sénancour was probably in Paris, super-
intending the publication of *Obermann*, but he was
not likely to be seen in the frivolous or fashionable
circles frequented by the English. A few of the visitors,
indeed, attended lectures,[1] listening attentively and
putting questions to Laplace, Lalande, or Cuvier, but
the great majority were bent on pleasure. Frascati,
Tivoli, the hotel Richelieu (the *roué's* old mansion and
grounds, now used not only for a hotel but for balls
and concerts), and the so-called Hameau Chantilly
were thronged, not to speak of the theatres, which
had a very profitable season. Molé, it is true, retired
in April 1802, dying in the following December, but
there were such tragedians as Talma, Raucourt, Contat,
Mars, and George, such dancers as Vestris, who was
about, however, to retire, such vocalists as Cherubini,

---

[1] One of these was Manning. At first, indeed, imperfect knowledge
of French deterred him, for Lamb wrote to him :—'Your letter
was just what a letter should be, crammed and very funny. Every
part of it pleased me till you came to Paris, then your philo-
sophical indolence or indifference stung me. You cannot stir from
your rooms till you know the language. What the devil! Are men
nothing but ear-trumpets? Are men all tongue and ear?'
But presently he says :— '. . . the god-like face of the First
Consul. . . . I envy you your access to this great man much more than
your *séances* and conversaziones, which I have a shrewd suspicion
must be something dull.' (S. Wheeler, *Letters of Lamb*.)
Among the lectures by which he profited were those on Chinese
by Joseph Heger, a German whom he may have previously met in
London.

I

such instrumentalists as Kreutzer. In February 1802 there was the opportunity of witnessing Duval's *Edouard en Écosse,* which (though intended only as a glorification of the Young Pretender, who in France was always styled Edward) was so boisterously applauded by royalists as applicable to the Bourbons, that Napoleon, present at the second performance, suppressed it. Blangini taught singing, and among his pupils were Miss Whitworth, Quintin Craufurd's wife and step-daughter, Lady Conyngham, Lady Annesley, and Lady Liddell. The *Journal des Dames* of May 10, 1802, speaking of the influx of parents anxious for their children to learn accomplishments, says :—' In what other European city could a pupil have two musicians like Garat and Plantade for singing, two professors like Staybelt and Puppo for the piano, two virtuosi like Bode and Kreutzer for the violin, two composers like Paesiello and Méhul for music, and a man like Deshayes for dancing?' Paris, moreover, in spite of the Revolution again set the fashions, and though its transparent dresses, 'worn with such grace,' says George Jackson, 'as to reconcile you to them,' had never, whether on account of modesty or climate, been adopted in England, the *Times* in 1801 described the way in which Parisian ladies wore their hair. Lap-dogs were frequently to be seen under the arms of promenaders, or in fine weather running at their heels.[1] Shoe-buckles and knee-breeches, though not wigs, had been revived, and foreign ambassadors were resplendent with decorations and diamonds; yet

[1] Holcroft, *Travels.*

'muddy boots and dirty linen were seen at Madame
Fouché's receptions,' 'the roughnesses of the Revolution,' says Jackson, 'not being yet polished off.'
Mademoiselle Bertin, Marie Antoinette's dressmaker,
had returned from exile.   Bonaparte, too, had imposed
costumes on all public functionaries, and Paris had
never seen more brilliant uniforms.   His two hundred
Mamelukes had been sent up to Paris to figure in the
review of the 14th July, which was then, as it is now
again, the national festival, and in honour of the peace
he reviewed 14,000 troops in the Carrousel.

Napoleon took particular note of the British military
uniforms at his receptions, and many British officers
witnessed a grand review by Moreau on the 8th
September 1802.   Maurice Dudevant, the future father
of George Sand, wrote to his mother :—

'All these young lords, who are soldiers at home, question
me with avidity on our army.   I reply by the recital of our
immortal exploits (in Italy), which they cannot sufficiently
admire.'

As for private and official festivities, visitors were
all anxious to see Madame Tallien, 'our Lady of
Thermidor,' now, as I have said, the mistress of the
army contractor Ouvrard.   Madame Récamier gave
musical parties at Clichy, she herself playing on the
piano.   Madame de Montesson, morganatic widow of
the Duke of Orleans, Madame Lebrun, wife of the
consul, and Madame Junot (Duchess d'Abrantès) also
gave entertainments.   At some of these Garat's inimit-
able voice was to be heard, though he no longer sang

in public.   Madame de Genlis, though not able on her
pension of 6600 f. to afford dinners, received callers.
Talleyrand had been, or was about to be, forced by
Napoleon to marry Madame Grand, as the only alter-
native to dismissing her, in order that ambassadors'
wives might visit his house, and he was very hospitable
to English notabilities, though there is no reason to
think that our Government had given him the £16,000
on which, as Francis Jackson wrote to Speaker Abbot,
he counted for having concluded peace.   Spain, however, had given him a like sum, and Jackson satirically
suggested that such presents would serve as a *trousseau*
for the lady on the arrival of the dispensation from
Rome.   But Talleyrand received a dispensation, not
from the vow of celibacy, but merely from the obligation of daily reciting the breviary.   Whitworth was
therefore mistaken in justifying his wife's acceptance
of Madame Talleyrand's invitations on the ground that
the church had sanctioned her marriage.

The *Times* of January 13, 1803, says :—

'Monsieur, or rather Madame, Talleyrand's dinners, exceed
all others in Paris ; about 80 persons sat down to the last
dinner.   On the table was placed every delicacy possible to
be had, and a servant in livery, belonging to the house,
behind every chair.   The second course, put on like magic,
more elegant than the first ; around the room, in niches
made for the purpose, were statues of the finest marble, each
supporting a basket on its head, holding a branch of lustres
of about ten lights each, altogether making more than four
hundred lights in the room; the furniture of velvet and gold,
corresponding with the other elegancies ; three rooms were
fitted up in this manner, forming a most complete suit.   A

very handsome salary is allowed to this Minister, exclusively for the support of his table.'

Talleyrand doubtless allowed his guests plenty of time to do justice to his sumptuous fare, whereas Napoleon unpleasantly hurried over his dinners in half an hour. He deputed prefects, however, to preside in his place at less expeditious state banquets.

Lechevalier, of the Foreign Office, who had lived in England and had taught French to Sir F. Burdett and his wife and her sisters, also laid himself out to be agreeable to British visitors. There was a rage for dancing, not dancing on a volcano ready to explode, as was said in July 1830, but on the ashes of an extinct one.

Conversation, on the other hand, as we learn from German visitors, languished. The salons of the old monarchy, where brilliant paradox and ruthless scepticism had flourished, found no successors. It was not safe to talk politics, for spies abounded, and even the Institute had to avoid philosophy, legislation, or sociology.[1] Riddles were consequently in vogue. But La Métherie, the mineralogist, and his guests ventured to condemn the tyranny of the Consulate, and Besnard relates how Lord Archibald Hamilton, after hearing one of these outbursts, exclaimed, 'Too fortunate Frenchmen! You have apricots, peaches, cheap and good wine, and yet you complain,' while, turning to Besnard, he whispered: 'A peach with us costs 4/ or 5/ and a bottle of champagne or burgundy a guinea.' The old nobility, indeed, such of them as had remained

----

[1] *Mémoires d'un Nonagénaire.*

or returned, were too impoverished to live in great style, but the *nouveaux riches*, financiers and contractors, had installed themselves in rural mansions, yet did not succeed in imitating the old aristocracy. They were lavish in some things, parsimonious in others. Stables, gardens, and woods were allowed to become slovenly. 'There is at present no veritable society,' says a contemporary, and nobody in the country kept open house.[1] 'Those people who chose to be presented at Bonaparte's court,' says Mrs. Villiers (afterwards Lady Clarendon), 'were invited to many magnificent dinners and assemblies (balls) given by the ministers, but as ourselves, with a very few other exceptions, did not feel inclined to pay homage to Bonaparte, the theatres and the entertainments given by foreigners were mostly our resources.'[2] Mrs. Villiers was certainly, as she says, an exception, as also were Montagu and Ryder, a future peer who declined to be introduced to Napoleon, for it was not till the renewal of the war that admiration turned to hatred and that Bonaparte became a bogey with which children were frightened. Even then no Englishman would have gone the length of saying, as a French ecclesiastic has done nearly a century afterwards, that 'Napoleon was the greatest enemy of God and of mankind. Would that his name could be effaced from human memories!'[3]   A royalist agent remarks :—

'M. de Calonne states that in England the enthusiasm for

[1] De Bray, *Revue de Paris*, February 15 and March 1, 1901.
[2] *Westmorland MSS.* (Hist. MSS. Commission).
[3] Mgr. Justin Févra, *Revue du Monde Catholique*, June 15, 1900.

Bonaparte is not only general, but carried to an extent which it is difficult to conceive. The Court and the city, the capital and the provinces, all classes of citizens, from ministers to artisans, are agreed to publish his praises and vie in chanting his victories and the lustre of his rule.'[1]

Yet Phillips's *Practical Guide during a Journey from London to Paris*, the first book of its kind, had said:—

'We shall only express our wish that the great man who has done so much for France and mankind may moderate his ambition and make the illustrious Washington his political model.'

Englishmen anxious to see republican forms and manners were satirically recommended by the *Times*, December 1, 1802, to lose no time in visiting Paris, or the whole ancient system of the court, with all its formalities and regulations, would arrive before them. 'The ladies of the old court,' it added,—

'are in great request in the circle of Madame Bonaparte, and several of the most pronounced royalists among the emigrants are already *bien acclimatés* at the *Thuilleries*. In the gardens of this palace, no persons are admitted to walk in the Jacobin costume. *Cocked hats* are indispensable to all who would not be turned out by the sentries. The high *ton* and extravagance of dress are generally restored, and the fashions at least are as Anti-Jacobin as possible. *Tu* and *Toi*, and *Citoyen*, which for some time have been banished to the Faux-bourghs and the Offices, are totally out of use in addressing the Consul or Ministers, and would pass for the grossness of disaffection at Court. In short, everything

---

[1] Remacle, *Bonaparte et les Bourbons*, p. 99.

is returning rapidly to that gaiety, splendour, and urbanity,
which is the characteristic of the nation. It was the
ingenious expression of a distinguished lady a few nights
since at the *Thuilleries*—that "she saw the whole of the
ancient monarchy excepting the Bourbons!"'

This reminds us of Victor Hugo's well-known
couplet:—

'Ce siècle avait deux ans, Rome remplaçait Sparte,
    Dejà Napoléon perçait sous Bonaparte.'

A letter from an officer published in the same journal
on the 9th February 1803 says:—

'Nothing can be more wretched or discontented than all
descriptions of people; all ruined except a few upstarts,
who are immediately self-interested in the present system.
It is completely a military government, and the country is
kept quiet by the bayonet alone:—taxed at half their
income, and more taxes to be laid on.

'The roads wretched—cut up by the artillery and ammuni-
tion-waggons, and in no places repaired, but a little picked
in on the straight road from Calais to Paris for Lord Cornwallis. Crowded with turnpikes, the produce of which is
applied to the public purse, and not to mend their ways.
The Inns, as formerly, dirty, and good eating and drinking
very dear. The lower classes are civil,—the higher very
haughty.

'Yet notwithstanding the distress and poverty of the
country, there are no less than 26 theatres open and crowded
every night in Paris, independent of shows, jugglers, etc.
Nobody can form an idea of what an *Opera* is, unless they
have seen the present style of one in Paris—so superb.

'The Bishop of Durham would expire at seeing the dresses
of the performers. The ladies are almost quite naked, and

really not covered enough to give the least idea of modesty. There cannot be anything so profligate, so debauched, or so immoral, as the ideas or manners of all ranks of people, particularly the higher class ; and poor Virtue and Decency are entirely banished their Calendars.

' The daughter of Madame Bonaparte sits every night in a crimson and gold box at the Opera.   The Consul in one directly below, with a gilded grating towards the audience, who see very little of him.   He leaves the house before the dropping of the curtain, and escorted by a strong guard of cavalry and torches sets off full gallop for Malmaison, where he sleeps.'

Another visitor is reported by the *Times* as describing Paris as ' more immersed in luxury than at any former period.   The theatres are every night full, and the political coffee-houses, unless on particular occasions, nearly empty.   Provisions of every kind are cheap and plentiful, and the best wine may be had at three livres the bottle.'

Whether by way of entertaining one another or of reciprocating French hospitality, some of the British visitors gave receptions and balls.   Maurice Dudevant speaks of Lady Higginson's balls, where he seems to have heard French nobles decrying their own country, and he warned Englishmen against judging France by this unpatriotic class.   He may have been one of Lord Robert Spencer's guests at Robert's famous restaurant. The Duchess of Gordon and Mrs. Orby Hunter were prominent for their entertainments, and a Paris newspaper mentions those of Lady 'Shumley,' a phonetic approximation to Cholmondeley.   Jerningham speaks of the Duchess of Gordon's balls, and of her addiction to playing at *hasard,* at which she rattled the dice, and whenever she lost exclaimed, ' God damn !' Eliza Orby Hunter, aged twenty-three, was apparently the wife of George Orby Hunter, who afterwards, living at Dieppe, translated Byron into French verse, and died in 1843.[1] The Orby Hunter family were owners of Croyland, Lincolnshire.

' Paris,' wrote Colonel Ferrier to his sister, 'is certainly the place of all others for young men. Plenty of amusement without dissipation; no drinking; if a gentleman was seen drunk here he would be looked upon as a perfect *bête.*'[2] If, however, there was less drinking than in London, there was clearly more gambling. John Sympson Jessopp left with the impression that debauchery abounded. With the natural English desire to see everything, he found himself one night, with his younger brother, in a magnificent gambling-house. Somebody who had lost heavily fell upon the croupier, snatched his rake from him, laid about him furiously, then hit out at a huge chandelier, with scores of wax candles in it, and frantically smashed it. There was terrible panic and confusion. One of the croupiers slipped out through a door leading to a staircase to fetch the police. Jessopp, plucking his brother by the sleeve, managed to get down the stairs and into the street, where they concealed themselves in a doorway. In a few minutes a company of gendarmes

---

[1] Charles Orby Hunter, probably his father, had died at Paris in 1791.
[2] Reichardt, however, comparing France with Germany, speaks of the increase of drinking, and of young men deliberately assembling for a carouse; he also speaks of gormandising.

hastened up, and leaving two of their comrades at
the door mounted the stairs, arrested every soul on
the premises, and carried them off to the lock-up.
The two young Englishmen, watching their opportunity,
hurried back to their hotel. The sequel they never
heard.[2] Francis Jackson, moreover, writing to Abbot,
described Paris life as an uninterrupted picture of
vulgarity and profligacy, and the *Times* of the 23rd
September says:—

'Paris, under the Regent of Orleans, was not so profligate
and corrupt as it appears to our best travellers at present.
Gambling, debauchery, intemperance, and the insatiable
desire after public spectacles, with all the vices in the train
of indolence and licentiousness, form the monotonous
indiscriminable character of the Citizens.'

Some of the visitors must have shared in the
stupefaction felt on the 21st January 1803 at seeing the
Madeleine draped in crape in memory of the anniversary
of Louis XVI.'s death, but they were as ignorant as the
rest of the world that this audacious celebration was
the act of a man of English parentage, Hyde de
Neuville. The Madeleine, as Holcroft tells us, was then
'a grand colonnade of lofty uncorniced pillars, rising
about roofless, half-finished walls.'

British visitors had the opportunity of mixing with
some of their countrymen. There was Paine, until his
return in September 1802 to America, where his friend
Jefferson had become President, and we have seen that
Redhead Yorke and Rickman renewed acquaintance

[1] Information kindly supplied by Canon Jessopp.

with him.   He had had to wait, not only for funds, but
for a safe passage without fear of British cruisers.
When Redhead Yorke with some difficulty recalled
himself to his remembrance, Paine thus unbosomed
himself:—

'Who would have thought that we should meet [again
after the lapse of ten years] at Paris? . . . They (the
French) have shed blood enough for liberty, and now they
have it in perfection!   This is not a country for an honest
man to live in.   They do not understand anything at
all of the principles of free government, and the best way
(for foreigners) is to leave them to themselves.   You see
they have conquered all Europe only to make it more
miserable than it was before. . . .

'Republic!   Do you call this a republic?   Why they are
worse off than the slaves at Constantinople, for they are ever
expecting to be bashaws in Heaven by submitting to be
slaves below; but here they believe neither in Heaven nor
Hell, and yet are slaves by choice.   I know of no republic
in the world except America, which is the only country for
such men as you and I.   It is my intention to get away
from this place as soon as possible, and I hope to be off in
autumn.   You are a young man, and may see better times,
but I have done with Europe and its slavish politics.'

Paine, it may be feared, experienced another dis-
illusion on recrossing the Atlantic.   Yorke does not
seem to have told him of his own change of politics.

Next to Paine in celebrity comes Helen Maria
Williams, an eye-witness of the Revolution, whose
reminiscences of Madame Roland must have been
interesting.   She was visited by Sharpe, Rogers, Lord
Holland, Kemble, Poole, and Mrs. Cosway, though some

English held aloof or even sneered at her.   Her attire
and manners were certainly open to ridicule,[1] and her
cohabitation with John Hurford Stone, the refugee
printer, even assuming a secret marriage, exposed her
to misconstruction.   Stone's brother William, ruined
by twenty-one months' imprisonment and arrested for
debt on his acquittal for treason, had also gone to
France, where he became overseer of a paper-hanging
factory. We shall hear of him again. There was the
widow of Sir Robert Smyth, who remained in Paris
after her husband's death.   She and her young
children had been painted by Reynolds, and one of
those children now married Lambton Este, a son of
Charles Este, by turns actor, clergyman, and journalist.
Smyth's old partner, James Millingen, son of a Dutch
merchant settled in London, had remained in Paris
after the Revolution, though his brother John Gideon
had become an English naval official.   He was afterwards an eminent archæologist, and his son Michael,
archæologist and physician, attended Byron on his
deathbed. Anastasia Howard, Baroness Stafford, an
ex-nun, had likewise stayed in Paris after her release
at the end of the Terror,[1] though her fellow-nuns
had in 1800 found a retreat in England. She died

---

[1] Reichardt, who met Bishop Grégoire and Kosciuski at her house,
describes her as wearing a cap with long flaps covering her cheeks,
and with a large bouquet falling down from her hair to her nose, so
that with her constant nods and gesticulations there were only
occasional glimpses of her eyes and mouth. He was bored, too, by
the poetical recitations of Vigée, Madame Vigée-Lebrun's brother.
Poole, however, was pleased at meeting so many *literati*, and Meyer,
canon of Hamburg, thought the hostess resembled Angelica Kauf-
mann.   [2] *Jerningham Letters*, 1896.

in 1807 at the age of eighty-four. Her nephew Charles Jerningham called on her, but though in good health, senility scarcely allowed her to recognise him. This reminds us of her co-religionists at the Austin convent. They, too, had survived the Revolution, and the Superior, Frances Lancaster, must have had much to tell Sir John Carr of how the nunnery was turned into a crowded political prison. Arabella Williams, daughter of David Mallet, author of *Northern Antiquities*, had had more recent troubles. She had spent most of her life in Paris, but visits to London to obtain her share of her mother, Lucy Estob's, property brought on her the suspicion of the police and she was arrested. The banker Perregaux and others had to exonerate her from the charge of espionage.[1] Another but more recent resident, representing the *demi-monde*, though that term had not yet been invented, was Mrs. Lindsay, the Ellenore of Benjamin Constant's *Adolphe*, that romance of the Werther and Corinne school, in which the heroine, depicted as a Pole who deserts her old paramour and her children by him, clings to a man anxious to discard her. We do not even know her Christian name, unless she was the 'Lady Florence Lindsay' whom Lady Morgan met at Florence in 1819. She is said to have been Irish on the father's and French on the mother's side; handsome and sprightly, she had been brought up in good society. She had lived in Paris from 1786 to 1792, and her confiscated tradesmen's bills, still in the Archives,[2] indicate that she was then the mistress of Comte de Melfort, a man

---

[1] F. 7, 6251, dossier 4980.   [2] T. 777 and 1640.

of Scottish Jacobite ancestry. Another of her lovers
was Vicomte Chrétien de Lamoignon, who, the last of
his family, was wounded at Quiberon, and after the
Restoration was created a peer. She left France in
1792, and in 1795 Chateaubriand made her acquaintance in London, where she was on visiting terms with
the French aristocratic exiles. He styles her *la
dernière des Ninon*. On his going to France in
disguise in 1800 she, having meanwhile returned to
Paris, met him at Calais, escorted him, and hired
temporary lodgings for him near her own house. She
paid half the rent and another friend the remainder.
Constant met her in 1804, and after passing an agreeable evening with her, received a letter in which she
said that they strikingly resembled each other, but
' this is perhaps one reason the less against our suiting
each other. It is because men resemble each other
that Heaven created women, who do not resemble
them.' [1] Constant would have married her, however,
but for her age and for her two illegitimate children.
Charles Constant, Benjamin's cousin, describes her as
intelligent but devoid of culture. In 1801 she translated into French Cornelia Knight's *Life of the
Romans*. It is commonly stated that she died at
Angoulême in 1820; but if so it was under an assumed
name, for I have ascertained that there is no Lindsay
on the register. Then there was Mrs. Harvey, *née*
Elizabeth Hill, naturalised in Tuscany, who in 1805
was arrested on an unfounded charge of complicity in
Georges' plot. Her daughter Henrietta, a miniature

[1] *Revue Internationale*, 1887.

painter, petitioned for her release and the restitution of
her papers, the petition being backed by Denon,
curator of the Louvre. Scipio du Roure, son of the
Marquis de Grisac and grandson of the Countess of
Catherlough, Bolingbroke's sister, may almost be regarded as an Englishman, for he had been educated at
Oxford. He eloped with a Mrs. Sandon, who fired at
her pursuing husband, whereupon du Roure was
prosecuted as the delinquent. A flaw in the indict-
ment secured his acquittal, but he had to take refuge
in France. He arrived in the middle of the Revolution
and was a member of the Paris Jacobin Commune,
but was imprisoned in the Terror. He was now
studying jurisprudence and translating Cobbett's
Grammar. He went back to London to claim his
mother's property and that of a half-brother named
Knight, and died there in 1822.

The war, putting a stop to British imports, had given
a stimulus to French manufactures, several of which
were carried on by Englishmen. These were mostly in
the provinces, and English tradesmen had scarcely yet
reappeared in Paris. Henry Sykes, for instance, unable
to continue selling Wedgwood's pottery in the rue
St. Honoré, had in 1792 started cotton-spinning at St.
Rémy, though he had originally applied for and obtained the use of the unfinished Madeleine as a factory.
The Convention, on the 29th April 1795, granted him a
site for the erection of cotton mills at La Magdelaine,
near Verneuil (Eure). He was joined in 1802 by his
future son-in-law, William Waddington, of Walkering-
ham, Notts, a descendant of Charles ii.'s Pendrells.

Waddington, the grandfather of the French statesman
of our day, apparently had a visit from his brother
Samuel, a hop merchant at Tunbridge, who had
published an answer to Burke's famous pamphlet, and
in 1801 had been sentenced to £500 fine and a month's
imprisonment for 'forestalling.' His fellow hop-mer-
chants gave him an ovation on his release.   Then there
was Christopher Potter, who had been an army
victualler and whose election for Colchester in 1784 led
to the Act disqualifying Government contractors from
sitting in Parliament.   His successful opponent was Sir
Robert Smyth, and the two rivals may have met in
Paris.   He reopened during the Revolution the porce-
lain factory at Chantilly formerly carried on by the
Condé princes, thus justifying his name—*nomen omen*
—but he had now removed to Montereau.   A police
report of the 8th March 1796 thus denounced him:

'The Anglo-Pitts purchase nearly all the national property
which is sold in the department of the Oise.   Their chief
broker is a man named Poter (*sic*), owner of the porcelaine
factory at Chantilly, a man who was deep in debt two years
ago, but who has now paid up and is worth more than two
millions.   He was twice arrested under the revolutionary
government.   This man was twice M.P. in England, and
belonged to the Court party.   There is no doubt that he
is in France the secret agent of Pitt, with whom he has
been closely connected since the Revolution.   He made
many visits to England in 1792 and 1793.   Since that
time he has remained at Paris or Chantilly, where he daily
makes purchases.'[1]

[1] A. F. iv. 1473.

K

This report was made by an 'observer' named Martin, whose chief, Marné, sent it in as usual to the Directory. That body, or probably Barras, who seems to have examined these daily reports, instructed Marné to inquire whether Potter really visited England in 1792-1793, whether there was any proof of his connection with the court party, whether there was any probability of his being Pitt's agent, and what purchases he had made. Martin replied to this veiled rebuke on the 13th March :—

'I have learned nothing further on Poter. My object was not to denounce him. I do not know him intimately. I have merely had to do my duty as observer, and to call attention to him, according to notices which have been transmitted to me by persons whom I believe to have no interest in calumniating him. My guarantee of all the facts is therefore solely for the purpose of my mission. It is then for the Government to watch any particular person. Here, however, is my reply to the various questions which have been submitted to me by citizen Marné, and which I subjoin.

'1. Poter paid visits to England in 1792 and 1793, without this implying that he was betraying our cause, for our relations with England were not suspended till the middle of 1793 if I remember rightly.

'2. The real fact, and which Poter cannot contradict, is that he was twice M.P., and that the kind of popularity which he had gained induced the Court to place him on the list of candidates in 1783 or 1784 for making him a Minister. Pitt was the successful man. After that he fought a duel with the latter.[1] Was it because he was not a Minister ?

---

[1] I can find no confirmation of this story. If there was a duel, it must have been with Thomas Pitt, Lord Camelford, but Christopher

Thus the question whether he had then thrown himself into the Court party remains to be solved. It would not perhaps be difficult to ascertain the fact, for it is well known that Fox, driven from office, became more popular than ever. It is also known that he drew the Prince of Wales into the Opposition.

'3. As to this I will repeat what I have said above. It is for the Government to order its agents to watch him. As for me I promise to neglect nothing in Paris, and if any positive facts reach me I will transmit them to the Directory. Only yesterday I ascertained where he lives and the places which he frequents.

'4. It is quite certain that Poter has made purchases besides his Chantilly factory. To ascertain this it will merely be necessary to apply to the Senlis district. I remember having stated in my report of the 16th (*sic*) that Poter eighteen months ago was in everybody's debt, and that now he had settled with everybody. This is perhaps what has given rise to the belief that he might have dealings with Pitt in France, for in fact his fortune at this moment is marvellous; but it may be the result of great speculations or of stock-jobbing, which in the last twenty months has made the fortune of so many.

'I think I have dwelt enough on this subject. I repeat that my sole object has been to do my duty as surveillant. I will add this. Formerly entrusted with powers by the General Security Committee in the department of the Oise, I ascertained that Poter did much good at Chantilly, that he professed republican principles, and that I had even occasion to render him justice before the committee against the persecution which for eleven months he had been undergoing from the Chantilly revolutionary committee.'

was probably confused with Thomas Potter, a member of Wilkes's Hell-fire club, who, elected as an anti-Pittite, joined Pitt, and in 1756 was appointed Paymaster of the Forces. The two Potters may or may not have been kinsmen.

These reports seem to have induced Barras to make Potter's acquaintance and to send him first to Malmesbury [1] in Paris in 1796, and next to London in 1797, with an offer to conclude peace for a handsome bribe. On his return he warned the Directory that one of its members regularly communicated its deliberations to England. These relations with Barras probably protected him from further molestation during the Directory, but on the 13th December 1800 a police bulletin again denounced him as an English emissary sent to ruin French pottery and hat-making.[2] In 1800 he was a first-class medallist at the Paris Industrial Exhibition, and in 1802 he was one of the gold medallists to whom Napoleon gave a dinner. His Montereau factory, an old monastery where he employed a hundred men, was burnt down in 1802. He probably remained in France till 1814; he died in England three years later.

Among the silver medallists in 1802 was White, a mechanical inventor, probably the uncle or grandfather of Dupont White, sub-Minister of Justice in 1848, President Carnot's father-in-law. The exhibits also included a filter by Smith, an Englishman, perhaps the James Smith who in 1813 succeeded to Stone's printing business.

There were of courset eachers of English. They included Robert, of whom Napoleon might have learned the language at the Paris military school, a lost oppor-

---

[1] Malmesbury, who did not take the overture seriously, says—'He came to me *avec des projets insensés.*'

[2] A. F. iv. 1329.

tunity which he regretted; Mrs. Galignani, *née* Parsons, who had married an Italian ex-priest, ultimately the founder of the newspaper bearing his name; and Samuel Baldwin, employed before the Revolution in the French Foreign Office, who was arrested as a spy in the Terror, and having been inscribed on a long list of prisoners for trial would, but for Robespierre's fall, have been guillotined. He had taught English to the Royal Family before 1789, and he was accused of associating with priests and receiving frequent letters from Calais. He latterly published English and Spanish lesson books, and died in 1804, aged seventy-nine. There were also Cresswell, Davies, Fox, Hickie, Boswell, Macdermott, who kept a school, Stubbs, who had a reading-room with such English newspapers as were allowed to enter France, and Roche, probably Hamilton Roche, teacher at the military school, whose son Eugenius became a journalist in London. There were also two maiden ladies named Haines, ultimately joined by a Mrs. Poppleton, who carried on a school. She was probably the wife or widow of George Poppleton, who had taught English. There was likewise the daughter of a Scotsman named James Mather Flint, the widow of the clever but unprincipled anti-revolutionary pamphleteer Rivarol. Flint and his wife settled about 1734 in France, where their daughter Louisa in 1768 translated into French one of Shakespeare's plays with Dr. Johnson's notes,[1] and Johnson wrote to her in French a letter of thanks, in which he humorously rallied her on detaining in Paris the

---

[1] Probably Letourneur's Edition.

sister of Sir Joshua Reynolds. Fanny Reynolds had
apparently gone to lodge with the Flints, for Northcote
is incorrect in stating that Louisa accompanied her
to France. Reynolds himself in the following year,
when visiting Paris, called on the Flints. On the death
of his wife, Flint, who had embraced Catholicism,
entered the priesthood and received a small benefice
which was supplemented by a pension of 200 francs from
the General Assembly of the Clergy. This pension he
enjoyed till the Revolution, and he must have died
before 1793, for his daughter alone was then arrested
as an Englishwoman. She had, it is true, in 1780
married Rivarol and had given birth to a son, but
Rivarol had long deserted her, leaving her and her
infant in such distress that the Montyon prize, much
to his mortification, was awarded in 1788 to a Frenchwoman who had kindly succoured them. Madame
Rivarol afterwards tried to maintain herself by translations from the English. Her faithless husband died
in Germany as an *émigré* in 1810, and her son Daniel
was now serving till his death in 1810 in the Danish
or Russian army. She herself survived till 1821. She
is not likely to have been hunted up by any of her
fellow-Britons in 1802 or 1814.

Nor were political refugees likely to be sought by
them, otherwise they might have made numerous ac-
quaintances. Most of them were Irish, but King
mentions two Englishmen, Ashley, an ex-member of
the London Corresponding Society, who had a flourishing business in Paris, and 'Hodgson,' a hatter, either
Richard Hodson, one of the Reformers prosecuted in

1794, or William Hodson, who in December 1793 incurred twelve months' imprisonment and a fine of
£200 for saying that the world would not be happy
till there were no more kings. Thoro was also one
Scot, Robert Watson, who had crossed the Channel
in 1798, secretary and biographer of Lord George
Gordon, alleged teacher of English (but more probably 'skimmer' of English newspapers) to Napoleon,
rescuer from rain and rats of the Stuart papers at
Rome; his career was full of romance, and it ended
in the tragedy of suicide at a London inn at the age
of eighty-eight. As for the Irish, some had been
long domiciled in France, while others had just been
liberated under a secret article, or at least a secret
understanding, of the Treaty of Amiens. They would,
according to French documents, have been executed
in Ireland but for the threat of reprisals against
General Sir George Don, who, as will be explained hereafter, had been arrested in France.[1] These ex-prisoners
included James Napper Tandy, given up by Hamburg,
along with James Blackwell, Hervey Montmorency
Morris, and Wm. Corbett, to Sir James Craufurd, but all
claimed by Napoleon as French officers.[2] Tandy landed
at Bordeaux in March 1802, and died there in the following year, not having been allowed to go to Paris. In
December 1802, describing himself as a French general,
he sent a challenge to Elliott, an English M.P., who
had spoken of him as an 'arch traitor,' and on Elliott
taking no notice of his letter he denounced him as

[1] F. 7, 1672.
[2] Hamburg was fined four millions by Napoleon for this act.

a coward.[1]   Morris, who had fought for Austria against
the Turks before fighting for the French Revolution, after
a visit to Paris returned to Ireland, but in 1811 rejoined
the French army.   Corbett had escaped from Kilmain-
ham prison, an episode utilised by Miss Edgeworth in
one of her stories.   He, too, joined the French army,
became a general, and later on helped to liberate
Greece.   Blackwell, who, a student in the Irish College,
had joined in the attack on the Bastille, was penniless
on now landing in France, and Napoleon first gave
him 6000 francs and then a pension of 3000 francs
' for his services to liberty,' Napoleon not having yet
ceased to talk of liberty.   In 1803 Blackwell commanded Napoleon's Irish legion, Corbett serving under
him, as also John Devereux,[2] who, though a conspirator of 1798, waited on Lord Whitworth with a
letter of introduction from Lord Moira.   He was permitted in 1819 to enlist recruits for Bolivar at Dublin,
the British authorities being doubtless glad thus to
get rid of restless spirits.   He became a general in
the service of Colombia, and in 1825 revisited Paris,
where, as a ' most active and dangerous man,' his
movements were suspiciously watched by detectives.[3]
Arthur O'Connor, nephew of Lord Longueville and
ex-M.P. for Cork, has been already mentioned.   He
married Condorcet's daughter, and latterly devoted
himself to agriculture and to his village mayoralty.

[1] *Times*, February 25, 1803.
[2] Kirwan in *Fraser's Magazine*, 1860 ; Fitzpatrick, *Secret Service
under Pitt.*
[3] Année, *Livre Noir*, 1829.

He just lived to see the French empire restored. Robert Emmet returned to Dublin in October 1802, and was executed for a fresh conspiracy. So also was Thomas Russell, who while a soldier in Ireland became acquainted with Tone and was won over to his views. Thomas Addis Emmet, Robert's brother, went in 1804 to New York, where he became a barrister. William James Macnevin likewise crossed the Atlantic.

Other Irishmen had been or were now employed in the French civil service. Aherne, an ex-priest, had served under Delacroix or Carnot. Nicholas Madgett was in the Foreign Office under the Directory, as also a nephew, Sullivan, who had been a professor of mathematics at La Flèche and had gone with Hoche's expedition to Ireland.[1] Edward Joseph Lewins, who had dubbed himself first Luines and then de Luynes, as though related to the French duke of that name, had been educated at the Irish College, Paris. Sent by the United Irishmen to France, he was employed by the Directory in missions and reports, and on the abandonment of French expeditions to Ireland he joined the Duc de Larochefoucault-Liancourt in industrial enterprises, to carry on which he applied for the reimbursement of his secret service expenses. Talleyrand endorsed this application.[2] He was afterwards the *soi-disant* Thompson who, according to Goldsmith, was employed in opening English letters at the post-office, for he had been originally in the

---

[1] *Dublin Review*, April 1890.   [2] F. 7, 1671.

Irish post-office. He subsequently had appointments
in the Foreign and Education Offices. He was still
living in Paris in 1824, but his son refused, doubtless
for cogent reasons, to give any information on him
to Madden for his history of the United Irishmen.
William Duckett, one of the instigators of the mutiny
of the Nore, had been employed by the diplomatic
committee of the Convention, but eventually turned
pedagogue. Patrick Lattin, so brilliant in conversation, according to Lady Morgan, as to reduce Curran
and Sheil to silence, had served in the Franco-Irish
brigade till 1791, and was in the carriage when
Theobald Dillon was murdered by his troops at Lille
in 1792. He had settled near Lyons, but occasionally visited Paris, where he died about 1849. But it
is not always easy to distinguish him from another
Lattin. John Fitzgerald, also a Franco-Irish officer,
had emigrated at the Revolution but returned in 1802,
and his dinners from 1823 to 1836 drew the best
British and French company.[1] William Putnam
M'Cabe, one of Lord Edward Fitzgerald's bodyguard
in 1798, was now starting a cotton mill near Rouen,
but sold it in 1806 to Waddington. He had hair-
breadth escapes from arrest on repeated visits to
England and Ireland, and died in Paris in 1821. He
had been intimate with Tone,[2] the funeral of whose
daughter Mira in March 1803 drew together all the
Irish refugees. Tone's son had entered the French

[1] *Fraser's Magazine*, 1860.
[2] W. T. Tone's autobiography appeared in a French review, the
Carnet, in 1899.

army, but after Waterloo went to America with his mother, who then married an old Scottish friend, Hugh Wilson of Bordeaux. In 1803 she took out a patent for clarifying liquids. Wilson, after a roaming life, ended his days at Santa Cruz in 1829.

The English, of course, found many foreigners in Paris, though except in the aggregate in much smaller numbers than themselves. The Russians were already noted for their prodigality. Swedes were tolerably numerous. The Germans were mostly economical. Among Americans were Rufus King, Livingston, Jay, the Ambassador at London, and the future president, Monroe. There was also Colonel James Swan, a native of Dunfermline, but one of the 'Boston tea-party,' whose contracts with the French Government had involved him in litigation with his partner Schweizer, and who, rather than meet what he considered an unjust claim, was to undergo twenty-two years' imprisonment in a Paris debtors' prison.[1] Count Rumford, the inventor, now likewise settled in Paris.[2] The visitor of highest rank was the Prince of Orange, afterwards suitor to our Princess Charlotte and ultimately King of Holland. His father had sent him from London to claim an indemnity for the loss of the statthalterate, and he appears to have succeeded in his mission. Charlotte's eventually successful suitor, Leopold of Saxe-Coburg, also visited Paris, but not till 1810, when he offered, it is said, to be

---

[1] *Atlantic Monthly*, September 1890. His tomb at Père Lachaise is no longer discoverable.

[2] *Atlantic Monthly*, February 1893.

aide-de-camp to Napoleon.   Higher destinies awaited
him.   The Russians and Poles included Count Zamoiski,
Count Potocki, Prince Troubetski, Prince Galitzin, and
Princess Demidoff, an accomplished dancer.   Nor should
we forget Kosciusko, who had failed to liberate Poland.
Shepherd found him in a cottage near the barriers,
with a small garden which he cultivated himself.   He
must have been able to relate Polish imitations of the
French Revolution—a massacre of prisoners, a revolutionary tribunal, pillages, and confiscations; but he
could claim credit for Stanislas having been honour-
ably treated as a captive, in lieu of having been executed like Louis xvi.   Possibly a South American youth,
Bolivar, the future Liberator, made his acquaintance.
There was also Madame de Krudener, the Delphine
of Madame de Staël's story, now famous for her beauty
and her gallantries, not yet for the mysticism which
was to captivate the Tsar Alexander and the Queen of
Prussia.   She was at this time enamoured of the
singer Garat, but was shortly to accompany her sick
husband who, before reaching Aix, his destination, died
of apoplexy.   Madame de Staël herself, described in
a police note as known for her love of intrigue, was
not yet banished from the capital outside which she
was miserable, and there was her satellite, Benjamin
Constant, not yet much known, though he had been
arrested in 1796 for declaring that France needed a
king.   A fellow Swiss visitor was Pestalozzi, the educationist, noted by the police as having an English
pension.   Another educationist was the German Campe,
who in 1792, along with Cloots, Paine, Priestley, and

others, had received French citizenship. He was surprised to find the Parisians taciturn and apathetic,
instead of being lively, talkative, and enthusiastic as
in 1792. Science was represented by Oersted, who,
however, was as yet merely a youth who had gained
a travelling scholarship.

Alexander Humboldt did not arrive from South
America till 1804, but his brother William, statesman
and philologist, was spending three years in Paris.
Germany also sent the Landgrave of Hesse Rothen-
burg and Princess Hohenzollern, the latter anxious to
purchase the field in which her guillotined brother,
Prince Salm Kyrburg, had been buried. Prince
Emanuel of Salm, apparently her uncle, accompanied
her on her pious mission. Adam Gottlob von Moltke,
a cousin of the famous strategist and like him a Dane,
was a versifier of the Klopstock school and was intimate with Niebuhr. On the outbreak of the French
Revolution he had styled himself Citizen Moltke.
He helped to draw up the Schleswig-Holstein constitution. Another Danish visitor was Baggesen, who
had witnessed the Revolution, imitated Klopstock and
Wieland, and enjoyed a pension from his sovereign.
Samson Heine, father of the poet, a Dusseldorf merchant, was a visitor on business, like several of his
Jewish co-religionists. His son was too young to
accompany him. Another business visitor was Johann
Maria Farina, who opened depôts for his 'veritable
eau de Cologne.' Frederic Jacobi, a friend of Richter,
went in vain quest of health. He revived his acquaintance with Count Schlabrendorf, whom he had

met in London in 1786. 'For eight years,' said Schlabrendorf, reviewing his revolutionary experiences, 'it
was here all a scuffle like a village beershop, everybody pitching into each other. Then came Bonaparte
with a "stop that." The first thing he did was to
blow out the candles. He wanted no questions settled,
but merely the stoppage of disputes. Liberty or no
liberty, religion or no religion, morality or no morality,
was all immaterial to him. Liberty and equality remain, and now nobody opens his mouth or strikes
another.' I may here remark that the comparison of
Bonaparte to Cromwell, obvious as it now appears to
us, was not made by any English observer, though
it did not escape German visitors. Jacobi also went
to see St. Martin, the disciple of Boehme and Sweden-
borg, who had known William Law in England in
1787, and regarded the French Revolution as a pre-
cursor of the Day of Judgment. St. Martin, who was
living in seclusion till his death in October 1803, said
to him, 'Everybody has told you I am mad, but you
see that I am at least a happy madman. If, moreover, some madmen should be fettered there are others
to be left unfettered, and I think myself one of the
latter.' A disciple of Jacobi, Jacob Frederic Fries,
who had been educated by the Moravians and was
ultimately a professor at Jena, was also a visitor. His
democratic opinions for a time occasioned his suspension from his post. Frederic Schlegel, an intimate
friend of Novalis, studied at the Louvre, was taught
Sanscrit by Alexander Hamilton, and lectured on
German literature and philosophy. He and his Jewish

wife, a daughter of Moses Mendelssohn, embraced Catholicism in 1803. Less eminent than his brother Augustus, he was an orientalist and art critic. Living with them at Montmartre was Holmino von Klenke, who had made an unfortunate marriage with Baron Hastfer, and having divorced him was destined to be but little more successful with a second mate, Chézy, to whom Schlegel, his teacher of Persian, introduced her. Helmine was cured of a violent headache by Mesmer, who sat beside her at dinner, and unobserved by the other guests made some passes over her forehead. Mesmer, unlike what happened to him in 1781 and 1785, attracted no curiosity. Helmine also met Hardenberg, the future Prussian statesman, Achim von Arnim, a poet and novelist, and Mademoiselle Rodde, daughter of a Swiss professor, and herself at seventeen adorned with a doctor's degree.[1] Reichardt, the composer, and Fabricius, the Danish naturalist, should also be mentioned. Dietrich Heinrich von Bülow, who had twice visited America, had there embraced Swedenborgianism, had been ruined by a glass speculation, and was now dependent on his pen, likewise visited Paris. An admirer of Napoleon, this historian and pamphleteer had had adventures, and was destined to have others. Julius von Voss, poet and novelist, was another visitor.

Last but not least among the German visitors comes Schopenhauer. His father, Henry Florian Schopenhauer, a Hamburg merchant, with his wife and son, went to London in July 1802. Leaving Arthur at

---

[1] Helmine von Chézy, *Unvergessenes*.

school with the Rev. Thomas Lancaster at Wimbledon, the parents travelled about England and Scotland. They got back to London in October, and after a six weeks' stay all three embarked for Rotterdam. Mercier, the prolific writer, showed them the sights of Paris. In January 1803 they proceeded to Bordeaux. Thence father and son returned to Hamburg, while the mother went to Toulouse, Toulon, Hyères, and Switzerland, an account of which trip she published. Pecuniary losses affected the father's mind, and in 1805, at the age of fifty-nine, he fell or threw himself into a canal. Griesbach denies that he committed suicide, alleging that he slipped through a trap-door in his warehouse into the canal. He was an habitual reader of the *Times*, a taste inherited by his son.

The Italians include Bartolini, sculptor of a colossal bust of Napoleon, and a daughter of Beccaria, the Italian philosopher, who had inherited his intelligence and love of liberty, and possessed beauty into the bargain. She had divorced her insane husband. Helen Williams in 1794-1795 had found her residing by the lake of Lugano. She seems to have settled in Paris in 1798, and Paine then made acquaintance with her. She presented Redhead Yorke with a portrait of her father, and Holcroft was now struck by her intelligence and affability. At her house he met Melzi, who had presented the keys of Milan to Napoleon on his entering that city, and who had scandalised lovers of liberty by accepting the vice-presidency of the so-called Cisalpine republic, though Napoleon soon superseded him by his step-son Eugène de Beauharnais. Another well-known Italian, though born in Paris, was Caraccioli, the author of *Pope Ganganelli's Letters* and many other works; but he was an octogenarian and died in 1803. Then there was Casti, canon and poet, an imitator of Boccaccio. Prince Jerome Moliterno Pignatelli had figured in Neapolitan politics, and was now conspiring to deliver the Neapolitan ports to England. Though Merry granted him a passport he was stopped at Calais and incarcerated in the Temple, along with his English wife or mistress, a Mrs. Dorinda Newnham, an Irishwoman,[1] possibly the wife of a London alderman and ex-M.P. She was again arrested at Rome in 1809, but liberated as being both ill and mad. It was thought, however, that she had been forewarned of arrest and had burnt her papers.[2] Ultimately both of them got to England.

How did the English demean themselves and what was the impression produced on both sides? Francis Jackson, writing on 2nd February 1802 to Speaker Abbot, says :—

'I only wish you would extend the efforts of your police to keep at home a parcel of disorderly women who come abroad without bringing anything with them that does credit to the national character. There is Lady C. (Cholmondeley), who is one day taken up by the police and carried to the chief lock-up for persisting to drive in the Champs Elysées at forbidden hours and through forbidden roads. Another day she quarrels with people at the masquerade. A third she invites a dozen Frenchmen and women to her

---

[1] She pretended, however, to be Dorinda Rogers, an American.
[2] A. F. iv. 1496 and 1498.

house and abuses them all for slaves. Then we have
Lady M. (Monck), whose dear friend would welcome H. M.
Williams and who gets into all the bad company in Paris.
You must suppose it is very bad when here it is reckoned
mauvais ton. You really should keep these people at home.
As for your swindlers, of whom there has been a nest here
for some time, they are not near so troublesome, for there
are swindlers in all countries and the police here is very
good.'[1]

There is evidently a little exaggeration here, but we
have already seen that Lord Whitworth shut his doors
against some of his countrymen whose inordinate
admiration of Napoleon was not conducive to the
maintenance of peace, since it must have given the
impression that there was a strong French party in
England, so that Napoleon might dictate his own
terms. Whitworth acknowledged that the Duke of
Bedford, fully alive to Napoleon's projects, conducted
himself very properly, adding, 'I wish I could say as
much of many of my countrymen and countrywomen.'[2]
Lady Oxford even considered Napoleon handsome—
an opinion, says a royalist spy, not shared by a single
Frenchwoman. The Duchess of Gordon, though
another of his admirers—pointing to his portrait she
would say to the wife of Consul Lebrun, 'Voilà mon
zéro (héros)'—went rather beyond the bounds of
politeness when, seated between Berthier and Decrès,[3]
Ministers of War and Marine, she said, 'I am always

[1] Lord Colchester, *Letters.* King speaks of the swarm of English
bankrupts and sharpers at Calais and Boulogne.
[2] Oscar Browning, *England and Napoleon in* 1803.
[3] Brother to Madame de Genlis.

frightened when I look at you (Berthier), but fortunately you (turning to Decrès) reassure me.'[1] This, however, might pass for one of her usual sallies, intimating that the French army was formidable, but not the navy. Yet Thibaudeau says :—

'Paris was infatuated with the arrival of these foreigners. It was a scramble among all classes to give them the best reception. It was the height of fashion to dine and amuse them and give them balls; the women especially were enamoured of the English and had a rage for their fashions. In short France seemed to eclipse itself before a few thousands of these proud and unprofitable foreigners, towards whom the attentions of hospitality were carried to a ridiculous excess. Frenchmen of the old school did not share this intoxication, but sighed over this forgetfulness of national dignity.'[2]

And Reichardt speaks of French fops parading English garments, horses, and dogs. Even Napoleon, he says, sent to England for horses and hounds. Frenchmen, with their keen sense of the ludicrous, were amused, he tells us, with the middle-class Englishman, who had never previously visited Paris. Caricaturists depicted him standing open-mouthed in front of public buildings, with the wife in insular toilette or grotesquely aping French fashions. A short play entitled *l'Anglais à Paris*, which was apparently never printed, doubtless made good-humoured fun of the visitors.

[1] Remacle, *Bonaparte et les Bourbons.*
[2] Thibaudeau, *Mémoires.*

At a theatre two of these were once so unceremonious as to take off their coats on a hot July night, whereupon there was a scene. They were obdurate, alleging that this was allowable in London,⁁ until a police inspector arrived and expostulated with them. Their habit of carrying umbrellas and their nankeen or black gaiters were, however, adopted by the French, but their beverages probably found less favour, albeit an English tea-warehouse had been opened, as also a beershop which boasted of its *aile* (sic) as especially suitable for cool or damp weather.

Vernet drew a caricature of the Duchess of Gordon as a stout woman holding her daughter by the hand. There were other family parties. 'English women,' says the *Journal des Débats* (Sept. 1, 1802), 'are readily to be distinguished. If their grave and becoming demeanour were not sufficiently marked, the group of children accompanying them would be more than enough to show the difference between them and Parisian ladies.' Although tradesmen were glad to see English customers, they missed the extravagant *milords* of old times. The Cholmondeleys, indeed, had astonished Calais by their lavishness, requiring five-and-twenty horses for their coaches to Paris, where they were doubtless equally prodigal, and Lord Aberdeen was also lavish; but most of the visitors haggled about prices, bought only cheap goods, and frequented cheap restaurants. Even rich nabobs seemed bent on spending as little as possible. A royalist agent, while remarking that all Europe was infected with the enthusiasm for Bonaparte and hastened to Paris to behold the great man at least once, says :—

'It is easy to see that curiosity alone attracts foreigners, especially the English. The proof is that they never make a long stay among us. They come to see the First Consul, attend the parade and theatres, visit the museums and other curiosities; then they leave. Paris is thus for foreigners merely a huge inn, where they come to examine the consequences of the Revolution and admire the masterpieces stolen from Italy and Flanders.' [1]

This is corroborated by a Weimar magazine, *London und Paris*, which speaks of the wealthiest visitors as apparently resolved on economising, beating down shopkeepers and chiefly frequenting the museums and other gratuitous spectacles, or gaping from morning to night in the squares and on the bridges. Campe speaks of a fortnight as the average stay, and accepting the obviously exaggerated calculation of a Paris newspaper that there were 32,000 English arrivals a month, he estimated that each spent 30 guineas and that Paris was the richer by 960,000 guineas a month. Reichardt estimated 20 guineas as the cost of the journey and of ten days' stay in Paris.

As for English impressions of France a few words will suffice. Most of the 'chiels' who took notes were struck with the liveliness of French society. The absence of roughness and hustling in the crowds at fireworks and regattas also then, as now, attracted notice. Eyre speaks of the readiness with which

[1] Remacle, p. 93.

Parisian crowds made way for foreigners. On the
other hand, the frequency of divorce and of *liaisons*
excited comment. King speaks of obscenity, immorality, and profligacy as universal in Paris, a remark
which we might attribute to British cant but for his
statement that he also saw drunken Englishmen reeling
in the Palais Royal arcades. The term *monsieur* had
been generally revived, though in the public offices
citoyen was still retained. Madame Récamier showed
visitors of both sexes her sumptuously furnished bed-
room. Pinkerton and Hughes were charmed with
the affability and grace of Frenchwomen, and Williams
wished France and England could bestow on each other
the one gaiety the other seriousness, while Miss Plumptree vindicated the virtue of the great majority of
Frenchwomen. Miss Edgeworth was struck by the
absence of beggars on the coach-roads—in Paris, however, carriages were beset by them—and by the good
manners of the lower orders. Forbes found the coach-
drivers so polite as to stop and allow their fair passengers to sketch the landscape. Eyre was delighted
with the Palais Royal, whereas Redhead Yorke styles
it a den of iniquity, and Miss Plumptree considered its
erection a greater sin of Égalité Orleans than even his
Jacobinical delinquencies.

Holcroft, who had a French wife and had paid
previous visits, tells us more than other writers of
comparative manners. He himself was taught a lesson
of politeness. He was leaning against the mantelpiece
apparently monopolising the fire, when a girl came up
and in lieu of saying 'You are in my way,' employed

the delicate periphrasis of 'I am in your way.' He took the hint and moved, but this was not all. She touched a cup and saucer on the mantelpiece, expecting him to remove it. He did not perceive her meaning, whereupon she took the cup and saucer and handed it to him. Again when a friend was lolling in a chair with his hands in his pockets and his legs stretched out, a French lady remarked to Mrs. Holcroft, ' Look at that Englishman, he is anything but squeamish.' Yet Holcroft saw Frenchmen in similar attitudes, not to speak of their spitting on the floor or pulling out white handkerchiefs bedaubed with snuff. The French were scandalised at the appearance at the Tuileries of an officer in Highland costume ; but Holcroft observed women in male attire in the streets and also at the theatres, where they thus evaded the regulation excluding women from the pit. He saw a married couple undistinguishable in point of dress, but he admits that the woman showed timidity and the utmost propriety. On another occasion, however, he sat behind a girl in male dress who, manifestly to attract his notice, pretended to be making love to a female friend by her side. Little girls, moreover, were frequently dressed as boys, while boys had all sorts of outlandish costumes. Naughty children were often threatened with being sent back to their nurses on the ground that they must be changelings, and putting children out to nurse was so universal that in eighteen months Holcroft, except among the poor, saw only two infants in arms in the streets. He found French politeness in several respects wanting. Shopkeepers were the reverse of obsequious, and when his heels were trodden upon or his coat soiled by a cane or umbrella carried under the arm he seldom received an apology. If, moreover, at a theatre a neighbour borrowed his copy of the play it would have been retained till the end of the performance if Holcroft had not asked for it back.

There were marriages and deaths among the visitors. Lady Catherine Beauclerk, daughter of the Duke of St. Albans, was married at the Embassy to the Rev. James Burgess, the Duchess of Cumberland being present; she died nine months afterwards at Florence. The Baroness Crofton's daughter was married to St. George Caulfeild of the county Roscommon, probably the ex-Guardsman and man of fashion who on the 2nd February 1803 appeared at Covent Garden as Hamlet. He was 'well-proportioned and genteel,' but too laboured in his attitudes and gesticulations. Richard Trench married Miss St. George. Lady Isabel Style died at St. Omer in December 1802, Champion de Crespigny in Paris on New Year's Day, 1803, and Luttrell in the same month. Sir Robert Chambers, ex-Chief Justice of Bengal, who had intended going south, died in Paris in May 1803, and was buried in the Temple Church, London. Mrs. Charles Ellis, granddaughter of the Earl of Bristol, Lady Mary Eyre, relict of Thomas Eyre and sister of the Earl of Uxbridge, Lady Anne Saltmarsh, and Colonel Alexander Malcolm also died in Paris or the provinces.

Before passing on to the renewal of the war, I may mention some of the return visits to London. These were sufficiently numerous for sheets of voting-papers on Napoleon's life-consulate to be sent over to the French Embassy. Let us hope that one of these was not filled up by tho most prominent visitor, Grégoire, Constitutional Bishop of Blois, who had sat in the Convention, but was happily absent in Savoy at the time of Louis XVI.'s trial. He was no doubt eagerly questioned on the events of the Revolution and on the horrors from which he had rather unaccountably escaped. He plumed himself on being the first Catholic prelate who since 1688 had promenaded in St. James's Park in full costume, and he wittily remarked to Fulton, 'The English are a magnanimous, hospitable, and kindly people, and the country would be enchanting if it had but pleased God to give it sunshine and French cookery.' Sir Joseph Banks showed him the sights of London. Madame Récamier was welcomed at London and Bath. She was noticed by the Prince of Wales, and made or renewed acquaintance with the Duchess of Devonshire, Lady Elizabeth Foster, the Marquis of Douglas, his sister the Duchess of Somerset, the Duke of Orleans (afterwards Louis Philippe), and his brothers. Her portrait was in great request, but she was mobbed in Kensington Gardens on account of her transparent French costume.[1] Her husband, the banker, joined her in London in May 1802. Madame Vigée-Lebrun, who had painted Marie

---

[1] Some French ladies, who were disagreeably crowded by public curiosity in Kensington Gardens, complained heavily of our want of *politesse*. They should remember, however, that they were not quite undressed in the fashion, and that the English ladies always walk out

Antoinette, went in April 1802 and stayed three years. The Prince of Wales and Lord Byron were among her sitters. Madame Tussaud, an artist of another order, settled permanently in London with her waxwork collections. Delille recited his verses, but was addicted to eating jellies meanwhile, which with his rapid pace made it difficult to understand him. He returned in August 1802, and had obtained or was about to obtain dispensation from deacon's orders so as to marry his housekeeper. Garnerin, the aeronaut, made a long stay, and ascending at Ranelagh Gardens alighted at Colchester. He made another ascent at Bath. Félissent, the worthless second husband of the great singer Mrs. Billington, had to her surprise followed her from Italy to London; but the Government, doubtless out of friendliness to her, expelled him under the Alien Act. Was he anxious to share the 4000 guineas which she was earning that season, or was he jealous, and not without cause, of the Duke of Sussex? Talleyrand shamelessly gave his brother, Colonel Archambaud (afterwards Duc de Talleyrand), a letter to the Prime Minister, Addington, requesting him to procure the payment of a considerable sum due to him while commanding a regiment of *émigrés* in English pay. Archambaud returned with the money, but the London newspapers revealing his *incognito* mission, Napoleon banished him from Paris, as also another Bozon, who had likewise fought against France but had since cringed to Napoleon. Fiévée, the press censor, was

with something upon their heads, however they treat the rest of their persons.—*Times*, April 19, 1803.

sent to write letters on or rather against England in the *Mercure de France*,[1] as also Colonel Beauvoisin, who on his return was ordered by Napoleon to write against Pitt, Cronville, and the Court. He was sent on a second visit with directions not only to write letters to his paper (apparently the *Débats*), and to send all anti-French pamphlets, but to 'find pretexts for traversing the whole coast from the Thames to beyond Plymouth, the Bristol Channel, Edinburgh and the Scotch coasts.' He was to 'have a fixed salary, and extra pay whenever he answers the expectations formed of his talents and fidelity.'[2] Beauvoisin, according to Goldsmith, was intimate with Despard, the conspirator. Bonnecarrère, Madame Bonneuil, who had previously had a mission to Russia, Madame Visconti, mistress of General Berthier, and Madame Gay, are also mentioned by Goldsmith as Napoleon's emissaries. Military men were also appointed by him as consuls at London, Bristol, Hull, Glasgow, Dublin, Cork, and Jersey; but a letter from Talleyrand to Fauvelet at Dublin, instructing him to make plans of Irish harbours, was intercepted, whereupon the English Government insisted on the withdrawal of these spies, a demand the more easily made by it as it had not itself appointed any consuls to France. A more legitimate visitor was Coquebert, a scientist and diplomatist who was deputed to discuss a commercial treaty, but failed to effect an agreement.

[1] Holcroft was told by a French lady, who sent for him to make this confidence and received him in her bath, that Fiévée was commissioned to bribe London newspapers (*Travels from Hamburg to Paris*). Holcroft believed that the mission was unsuccessful.

[2] Napoleon, *Correspondance*.

Some of the visitors were of an undesirable class, for in September 1803, when a royal proclamation ordered a general expulsion, the *Times* said :—

'What did France send to us? With the exception of a few persons who came on commercial speculations, she sent a multitude of adventurers, who were starving at home and hastened hither, impelled by the reports of our riches and the simplicity of our character; and in return for the wealth which our nobility and gentry carried over to their country, they came among us with no other possessions than their vices.'

Shall we reckon among French visitors Maurice Drummond, a descendant of the Jacobite Drummonds, who took over with him his wife, daughter of Lord Elphinstone, and his daughter Clementina, destined as Lady Clementina Davies to write *Recollections of Society*? She went at Edinburgh to a school kept by the sister of Professor Playfair, and her brother was born in 1807 on British soil. The latter, in 1841, proved his right to the French title of Duke of Melfort and Perth, while in 1853 an Act of Parliament, reversing the attainder, restored to him his ancestral British title of Earl of Perth and Melfort. He survived till 1902, when, his son and grandson having predeceased him, the earldom passed to Viscount Strathallan.

A less doubtful British immigrant was John Gamble, probably brother of the James Gamble who witnessed the Revolution. He had been in partnership as a paper-maker at Essonne with Jules Didot St. Léger,

who had married his sister Maria.[1]   Accompanied by
Nicolas Louis Robert, the Essonne overseer, inventor
of a machine for endless paper-making, he started
paper mills in 1801 at Frogmore, Herts, but these did
not succeed.   Didot himself, however, was more fortunate at Two Waters, Hemel Hempstead, where he
remained from 1802 till 1816.

[1] See my *Englishmen in the French Revolution* and *Paris in* 1789-94.

IV

CAPTIVITY

IT is not my purpose to discuss the causes of the renewal of the war. M. Martin Phippson, in the *Revue Historique*, March to June 1901, contends that though England, owing to Addington's incapacity, was seemingly the aggressor, Napoleon was really so, albeit desirous at the last moment of postponing the rupture till his armaments were completed. Of all the explanations of the rupture the strangest, yet the most recent, is that of M. Albert Sorel, who, quoting some anonymous English writer, represents the renewal of the war as necessary to the English ruling classes in order to avert the establishment of a government like the French.[1] The truth is that all reflecting Englishmen perceived Napoleon to be a tyrant, and Paine, as we have seen, regarded Frenchmen as worse off than the slaves of Constantinople.

[1] *Révue des Deux Mondes*, Sept. 1, 1902, p. 115.

174

The treaty of Amiens, moreover, had never been more than a truce. Whitworth had never appeared to instal himself for a permanency, and English visitors consequently complained of his want of hospitality. On the 13th March 1803 Napoleon rudely apostrophised him at Joséphine's reception. Whitworth's own account of this has been published by Mr. Oscar Browning, but Napoleon's version addressed to Andréossi, which seems to have been overlooked in England, is to be found in his correspondence. It reads thus :—

'The First Consul being at the presentation of foreigners which took place to-day at Madame Bonaparte's, and finding Lord Whitworth and M. de Markoff side by side, said to them, "We have been fighting fifteen years (*sic*). It seems that a storm is brewing at London, and that they want to fight another fifteen years. The King of England says in his message that France is preparing offensive armaments. He has been misled. There is no considerable armament in the French ports, all having started for St. Domingo. He says that differences exist between the two Cabinets; I know of none. It is true that England should evacuate Malta. His Majesty is pledged to this by treaty. The French nation may be destroyed but not intimidated."

'Going round and finding himself alone with M. de Markoff, he said in a low tone that the discussion related to Malta, that the British Ministry wanted to keep it seven years, and that you should not sign treaties when you would not execute them. At the end of the circle, the English minister being near the door, he said to him : "Madame Dorset has spent the bad season at Paris ; I ardently hope that she may spend the fine one ; but if it is true that we are to have war, the entire responsibility in the eyes of God and man will be on those who repudiate their own signature and refuse to execute treaties." '

This storm blew over, and on the 30th March the young Duke of Dorset, the Harrow schoolboy, set off to spend Easter with his mother, his two little sisters, and his step-father at Paris. It was also stated that the Embassy was about to be newly furnished. But in April matters again looked threatening. Madame de Rémusat tells us that people collected outside the British Embassy, to judge by the preparations for departure whether there was to be peace or war. Whitworth[1] left Paris on the 12th May and landed at Dover on the 20th. His staff met with some obstacles. Talbot, on his way to Calais, was stopped at St. Denis because his passport had expired. He acknowledged that he ought to have renewed it, but the Prefect of Police, on being consulted, said he was exempt from the decree, and after a few hours' delay Talbot, who admitted that he had been courteously treated, proceeded on his journey.[2] Mandeville not being allowed, probably for the same informality, to embark at Calais, returned temporarily to Paris. Hodgson, the chaplain, and Maclaurin, the physician to the Embassy, also encountered difficulties. On the 6th May it had been announced in the House of Commons that Andréossi had asked for his passports. On the 17th messages to both Houses and a notification in the *London Gazette* dated the 16th announced

[1] A police note charges him with having transmitted letters to and from *émigrés*.

[2] A. F. iv. 1327.

an embargo on all French and Dutch vessels in British ports, together with the issue of letters of marque. On the 19th two French vessels laden with timber and salt were captured off Brest. On the 23rd a decree was communicated to the French Chambers providing that all Englishmen enrolled in the militia or holding commissions in the army or navy should be detained as reprisals for this embargo and capture prior to the declaration of war on the 18th. The decree was even extended by being made applicable to all persons between eighteen and sixty, even if, like clergymen and others, not enrolled in the militia. Talbot before leaving wrote a letter of remonstrance to Talleyrand, who stated that Talbot having no longer any official status he could not reply.

The only precedents for this detention were the arrest in 1746, without any apparent reason, of all the English in Paris on the return of the Young Pretender, and that of all Englishmen in France in 1793 as hostages for Toulon. Thomas Moore heard Lord Holland in 1819 justify Napoleon, but Mackintosh maintained that the seizure of vessels was warranted by international law, and a French jurist, Miot de Mélito, describes the detention as a 'violent measure unusual even in the bitterest wars,' while Henri Martin, the French historian, charges both Governments with having violated international law. The truth is that Napoleon acted in a passion, and as in the case of the Duc d'Enghien was too proud ever to acknowledge a mistake. As to an embargo, he himself as early as the 13th May had despatched orders for the seizure

M

of British vessels in Holland, Genoa, and Tuscany.   If,
moreover, we are to believe Madame Junot, Napoleon's
decree was due to his having been informed that Colonel
James Green had in a café threatened in his cups to
assassinate him, and though Junot, being acquainted
with Green, vouched for his having left Paris prior to
the date of the alleged threat, Napoleon refused to
cancel the decree.   So swiftly was it enforced that
the *Prince of Wales* packet and the cutter *Nancy*,
which had made their usual passage from Dover to
Calais, were seized and their crews detained.   When
a few weeks afterwards Napoleon visited Calais, Captain
Sutton, of the *Prince of Wales*, petitioned him for
release, but he met with a peremptory refusal, and
Napoleon, on the two vessels being pointed out to
him in the harbour, said, ' You have plenty of mud
there; let them lie and rot.'

The aggregate number of the British captives, represented by the French as seven thousand five hundred,
was really only seven hundred, four hundred of them,
according to Sturt, being small tradesmen.   Napoleon,
according to Maclean, was much disappointed at the
smallness of the haul.   Everything indeed had been
done to induce the visitors to stay.   The *Argus* had
on the 10th May remonstrated against any fear of
detention as in 1793, France, it said, being no longer
under a Robespierre, and provincial authorities had
given assurances that expulsion with reasonable notice
was the worst that could befall.   It was unfair,
however, to accuse Napoleon of having 'enticed' the
English to remain.   His assurances of safety were

probably sincere at the time, but his moral sense did not impress upon him the sacredness of such a virtual pledge. He had no scruples as to suddenly changing his mind to the detriment of persons who had trusted him. Most of the visitors, however, had deemed it prudent to return home while the issue was still uncertain. As late indeed as May arrivals in Paris had continued. From May 10th to 19th there were 48, and from the 20th to the 29th there were 38, but in the next ten days the number fell to 17 and in the following ten days to 6. Most of these visitors, moreover, must have come up from the provinces on their way home, while others came to fetch relatives. There were some narrow escapes. Sir William Call was just in time to leave Geneva, and Miss Berry and Mrs. Damer, warned by Lord John Campbell, hurried away from that city, forgetting or possibly not thinking it safe to pass on the warning to others. The Duke of Bedford, the Duchess of Gordon and her daughter, and Sir Harry Featherstonehaugh left Paris four days after Whitworth. The son of Sir G. Burrell and a companion escaped by making their valet pass for an American and themselves for his servants. Young Edgeworth, on the other hand, received his father's letter of warning just too late, and was detained till 1814, though his companions, Roget as a Swiss and the Philips boys as below the age, obtained exemption. Yet not only had men been detained when over sixty, but some youths of ten or twelve, and therefore well under the limit of sixteen, had been stopped on the plea of their producing no certificates of birth. Augustine

Sayer, aged thirteen, whom his parents had apparently placed in a school, was not allowed to return home, but was forced to maintain himself by tuition. He was eventually physician to the Duke of Kent and to the Lock Hospital, dying in 1861. He may have been one of the English boys sent to Dubufe's school, for Dubufe, a member of the London Society of Arts, contradicting a statement that Protestants were refused admission to French schools, mentioned that he had received such pupils. John Charles Tarver, the future educationist and teacher of French at Eton, might surely, however, have been sent to his parents in London between 1794 and 1802, even if this was impossible after 1803. Farel, the engineer, in whose care he had been left by them on their release from captivity at Dieppe after the Terror, had virtually adopted him. Born at Dieppe in 1790, he had practically been naturalised, and Farel in 1805 got him into the French civil service. He remained in it till March 1814, when, obtaining leave of absence, he went to London and found his mother, brothers, and sisters still living; but he returned to France during the Hundred Days, intending apparently to resume his official post. Disappointed in this hope, he recrossed the Channel and found a more distinguished career open to him.

Before entering into details respecting the captives, I should speak of the unusual bitterness given to the war by Napoleon. Anglophobia, indeed, had been displayed by him even during the peace. The publishers of the *Almanach National* were sharply rebuked for proposing to insert 'Angleterre' with its royal family at the head of the alphabetical list of foreign powers. They had to relegate it lower down as 'Grande Bretagne,' and curiously enough British representatives at international Congresses are to the present day seated according to this nomenclature. Napoleon, moreover, during his tour in Normandy scolded his minister Chaptal for speaking of '*jardins anglais.*' 'Why,' he vehemently exclaimed, ' do you call them English gardens ? Do you not know that this style of gardening came to us from China, that it was brought to perfection in France, and that no good Frenchman can credit England with it ? Bear in mind that " French gardens " is the only proper term for them, and never again grate on my ears with " English gardens." '[1]

His animosity was naturally intensified on the resumption of hostilities. The theatres were forbidden to perform pieces containing allusions complimentary to England, while plays of an opposite character were ordered to be performed not only in Paris but at Boulogne, Bruges, and other ports where troops were being collected for the invasion. A corps of Irish interpreters was formed, and Chaptal was directed to get some invasion songs written and set to music. Pamphlets demonstrating the facility of the invasion or vilifying the English were likewise published. One of them was entitled, ' The English people, swollen with pride, beer, and tea, tried by the tribunal of reason.' This was a reprint of Montlosier's articles, but issued without his consent. Caricatures were also multiplied.

[1] Remacle, *Bonaparte et les Bourbons.*

One of them represented George III. as dragged on the
ground by his hair by a French soldier. His crown
tumbles off, and the soldier, striking him with his fist,
says, 'Look to thy crown and defend thy coasts.'[1] The
Bayeux tapestry was brought over to Paris to suggest
the practicability or imminency of a landing in England,
and the Joan of Arc celebration at Orleans, suspended
since the Revolution, was revived. Even indeed in
February, three months before the rupture, Napoleon
had emphatically approved, if not suggested, the
erection by the Orleans municipality of a statue of
the heroine. This gave the *Times* a text for comment-
ing on the anomaly of the glorification by a usurper
of the maiden who restored the French crown to its
rightful owner. Napoleon might, however, have
rejoined that he had not usurped the crown, but had
picked it out of the gutter of the Revolution. The
teaching of English in schools, too, as Lamartine
testifies, was forbidden. Yet it is but fair to say that
French was discouraged, as Lord Malmesbury tells us,
in English schools, and that the *Times* of January 4,
1803, contained the following curious article:—

The political ill-consequences of the spread of the French
language throughout Europe are admitted ; and we do not
conceive that its bad effects upon the morals and character
of other countries will be disputed. We have no hesitation
to add, that a nation which adopts the language of a superior
is prepared to admit its yoke. There is no better or quicker
road to dominion, than by imposing the necessity, or com-
passing the mode, of making a language general. In this

[1] Remacle.

word are comprised the ideas, character, and love of the people whose idiom you prefer to your own.

We never heard it alleged as *unwise* in the Government of *China*, to intercept all communication between its subjects and foreigners.

Except as a *first step* and beginning of mischief, all apprehensions from the representation of a French Comedy are ridiculous. It is as the *mali labes,* the first spot and eruption, that we are induced to contend against anything so contemptible as the pic-nickery and nick-nackery—the pert affectation, and subaltern vanity of rehearsing to an audience that cannot understand, in a language one cannot pronounce!

Does any one advantage result to the community of Great Britain, from the practice of teaching French indiscriminately to every girl whose parents can send her to a boarding-school?

Does any advantage result from its being taught to shop-keepers' sons, at a day-school, for fear foreigners should not pawn or buy, for want of understanding them?

Are not the great part of the female sex, and of the uninformed part of ours, exposed, by this practice, to the moral and political corruptions of another country? Is not the business of French Emissaries facilitated by the half-understanding of low and ignorant Englishmen?

Ought a girl to be able to read any book that her father cannot? Ought she to converse in a gibberish, which her mother cannot detect?

Ought the mass of a virtuous and happy people to be educated to form ideas different from the manners, habits, and institutions of their own country? Ought it to be in the power of an enemy to poison their minds, corrupt their principles, and seduce them from their allegiance and religion?

Napoleon's letters show how jealously he watched over the detention of the English, and over everything relating to England. Thus in 1806 he ordered all Englishmen to be expelled from the Papal States, and this order perhaps accounts for Coleridge's belief that he had a narrow escape from being seized on account of his articles in the *Morning Post*. It is extremely unlikely, however, that Napoleon ever heard of Coleridge. He likewise decreed that English civilians found in any country occupied by his troops should be prisoners, and all English property or merchandise confiscated. Even any neutral vessel which had entered an English port was also to be forfeited. Lord Oxford, Lord Mount Cashell, and General Morgan would have been arrested at Florence but for the refusal of the Queen Regent to act as Napoleon's policeman. Again in 1806 Napoleon writes, 'I do not know why English prisoners have been placed at Arras; no doubt to be near home so that they may escape.' He writes eight months later from Posen: 'Issue a circular and take measures that throughout the Empire all letters coming from England or written in English and by Englishmen shall be destroyed. All this is very important, for England must be completely isolated.' In 1807 he complains that English prisoners still received letters. Two years later, on a report that the English at Arras and Valenciennes were meditating escape, he ordered their removal further inland. This measure was extended in 1811 to the prisoners at Brussels. The daily police report, which constantly spoke of the English prisoners, was evidently scanned by him, even when absent from Paris, with great attention; and seemingly anxious that no other eye should see these documents, he directed that during his absence in Russia they should be destroyed. There is consequently a gap of four months in 1812. Even to the last the prisoners were never forgotten by him, for on the 6th January 1814 he ordered their removal from Verdun to Orleans, manifestly to prevent their release by the allied armies. Only in one instance do I find his severity relenting. On the 12th November 1812 at Givet he remarked English prisoners (captured soldiers or sailors, of course, not *détenus*) who had been set to repair a swivel bridge. Eight or ten of them jumped with alacrity into a boat to help to make the mechanism work. He directed that these men should be picked out, presented with 100 francs each, and sent back to England. An English clergyman at Givet who had petitioned for a three months' visit home was to escort them. A petition from another Englishman there was also to be favourably considered. It is pleasant to find Napoleon for once good-humoured and generous.[1] When, in 1812, he directed that the smuggling of coffee and sugar into Corsica by English vessels should be winked at, and that sugar and coffee seized in British bottoms should not, like British manufactured goods, be burnt, he was obviously inspired by more selfish considerations. French fishing-boats were forbidden to pass the night out at sea, lest they should smuggle English goods, yet they were authorised to smuggle (the French had

---

[1] England in like manner released in 1810 eighty-four sailors of a captured privateer who had rescued a shipwrecked British crew.

adopted the word *smogler*) spirits into England.   Fishing-boats on both sides were unmolested, unless indeed
they had clandestine passengers on board; and the
Times, running a light cutter in the Channel, procured from them Paris newspapers.   Letters were probably conveyed occasionally in the same way.   England
had not retaliated against French products, for in 1807
the *Monthly Review* appealed to British patriots not
to continue spending a million and a half a year on
French brandies and other goods.   But Cancale must
have been unable to continue sending its oysters, one
hundred and nineteen millions of which had been forwarded in the twenty months of peace.   The export
of oysters from Granville and St. Malo was, however,
permitted by Napoleon in 1810.

The Irish refugees, whom Napoleon, as we have seen,
had offered Cornwallis to expel, now became his cats-
paws.   In July 1803, while declining to see Arthur
O'Connor, he deputed General Truguet to treat with
him and Berthier to advance him small sums of money.
He promised to send 25,000 troops to Ireland, and
if 20,000 Irishmen would join them he pledged himself to make Irish independence a condition of peace.
But he found that the Irish refugees or emissaries
were split into two parties, not always on speaking
terms, O'Connor accepting, the Emmets rejecting, the
idea of a French protectorate.   In July 1804, having
read a memoir by the Emmets, Lewins, and other
exiles, he decreed that all Irishmen accompanying
the projected expedition should be considered Frenchmen, and if not treated when captured as prisoners

of war reprisals would be exercised.[1] Robert Emmet
had had an audience of Napoleon previously to the
peace, and an Irish legion was formed in November
1803. MacSheehy organised it at Brest, and on
the Emperor's coronation it was presented, like the
French regiments, with an eagle and colours. Irish
dissensions, however, are proverbial, and a duel between MacSheehy and O'Mealy led to the former
being transferred to a French regiment and to the
latter resigning and apparently returning to Baltimore. In 1806 the legion was ordered to Landau
and had to pass through Verdun.

The governor [says Myles Byrne] took upon himself to
lodge the Irish legion in a suburb, lest its presence might
not be agreeable to the British prisoners. At daybreak
he had the drawbridge let down and the gates opened to
let the legion march through before the English prisoners
could have light to see and contemplate our green flag and
its beatific inscription, so obnoxious to them, 'the independence of Ireland.' Our march, however, through the town
at that early hour attracted great notice. As our band
played up our national air of Patrick's Day in the Morning
we could see many windows opened and gentlemen in their
shirts inquiring across the street in good English what was
meant by this music at such an early hour.

Some months later the legion was ordered to Boulogne, to be ready for the invasion of England, and
at Arras 'the governor,' says Byrne, 'had the good
sense to make the English sleep one night in the
citadel until we marched out in the morning.' The

---

[1] *Correspondance.*

legion was eventually sent to Spain. The experiment
of inviting English prisoners to join it did not succeed,
and in 1810 Napoleon stopped it. 'I do not want
any English soldiers,' he wrote; 'I prefer their being
prisoners to answer for my prisoners in England;
moreover the majority desert.' This had apparently
happened in Spain. In 1811 Napoleon directed Clarke
to send for O'Connor and his fellow-exiles in Paris
and try to revive an insurrection. He was ready to
send 30,000 troops if sure of a rising and if England
continued to send forces to Portugal. O'Connor
accordingly sent Napoleon a preliminary memoir,
whereupon in September he commissioned Clarke to
despatch agents to Ireland.

In spite of his ostentatious preparations Napoleon
told Metternich in 1810 that he had never been mad
enough to think of invading England unless in the
wake of an insurrection, the Boulogne army being
all along aimed at Austria. The latest and fullest
French writer on the subject, Colonel Desbrières, from
an examination of the confused orders and counter-
orders, so unlike the rest of Napoleon's plans, comes
to the same conclusion.[1] All that Napoleon could
have intended was to disquiet England, and thus prevent her from despatching troops to the Continent.
This was legitimate strategy, and he was obviously,
moreover, as much entitled to use the Irish as pawns

[1] *Projets de Débarquement*, 1902. Napoleon mystified his subordinates as well as the foreigner, for on the 22nd August 1805 he wrote to
Admiral Villeneuve, ' England is ours. All is embarked. Appear
for twenty-four hours and all is ended ' (*Eng. Hist. Rev.*, October
1903).

as England had been to use the Vendeans, but his manufacture of counterfeit notes is less excusable. A manufactory of forged notes in Paris, enshrouded in mystery, was superintended by Lale, a clerk in tho engraving department of the War Office, Fouché, Savary, and Desmarest being the only confidants of the secret. A Hamburg Jew named Malchus and two Frenchmen, Blanc and Bernard, were sent to buy merchandise with the notes. They were instructed to go to Scotland and Ireland, so as to disappear before the fraud was discovered. They were ostensibly told to destroy what they bought, but they naturally preferred smuggling it into France, and this was winked at, so that they made large profits. The fraud was, however, soon discovered. Malchus was hanged. His confederates escaped in an English smuggling boat which was captured by a French revenue vessel. They were at first imprisoned at Boulogne, but Savary promptly ordered their release, together with funds to return to Paris for further employment. Napoleon, at a later date, practised the same trick on Russia and Austria. On the restoration of peace with the latter in 1810, he offered an excuse or rather defence of the act to Metternich. He had at that time just ordered Fouché to resume the forgery of English notes.[1]

Napoleon, it may be remarked, attributed the rupture of 1803 to his refusal to conclude a commercial treaty

[1] See a full account of this in *Humanité Nouvelle*, July to September 1899; Allonville, ' Mém. Secrets '; Metternich, ' Mémoires '; Lecestre, ' Lettres de Napoléon,' containing letters on this subject which were suppressed in the collection published by Napoleon III.

'which would necessarily have been detrimental to the
manufactures and industry of his subjects,'[1] and he
never relaxed stringency in excluding British merchandise. As late as 1810 such goods were seized and
burned at Roscoff, Bâle, and Strasburg, though the
prefect of Strasburg suggested that textiles should be
utilised in hospitals and ambulances. The war thus
gave a stimulus to French manufactures, except to
those hampered by want of raw materials. The ports,
however, suffered severely through the English blockade,
especially Nantes and other towns which had had a
large trade with the West Indies. During the short
peace Nantes had sent out merchantmen, and sixty
of these, unable to get back, were captured. Marseilles
also suffered, but the blockade could not entirely stop
its trade.

Even some Englishmen long resident in France were
declared prisoners and had to plead for exemption.
Chalmers, a Bordeaux merchant, Scottish on the father's
side, French on the mother's; James Macculloch, who
had been in Brittany for thirty-five years; James Smith,
Stone's successor as printer; and James Milne, who
taught cotton-spinning at the Arts et Métiers, were in
this position. Chalmers found naturalisation the only
resource. Smith and Milne, perhaps also Macculloch,
were struck off the list of captives. As a rule rich
residents as well as manufacturers and artisans were
unmolested, for Napoleon was not insensible of the
advantage thus accruing to Parisian tradesmen. Thus
Francis Henry Egerton, brother and eventual successor

[1] Talleyrand's letter to Fox, April 1, 1806.

of the Earl of Bridgewater, an eccentric clergyman or
ex-clergyman of whom we shall hear anon, was not
disquieted. According to a French writer he had
created a scandal which necessitated expatriation, but
this assertion I have not been able to verify. His chess
parties in 1807 excited much notice. In 1813 he
visited Italy. Quintin Craufurd was also unmolested,
along with his *quasi*-wife Mrs. Sullivan, who, according
to a French police register, was originally an Italian
ballet-dancer, married John O'Sullivan, Under-Secre-
tary for War and the Colonies, and eloped with
Craufurd. Another version, however, states that she
had been the mistress or morganatic wife of the King
of Würtemberg, on whose legitimate marriage she
withdrew with her daughter to Paris, subsequently
marrying Sullivan. What is certain is that she had
cohabited with Craufurd in Paris as long ago as 1787,
for in that year she had had to fetch him home at
9 A.M. from the British Embassy after a whole night at
the card-table. Nothing worse now befell Craufurd
than a robbery. Madame de Genlis writes on the 23rd
March 1811 to her adopted son, Casimir Becker :—

That poor Mr. Craufurd was robbed yesterday while he
was playing whist at Madame de Talleyrand's. All his
superb jewels, caskets, rings, gold medals, 300 louis d'or, etc.
The window was opened by means of a hole cut in the
shutter, and the desk was forced. But it is believed from
several indications that what was done to the window was
merely a feint and that the thief belonged to the house.[1]

Even Craufurd, however, being uncle, as we have

[1] *Lettres de Madame de Genlis.*

seen, of two British diplomatists, incurred the suspicions of Fouché's spies, for their report of the 22nd May 1804 says :—

It may be supposed that this old man, now *blasé*, has no longer the activity which formerly rendered his house at Frankfort a centre of political movements very hostile to France, but he is still under the influence of Madame Sullivan, that foreigner of easy virtue who facilitated the departure of Louis XVI. and started the same day for Brussels.[1]

Talleyrand's protection nevertheless ensured him against molestation, and he was even permitted to procure books from England.   In 1816 he obtained the restitution of his papers,[2] seized, like his other effects, in 1793, and he claimed 2,230,000 francs compensation for his losses.   A smaller sum was probably awarded him.   He continued living in Paris till his death in November 1819.   A painful episode disturbed his last months.   Sir James Craufurd went over, and as far as can be judged endeavoured to extort from the sick uncle a will or a bequest of £48,000 in his favour. Though forbidden entrance, he flourished pistols in the faces of two servants and forced his way in.   He next prosecuted Mrs. Craufurd and several of her fashionable friends for spreading reports of his conduct, and in court he indulged in such personalities that he had to be expelled.   He also charged the servants with assaulting him, but this, like the other accusations, was dismissed, and he was eventually twice sentenced by default to

[1] A. F. 1493.   [2] T. 1910.

six months' imprisonment for libellous pamphlets, in one of which he accused Mrs Craufurd of bigamy.[1] Quintin Craufurd was very charitable to the poor of Paris. Though primarily a man of fashion, he ranks as an author by works on India, Mary Stuart, and Marie Antoinette, some of them in French. His widow, retaining to the age of eighty-four her vivacity and charm, died in Paris about 1832. Her daughter[2] married Count Albert d'Orsay, one of Napoleon's generals, and thus became the mother of Count Alfred d'Orsay, the handsome fop, spendthrift, and amateur painter, who in 1827 married Lady Harriet Gardner, step-daughter of the famous Lady Blessington. Sir James (latterly Sir James Grogan) Craufurd died in 1839.

Fraser Frisell, who, except for a brief visit to his native Scotland in 1802, had lived in France since 1792, was likewise allowed full liberty.

Americans, it may be mentioned, were liable to be arrested as English, for the latter sometimes attempted to pass themselves off as Americans. George Matthew Paterson, a cousin of Madame Paterson-Bonaparte's father, was detained as a British subject. He had, indeed, been born in Ireland. He was sent to Valenciennes, and then to Lille, whence he wrote letters to Madame Paterson-Bonaparte complimenting her on her marriage with Jerome and desiring to make her acquaintance.[3] William Russell was at least half American. He had got up the Bastille dinner at Bir-

---

[1] *Moniteur*, 1819-1820.   [2] See p. 220.
[3] *Correspondence of Jérôme Bonaparte.* Baltimore, 1878.

mingham in 1790, whereupon his house was burnt down
by the mob. He had gone to America in 1795, but in
1802, being in France on his way to England, he was
detained till 1814.

Junot, who as Governor of Paris had to carry out the
order of detention, was, according to his wife's memoirs,
very reluctant to do so, and consented only under great
pressure. He seems, indeed, by all accounts to have
been inclined to leniency, and Forbes tells us that he
suggested his obtaining exemption by pretending to be
a sexagenarian. For a time some captives were allowed
to remain in Paris, but this did not last long.
Napoleon, in this as in other cases, interested himself
in the smallest details. On the 3rd July he ordered a
hundred of the English in Paris to be sent off. They
were allowed to choose between Melun, Meaux, Fontainebleau, Nancy, and Geneva, only twenty-five, mostly
Irishmen, being permitted to remain in Paris. He
complained too of having found English at Boulogne
and Calais. Accordingly forty-eight hours' notice was
given them—that is to those not of the age to be
prisoners—to embark for England or to remove into
the interior. On the 7th July Napoleon gave orders
that the English officers should be sent to Fontainebleau or some other town: only forty were to remain in
Paris; 'the presence of so great a number of English in
Paris cannot but cause and does cause great mischief.'[1]
On the 23rd November he ordered that officers, old
men, and men with wives and children should be

---

[1] *Correspondance.*

interned at Verdun. The prisoners at Fontainebleau, Phalsbourg, and Marsal were accordingly transferred thither. Persons giving cause of complaint were to be confined at Bitche,[1] Sedan, or Sarrelouis, while privates and sailors were to be imprisoned at Charlemont and Valenciennes.

Verdun was obviously chosen because its distance from the sea rendered escape difficult. It was a town of ten thousand inhabitants, and the influx of English, mostly in affluent or at least easy circumstances, was a windfall for it. A French newspaper compared them in fact to sheep enclosed in a fold to manure the soil, and it suggested that other towns should share the advantage. The mayor of Metz, indeed, applied on behalf of that city, but ineffectually. Verdun retained a kind of monopoly, a regulated monopoly, for Napoleon in one of his letters (Nov. 24, 1804) warned the municipality that unless it kept down the price of lodgings, which had risen from 36 to 300 francs a month, the English would be sent elsewhere. Some of the army or navy officers and captains of merchantmen captured during the war were, of course, without means, and they had the option of gratuitous accommodation in the barracks. Another reason for the choice of Verdun may have been the absence of any upper class with whom the captives could mix, whereas at Nancy, the former capital of Lorraine and still a kind of provincial Paris, they had much more congenial surroundings. Austrian and Russian prisoners there joined them in 1804 in celebrating Carnival. The number of

[1] Now German territory and spelt Bitsch.

captives at Verdun from 1803 to 1814 varied from six to eleven hundred, but the highest number included captives made at sea or on battlefields. They procured remittances from England through Perregaux, the Paris banker, and some obtained permission for their families to join them. They had to give their parole not to escape as a condition of being allowed to hire their own lodgings, a breach of parole entailing incarceration. They had to answer to the roll-call morning and night. They beguiled their captivity as best they could. There were amateur theatricals, cock-fights, and horse-races. The prisoners were described by the *Argus* in January 1804 as 'playing, dancing, singing, and drinking all day long.'

Two clubs were formed, one English at Concannon's house,[1] the other Irish at Carron's, but the latter was broken up on account of Hibernian quarrels in 1807. Lady Cadogan gave entertainments, and on the Prince of Wales's birthday in 1804 Mrs. Concannon issued a hundred and twenty invitations to a ball and supper, when the costly toilettes of Mrs. Clive, wife of Colonel Robert Clive, and those of Mrs. Annesley, were much remarked. In 1807 the townspeople were invited by four captives to a masquerade ball.[2]

'Young Englishmen,' wrote George Call in his diary, after passing through Verdun in 1810, 'are much the same whether prisoners or at home, playing, driving,

---

[1] Concannon was ultimately allowed to visit Vienna and to reside near Epernay.

[2] At Fontainebleau also there was a theatrical performance for the benefit of the penniless captives, Concannon writing the prologue.

and shooting each other (*sic*) . . . One might fancy
oneself in London.' The richer prisoners gave monthly
subscriptions for their poorer brethren or for schools,
and the Birmingham Quakers in 1807 opened a subscription for them, an example followed in 1811 by
London. The English Government, moreover, at the
instance of Robson, sent £2000. Dr. Davis gave
gratuitous medical services to the poorer prisoners.
Maude and Jordan held Church of England services
in the college hall, and solemnised marriages the
validity of which was afterwards disputed. When
fellow of Queen's College, where he died in 1852,
Maude used to relate his experiences.[1] Captivity re-
veals character, and there was not unbroken harmony
or unalloyed respectability. Some speedily got into
debt, and the authorities had to consider whether imprisonment for debt could be resorted to. This seems
to have been at first settled in the negative. Lord
Barrington, in June 1804, gave a Frenchman a draft
on London which was dishonoured. The holder thereupon sued him and obtained judgment, but on appeal
this was reversed, on the ground that being detained
Barrington could not have arranged for an extension
of time. Ultimately, however, we find arrests for debt
made, and in 1807 Napoleon ordered that such judg-
ments should be enforced. Waring Knox was in a
debtors' prison at Saargemünd when, on the intercession of the Grand Duke of Berg, he received permission to live at Melun, provided his creditors agreed
to his exit. While in prison for debt at Valenciennes

---

[1] *Notes and Queries*, November 18, 1899.

in 1811, he asked for 200 louis and a passport that
he might go to England, where, having been brought
up with the Prince Regent, he could procure a confidential post and could discover and reveal the secret
projects of the British Government. General Clarke,
whose Irish extraction and knowledge of England,
where he had found his first wife,[1] made him a good
judge of such applications, believed, however, that he
simply wanted to escape from his numerous French
creditors. Whether the offer was sincere or not it
was almost equally contemptible. Yet we ultimately
hear of his giving his poorer countrymen a daily
meal at Valenciennes, where he died in a debtors'
prison in December 1813, just before release would
have come. It is significantly stated that Sir William
Cooper and Lady Cadogan, on being allowed to quit
Verdun for Nancy, left no debts behind them, whereas
half a dozen others had left half a million francs un-
paid. Police reports of 1804-1805 mention one Wilson
as behaving indecently with his French mistress at
the theatre, and striking the officer who reprimanded
him. He was deservedly sent to Bitche. Wilbraham
was charged with forgery and with swindling his fellow-
countrymen. We hear, too, of a duel between ' Gold '
(Valentine Goold, or Francis Goold, a surgeon ?) and
Balbi, the keeper of the gaming-tables, in which the
latter was wounded. ' Gold ' was consequently confined in the fortress, but Napoleon (this proves that
he looked into everything) ordered his liberation. ' A
prisoner of war,' he said, ' may fight a duel.' One of

---

[1] Elizabeth Alexander, divorced by him in 1795.

the brothers Mellish, interned at Orleans, actually challenged the prefect to an encounter. A duel in 1806 between Captain Walpole and Lieutenant Miles, both of the navy, in which the latter was killed, probably arose out of a gaming quarrel. In the gaming-room figured the notice, 'This bank is kept for the English; the French are forbidden to play at it.'[1]

The gaming-tables, Lord Blayney was told, cost the English prisoners £50,000 a year, but they were eventually closed. A Captain Cory, in one of his drunken fits, assaulted a French soldier. Colonel William Whaley, probably the brother of 'Jerusalem' Whaley, who indulged in quarrelling, duelling, and betting, was in 1808 sent to Moulins. He is described as 'notorious for immorality and extravagant conduct, and capable of the most desperate enterprises.' The English Government had refused him a passport for France, but he had managed to get there, and after six months' incarceration in the Temple at Paris, where he excited a mutiny among the prisoners, had been sent to Verdun. There in 1811, to revenge himself for a refusal to receive him, he denounced Blayney as having clandestinely procured plans of French fortresses. The charge was investigated and declared unfounded. There were other men base enough falsely to denounce fellow-captives. Morshead and Estwicke in 1808 were fined 20,000 francs for calumny and swindling. Sir Thomas Wallace was denounced out of revenge by MacCarthy as being deep in debt and meditating escape or suicide.[2] In August 1813 there

---

[1] Lawrence, *Picture of Verdun*, 1810. [2] F. 7, 3716.

was a scuffle between prisoners and townsmen, which gendarmes had to repress. Hutchinson, a teacher of languages, was sent to Bitche for insulting a French officer. A Captain Hawker and a man named Raineford, who entered a jeweller's shop on pretence of paying a bill, and seriously assaulted him, were sentenced in 1808 to twelve and six months' imprisonment respectively. 'Restless spirits,' says Call, 'do their best to compel the French to treat the prisoners harshly.'

Some captives, indeed, brought punishments on themselves. Thomas Devenish, having inveighed against Napoleon, was sent to Doullens fortress, but after a time was allowed to return, and Brodie, who had taught English at Blois, audaciously sent General Wirion, the commandant at Verdun, a letter of diatribes against Napoleon, for which he was relegated to Bitche. A surgeon named Simpson, who at the theatre hissed a bust of Napoleon and next day boasted of the act, pleaded inebriation, but was consigned to the fortress. On the other hand Neilson, captain of a merchantman, obviously tried to curry favour by naming his infant Napoleon, and Felix Ellice, a prisoner at Thionville, composed four sonnets and an ode on the birth of the King of Rome. Williams, imprisoned at Bitche, who had been employed by the Admiralty till 1799, but had apparently been dismissed, offered in 1804 and again in 1808 to detect the spies acting for England, but his overtures were refused, it being believed that the spies had been changed. Two navy lieutenants were imprisoned for fourteen days in 1805 for striking a French officer. A Captain Bannatyne and two officers got up theatricals on the plea of intending to pay debts, but in reality, it was said, to swindle their countrymen. Captain Nanney was sent to Arras for seducing a townsman's wife, but escaped in August 1809. Gentlemen's servants are not always of exemplary behaviour, and we hear of ten valets being packed off from Verdun.

These black sheep were of course exceptions, and we hear on the other hand of Colonel Reilly Cope indulging in botanising, of Forbes having his daughter taught to dance, and of Captain Molyneux Shuldham constructing a carriage propelled by sails at seven or eight miles an hour. Horses, however, being frightened by this monster, and a cart being overturned by it, it was hissed and stoned by the peasantry. Shuldham also invented a boat which, placed on a kind of skates, slid over the ice.[1] He and others likewise amused themselves with rowing, but anglers complained that they frightened away the fish, and the pastime was consequently forbidden.

General Wirion, the commandant of Verdun, had clearly no enviable position. Not only had he to keep the captives in order and prevent escapes, but he had to deal with a swarm of French adventurers of both sexes who sought to make money by facilitating escapes. It was accordingly ordered in July 1805 that all suspicious women should be expelled, and that no passports should be allowed to Verdun unless good reasons were shown. Frenchmen, like foreigners,

---

[1] A. F. iv. 1504. Folkard, *The Sailing Boat*, 1853.

could not then go freely from one town to another.[1]
Women who had caused quarrels among the captives
were expelled, but some of them then settled in the
neighbouring villages. An honourable commandant
would have found his post unpleasant and irksome, and
Wirion, the son of a pork butcher, was not even an
honourable man. He recognised Lord Barrington's
mistress, Madame St. Amand, who was at first passed off
as his wife, by calling on her, and he took money for
winking at illicit amours. He is said to have recommended housekeepers or mistresses who were his spies,
and in one case an Englishman who had foolishly
told his mistress his plans of escape was betrayed
by her. Wirion may have thought this a legitimate
stratagem, but he likewise unblushingly levied black-
mail, and his subordinates followed suit. He would
invite himself or be invited to dinner with the wealthier
captives, and they would allow him to win from them
at cards, in order to obtain small favours or to avoid
being sent to Bitche, to which they were liable at
his mere caprice. He inflicted a fine of 3 francs on
men failing to present themselves at the roll-call morning and night, but not finding many able to pay 6 francs
a day for late rising and an evening promenade he com-
muted this for 6 francs or 12 francs a month. In the
winter of 1804, however, he made one roll-call a day
suffice, and allowed exceptionally good prisoners to
appear only every fifth day.[2] He received, according to Sturt, 600 francs or 1000 francs a month from
the gaming-tables as the price of his protection, and

[1] A. F. iv. 1495.   [2] A. F. iv. 1491.

he is said to have extorted no less than 136,000 francs
from a prisoner named Garland.

Wirion's gendarmes got up lotteries for articles which
sometimes did not exist, and prisoners had to take
tickets as the price of small favours.   Complaints of
his extortion were unavailing until the appointment
as Minister of War of General Clarke.   Wirion was
thereupon summoned to Paris in 1810, and rather
than face a court-martial he shot himself in the Bois
de Boulogne.   No French newspaper, indeed, records
this, and though affirmed by Lord Blayney, who arrived
at Verdun shortly afterwards, I should have felt doubts
of its accuracy but for finding a passage in *Letters
from the Cape*, a pamphlet dictated by Napoleon at
St. Helena in 1817.   It says:—

The English prisoners detained at Verdun were treated
with great attention (*sic*), and a French officer who commanded that depôt having been guilty of some extortions
upon them, an inquiry was in consequence ordered by the
Emperor, and the culprit was so much afraid of his anger
that he committed suicide.

I have, moreover, discovered in the police bulletin of
April 8, 1810, the following record:—

General Wirion went yesterday morning at ten o'clock in
a hackney coach to the Bois de Boulogne.   Alighting a few
steps from the Porte Maillot, he blew out his brains.   Upon
him was found a letter to his wife and another to the doctor,
asking him to attend to her in these sad circumstances.   It
appears that impatience at the apparent tardiness of the
commission deputed to investigate the complaints against
him was the reason of the suicide.[1]

[1] F. 7, 3767.

Wirion's chief subordinate and successor, Colonel Courselles, though far from immaculate, was more cautious and moderate in his extortions. He confined himself to a monopoly of the wine supply, charging exorbitant rates, and to paying the allowance to the poorer prisoners in *livres tournois* in lieu of francs, thus clearing a profit. Courselles, in his turn, was called to account, but he threw the blame on his subordinates, one of whom, Lieutenant Massin, shot himself through apprehension of a court-martial. He had simply by Courselles' orders destroyed incriminating documents, but thus thrown over by his chief he left a note stating that though innocent he could not face threatened dishonour. It is satisfactory to learn that Courselles was likewise removed, that his successor was so upright a man that on his death in 1813 all the English attended the funeral, and that the next commandant was still more indulgent, allowing captives to live not merely in the outskirts of Verdun but in neighbouring towns.

The captives were popular at Verdun. Some of the inhabitants were suspected of allowing letters under cover to be directed to them in order to evade their being opened and read. It is true that a boy five years old, on being jocularly asked by Eyre whether he would go with him to England, replied, ' No, all Englishmen are bad '; but when in 1805 a hundred and seventy of them were transferred to Valenciennes, Givet, and Sarrelouis, two hundred inhabitants collected to see them off. Women shook hands, even gave kisses, and exclaimed, ' Poor young fellows ! ' a proof, says Wirion, that the prisoners had gained great influence and that their removal was urgent.[1]

Three M.P.'s being among the captives, it will naturally be asked whether they retained their seats. They could not or did not resign, but in those days a constituency did not suffer much from going without a representative. The next general election did not take place till 1806. Lord Yarmouth was then re-elected for the Irish pocket borough of Lisburn, and continued —we can hardly say to sit—for it. In 1822 he was called to the Upper House. Lord Lovaine, in like manner, remained member for Beeralston, Devonshire. He was even nominated in 1804 a Lord of the Treasury, and in 1807 an India Commissioner. Thomas Brooke was likewise again re-elected for Newton in 1806, but he, as we shall see, had escaped from Valenciennes. Green, who is described in the police register as a man of letters, and Sturt were not re-elected. Tufton, who with his brother Charles was detained at Fontainebleau, and Thompson, who at Orleans inveighed against Napoleon, had ceased to be M.P.'s.

One of the privations of detention was not merely the censorship exercised over correspondence but the total deprivation of English newspapers. Even before the rupture, indeed, only one paltry Sunday paper in the pay of Napoleon[2] was allowed to pass through the post-office, though the Embassy of course could be subject to no such restriction, and other journals could be clandestinely perused. Napoleon in August 1802

[1] A. F. iv. 1502-1504.
[2] *Bell's Weekly Messenger*, according to Maclean.

rebuked Talleyrand for allowing English newspapers to reach 'a large number of persons' by being addressed under cover to the Foreign Office,[1] and Galignani's newly opened reading-room must have undergone unforeseen restrictions. When the war broke out Napoleon repeated his order that reading-rooms should be allowed only one particular English paper, which was supplied them gratuitously. Madame de Rémusat says he had, however, largely subsidised English journalists and writers, apparently to little purpose, but this may be considered an exaggeration. Galignani's *Monthly Repertory of English Literature*, started in 1807, did not compensate for the absence of newspapers. Even the *Morning Post*, though siding with France, was not admitted.

As long as the *Argus* lasted the captives were fain to subscribe to it, for 'infamous' as Forbes styles it, it gave copious extracts from the London press, but in 1810 Napoleon suppressed it, and the prisoners became dependent on the meagre and carefully manipulated intelligence of the Paris papers. In 1804-1805 several prisoners had sent the *Argus* letters and verses in favour of peace, hoping thus, perhaps, to procure release.

For a time the captives were buoyed up by the expectation of being exchanged for French soldiers and sailors, the balance of numbers being always largely against France; but the British Government refused to exchange combatants for civilians, as this would have been a recognition of the validity of the deten-

---

[1] Brotonne, *Lettres de Napoléon.*

tion. In the autumn of 1805 the prisoners petitioned the Electress (afterwards Queen) of Würtemberg, Princess Royal of England, to intercede for them, but she did not venture to comply, sending word that the matter was one for the two Governments.[1] There was again a gleam of hope in 1806, when, as we shall presently see, Lord Yarmouth went to Paris to negotiate, but the sky was soon overcast. The temptation to escape became stronger as time elapsed and as it became clear that the fall of Napoleon would alone bring liberation. Some broke their parole. Others thought they satisfied honour by sending word just before starting that they withdrew their parole. Sir James Craufurd, who had been allowed to go for two months to Aix-la-Chapelle to take the waters, did not return, but got round to England by Sweden, justifying himself on the ground that his wife was ill and that a lucrative post had been given to another man in his absence. The police bulletin scouted his alleged anxiety for his wife (a daughter of General Gage), stating that he had scandalously treated her, that she had consequently gone home, and that he had been living with a mistress.[2] Lord Yarmouth was informed by a correspondent that the King turned his back on Craufurd at a levée, telling him that prisoners ought to keep their parole; the letter added that Craufurd was uni-

---

[1] A. F. iv. 1495.
[2] A. F. iv. 1491. The mistress was probably the lady for whose arrival from Paris he had waited at Calais in 1803, thus losing his chance of escape. His breach of parole led to many English at Aix-la-Chapelle and elsewhere being relegated to Verdun.

versally despised in England.[1] A later report, however, represented him as receiving £1000 a year from the Government, and the Duke of York was reported to have said that in such arbitrary detention the parole was not binding. Colombine de Jersey, allowed a month in England, also did not return. Lord Archibald Hamilton escaped in January 1804. Sir Beaumont Dixie disappeared from Verdun in September 1804, leaving his clothes on the river bank as though he had been drowned; but he had falsified a passport and had been assisted by neighbouring villagers in his flight.[2] He was, however, recaptured and sent to Bitche, for attempts to escape or other misdemeanours entailed removal to that or some other fortress. 'There,' says the late Mr. Childers, 'the younger members of this unlucky colony appear to have amused themselves *more Britannico* in cutting deeply their names and descriptions on the outer stone walls of the barrack which formed their prison, and I read more than one name belonging to well-known English, Scottish, or Irish families.'[3] Fox and Addison, doctors on board merchantmen, let themselves down by a rope from Verdun citadel, but being unable to get across the canal at the foot they had to give themselves up. Two other doctors, Thomas Clarke and Farrell Mulvey, were likewise recaptured and sent to the fortress of Metz, Mulvey, however, in 1806 being allowed to return

[1] A. F. iv. 1491.
[2] Allonville states that Frenchmen, indignant at the detentions, assisted escapes.
[3] *Nineteenth Century*, May 1888, art. Niederbronn.

on parole to Verdun.   Three surgeons, Baird, Cameron,
and Hawthorn, escaped.   In 1807 a midshipman named
Temple escaped by crouching at the extremity of a
carriage, so as to be concealed by two women, his
French mistress and her maidservant.   The carriage
got to Strasburg, where the mistress, being a native
of the town, obtained a passport, and Temple was
smuggled in the same manner to Austria, whence he
wrote to Colonel Arthur Annesley expressing a hope
that nobody had been molested as an accomplice.   Unfortunately he was not equally solicitous or scrupulous
with regard to his creditors, for he left so many debts
behind him that some of the principal prisoners, revolted
by his dishonesty, forwarded a memorial to the British
Government, praying for his dismissal from the navy.
Annesley himself, whose honeymoon had ended in
captivity, got away in December 1811.   A Dr. Alderson,
married to a Frenchwoman, not obtaining an answer
to an application for a visit to England to recover £400,
took French leave, but his large farm near Lille was
consequently confiscated.   Leviscourt, a navy lieutenant,
who after several years at large on parole had been
confined in the fortress and was no longer on parole,
endeavoured to escape, but being recaptured was
dragged by gendarmes through Verdun, with a heavy
cannon-ball fastened to his leg.   Worsley, the schoolmaster, escaped from Mons to Holland.   James Henry
Lawrence, son of a Jamaica planter and himself a
Knight of Malta, escaped in 1810 by pretending on
the road to be a German.   He had lived several years
in Germany, and had published in German a Malabar

story, which on his arrival in England he issued in English, as also a *Picture of Verdun*. He subsequently led a roving life, chiefly on the Continent, and died in 1840. His father remained a captive. Another foreign knight, of the Order of Maria Theresa, Baron Charles Blount, obtained permission to reside at Bonn, but went to Cleves and fled. He was, however, recaptured and sent to Coblentz fortress. From Valenciennes there were forty escapes, and Lawrence says, ' Every morning those who came upon the promenade inquired who had decamped in the preceding night.' Fortunately there was yet no electric telegraph to give the hue and cry. Colonel Hill, of the Shropshire militia, probably a brother of Lord Hill, escaped and rejoined his regiment. Brooke, M.P. for Newton, Lancashire, quitting a large dinner-party at Valenciennes in October 1804, audaciously drove through the town with his French valet, who had obtained a passport for two merchants, and safely reached Cologne. Francis and Thomas Jodrell waited in December 1803 on the commandant of Valenciennes, told him they withdrew their parole, and drove off. Colonel Smyth accompanied them. All three were recaptured in the duchy of Berg, albeit Bavarian soil, and Napoleon had ordered a court-martial, but they giving a sentry the slip got clear off. Francis was High Sheriff of Cheshire in 1813 ; Thomas was killed at Rosetta in 1807. Philip de Crespigny, who had been married at the Danish Embassy in 1809, escaped from St. Germain in 1811. Wright, a midshipman, brother of the unfortunate Captain John Wesley Wright, facilitated the escape of a friend by holding the rope with which he descended from the ramparts at Verdun, whereupon he was consigned to the fortress. So also was Knox, he having become surety for a Captain Brown, who escaped but was recaptured.

Wirion, by Napoleon's orders, gave notice in 1805 after three escapes that the captives must be responsible for one another if they wished to be treated as men of honour, and that at the first escape all would be sent to fortresses. In 1806, moreover, a reward of 50 francs for the capture of any fugitive was offered at Valenciennes. It was very hard on the sureties to be shut up in a fortress if the men for whom they were answerable did not return on the expiration of their leave of absence, but this may in some cases have been preconcerted. When in 1807 the Arras and Valenciennes captives were removed to Verdun, Wirion gave warning that the first man attempting to escape would be shot, such being the legal punishment for breach of parole. This excited murmurs against terror and tyranny. Yet very shortly afterwards he reported escapes, and it does not appear that he ever enforced his threat, although Napoleon in January 1811 ordered that attempted escapes should be punished with death and that the sentences should be placarded.[1] It is obvious, indeed, that England would have threatened reprisals. Sentences of six years' confinement in irons were, however, inflicted on private soldiers and sailors, for I find that in 1812 Thomas Hudson, who by means of a forged passport had attempted

[1] Brotonne, *Lettres de Napoléon.*

in 1808 to escape from Metz, had the remainder of
the penalty remitted on the ground that he had been
instigated by a fellow-prisoner.[1]   Had such punishments been imposed on captives of higher status
England would manifestly have retaliated.   Alexander
Don, heir to a Scottish baronetcy, escaped from Paris
in 1810.   In 1808 he had been required to leave that
city for either Verdun or Melun, but must have
obtained leave to return.   An Italian lady, claiming
to have been married to him in Paris, but suspected
of being merely his mistress, was living at Florence
in 1812.   He became intimate with Sir Walter Scott,
who speaks of his literary and artistic tastes, his lively
manners, his love of sport, and his oratorical powers,
while Lockhart describes him as courteous, elegant,
accomplished, and the model of a cavalier.   He was
latterly M.P. for Roxburghshire, and died in 1826 at
the age of forty-seven.   His uncle, General Sir George
Don, had been captured and detained at Lille in 1799,
when he went with a flag of truce to General Daendels
bearing a proclamation from the exiled Statthalter.
The French Government threatened to shoot him
in reprisals if Napper Tandy and his companions were
executed.   An exchange for Don with Tandy was
declined by England, as also an exchange with a
French general.   England in 1800 claimed his uncon-
ditional release, on pain of imprisoning the French
generals at liberty on parole.   His wife, seeing no
prospect of his release, applied for a passport to
join him.   He continued a captive till June 1800.

[1] A. F. iv. 1234.

John, afterwards General Sir John Broughton, a Staffordshire baronet's heir, got off in the guise of a courier.

Two sailors named Henson and Butterfield escaped from Verdun, traversed all France, and reached the Mediterranean coast, but were there arrested and sent to Bitche. Philip Astley, the circus owner whose arrival in Paris has been mentioned, obtained a passport for Savoy on pretence of wishing to open a circus there, but he went on to Italy and thence escaped. He was destined to revisit and be buried in Paris in 1814. James Callender or Campbell of Ardinglas, endeavouring to escape, was sent to Ham, the fortress in store forty years later for Louis Napoleon. While there he became the successor to a cousin's estates of £3000 a year, but it was several years before he heard of it. He offered to present his horse to Napoleon, thinking thus to be liberated, but Napoleon insisted on his fixing a price and then sent him double the sum. Campbell revisited Paris in 1815 and was sent by Napoleon to the Conciergerie. This was probably at the instigation of his alleged wife.[1] Captain Charles Cunliffe Owen, father of Sir Philip of South Kensington fame, seems in 1811 to have shammed lunacy and was consequently placed in an asylum at Valenciennes.[2] He had cut a vein, but not dangerously, and had denounced an imaginary plot for seizing Belleisle. He was transferred to a private asylum in Paris, whence in July 1812 he escaped. Captain Francis Tulloch, who in 1808 had been removed from

[1] See p. 67.   [2] F. 7, 3773 and 3776.

Cambrai to Verdun, effected his escape in December 1810.

John Harvie Christie, who had gone to France to economise, after spending three weeks in Paris repaired to Bordeaux. Returning after two months to the capital, he found that arrests had just been ordered. He went to the Norman coast, hoping to embark as an American, but was apprehended at Fécamp, having unluckily in his possession a manuscript copy of satirical verses on Napoleon and Josephine.[1] He was tried on the charge of espionage, and though acquitted remained a prisoner. Henry Dillon and Lynch were arrested at Caen in 1809, and Poppleton, the teacher of English, who with three Frenchwomen had abetted their escape, was sent to prison for two months.[2] John Giffard, arrested in 1811 on the point of embarking at Honfleur, was consigned to a lunatic asylum. William Throckmorton, a friend of Miss Berry, was also recaptured at Honfleur in the same year. Another fugitive bore the appropriate name of Hurry, and Wirion being just then absent, his subordinate Courselles was suspected of having been bribed. Hurry was a freemason, and with a hundred of the captives had been admitted into the Verdun lodge. Wirion recommended that such admissions should be forbidden, for a French mason had confessed in private conversation that he should have felt bound, had Hurry applied to him, to facilitate his escape.[3] But non-masons also promoted escapes, for filthy lucre's

[1] A. F. iv. 1237.　　　　[2] F. 7, 3763.

[3] F. 7, 3716.

sake. Indeed this became a trade, and in 1811 two captains at Bruges were arrested for visiting the *dépôts* and offering passports.[1] In 1809 six inhabitants of Arras were prosecuted for facilitating the escape of an English lord, and at Verdun a breach was discovered in the walls just in time to prevent escapes. These had been so numerous among captains and officers of merchantmen that, with the exception of those above fifty years of age or those having their wives with them, they were ordered to sleep in the citadel. Permission to go outside the town within four miles was also revoked, but was afterwards renewed on condition of mutual suretyship. Augustus Bance, at Valenciennes, applied for French citizenship and for permission to open a soap factory at Antwerp. The latter application was refused, on the ground of Antwerp being too near the frontier, but while the naturalisation question was pending he escaped.

Mogg and three companions escaped from Arras in 1810, concealing themselves in the day-time and guided at night by the moon towards the coast. In a wood near Boulogne, they cut down trees and made a small boat, which a layer of suet rendered watertight, and they had brought sails and rope with them. They were, however, discovered. The authorities ordered the boat to be launched as an experiment, and there was not the slightest leakage. The men's ingenuity was admired, and they told the police inspector that if the Emperor was informed of their daring scheme he would certainly grant them their

[1] F. 7, 3773.

liberty.　One of them was accordingly taken before
Napoleon, who asked him whether his motive had
not been a desire to rejoin a mistress.　'No,' he
replied, 'it was to see my aged mother.'　Thereupon
Napoleon, remarking that she must be a good mother
to have such a son, released him, giving him a small
sum for his mother.　We are not told whether his
companions were also liberated.　Equally venturesome
was William Wright.　He became interpreter to
General Brabançon, and ultimately contrived to get
on board an English flag-of-truce vessel.　He crept
into a trunk till the usual search before departure
was over, and after passing an hour in this uneasy
posture was safe.　In his *Narrative of the Situation
and Treatment of the English arrested by order of the
French Government*, Wright states that at Valenciennes
an English hotel-keeper, King, who had resided there
for twenty years, was very kind to his captive countrymen.　Prisoners without money, says Wright, were
harshly treated, but the officials were open to bribes.
William Hamilton, according to a Boulogne tradition,
was assisted in an unsuccessful attempt to escape by
his jailer's daughter, whom he afterwards married.
He had entered the navy in 1803, and was captured
in 1805.　In 1817 he was appointed Consul at Flush-
ing, in 1818 at Ostend, in 1820 at Nieuport, and in
1822 at Boulogne.　He was knighted on his retirement
in 1873, and died in 1877, aged eighty-eight, being
probably the last survivor of Napoleon's prisoners.

　　Stewart Kyd, the ex-radical, and Dr. Barklimore
escaped, but the two bankers, Boyd and Benfield, had

to undergo the full time of detention. Benfield died in Paris, in straitened circumstances, in 1810. One of his daughters married Grantley Berkeley. According to a police bulletin Benfield was a nullity, whereas Boyd was acquiring a thorough knowledge of French institutions. He arbitrated on a claim against the French Government by Schweizer, Swan's partner and antagonist, who pronounced him to be a man of great culture and acknowledged probity. He also wrote pamphlets on financial subjects. He was indemnified for French confiscation, and from 1823 to 1830 was M.P. for Lymington. He died in 1837. Another man who made good use of his time was Tuckey, who, captured in 1805, compiled a maritime geography in three volumes. He had previously published an account of a voyage to Botany Bay with a cargo of convicts. He died while exploring the River Congo in 1816.

In several instances besides those already mentioned detention was followed up by actual incarceration. James Smith, the filter-maker, was sent to the Temple in 1804 for talking against the French and extolling the defences of England, to which he had paid frequent visits.[1] Colonel Stack was charged in the same year with espionage. It is even alleged, but this cannot be verified, that he was condemned to be shot as an accomplice of the Duc d'Enghien, but was reprieved. What is certain is that he spent three years in Bitche citadel, afterwards remaining a prisoner at Verdun till 1814. Colonel William Edwards, a Jamaica planter,

[1] A. F. iv. 1490.

brother I think of Bryan Edwards, M.P., was imprisoned seven years on suspicion of having facilitated
escapes. The youngest of his twenty-nine children,
born at Bruges in 1800, was Milne Edwards, the
eminent French naturalist.

We now come to the liberations and permissions
to visit or settle in various towns, for each of which
Napoleon's express sanction was necessary, and we
may begin with Lord Yarmouth, since he owed his
liberty to negotiations, albeit fruitless, for peace. He
had become a prisoner under trying circumstances.
He went over to fetch his wife and children just as
the rupture had occurred, and he inquired at Calais
whether he might safely land. He was answered in
the affirmative, yet no sooner had he done so than he,
with all his fellow-passengers, was declared a prisoner.
Curiously enough, however, he professed to consider
the detentions as justified by the embargo in England.
He was sent to Verdun, but it was alleged in March
1804 that he had been seen in Paris. Wirion, reproached with laxity on this account, denied, however,
that he had gone further afield than Clermont on an
affair of gallantry. He had been exempted, indeed,
from the twice-a-day roll-call till all exemptions had
been abolished, and he had also been allowed to go
out shooting; but Wirion urged that permission to
go outside the town tended to prevent escapes by
rendering them dishonourable, and if such permissions
were to be refused the garrison should be strengthened,
the walls being so dilapidated that egress was easy.[1]

[1] A. F. iv. 1328.

Yarmouth's mother had been in favour with the Prince of Wales, and he himself had then, as a youth, been admitted to Carlton House. When, therefore, Fox in 1806, on the death of Pitt, became Foreign Secretary, the Prince asked him to intercede with Talleyrand for Yarmouth's release. Napoleon is said to have imagined that Fox was himself interested in Yarmouth. He consequently not only gave Yarmouth unlimited leave of absence, but suggested that negotiations should be opened through this channel. In August 1805 Yarmouth had already been authorised to quit Verdun for six months and to live near, but not at, Paris. He announced that he chose Versailles, but nevertheless joined his wife in Paris. This contravention was reported by the police, but was winked at for a time.[1] In September, however, he was ordered to repair to Melun. In May 1806 he was allowed, together with Lord Elgin, General Abercromby, and Captain Leveson-Gower, to embark at Morlaix for England. He returned *via* Calais in June with credentials authorising him to negotiate. He was not a novice in diplomacy, for in 1793 he had been sent on a mission to Prussia, charging only his expenses. The police bulletins show how closely all his movements were now watched. They tell us how he went to the Opera, and how he wanted to buy French rentes to the amount of a million francs at one stroke, but could only purchase first 100,000 francs and then 500,000 francs. He called on Quintin Craufurd, Mrs. Sullivan being a friend of Lady Yarmouth, and he was said to be in love with

[1] A. F. iv. 1494.

her daughter, the so-called Mademoiselle de Dorset.[1] In case of the success of his mission he was said to intend buying up all the French brandy in the market and selling it at triple price. A man of pleasure and an art connoisseur, Yarmouth could scarcely be much of a diplomatist, and in August Lord Lauderdale was sent to join him. He was believed to feel annoyance at this. Lauderdale, as we have seen, was a follower of Fox and had always advocated peace. At the end of August Yarmouth was recalled, announcing, however, that he should return in January, and hoped then to conclude peace, but Lauderdale had really superseded him. Lauderdale nevertheless had committed a mistake at the outset. He had asked to be presented to Napoleon, and had had to be told that it was not customary for a plenipotentiary of a country still at war to be allowed an audience, yet it was evidently no fault of his if the negotiations proved abortive. According to a French writer who had studied the documents of the French Foreign Office,[2] Yarmouth on the 17th July submitted to Champagny a draft treaty by which England gave up Sicily to Joseph Bonaparte and recognised Napoleon's conquests in Holland, Germany, and Italy; but Napoleon, instead of closing with so advantageous an offer, awaited the result of his negotiations with Russia. All August was consequently wasted in futile discussions of formalities, and when the Russian

[1] There is a mystery about her paternity, but there seems to be a hint that she was a natural daughter of the Duke of Dorset.

[2] M. Coquelle, paper read at the Congress of French Learned Societies at Paris, 1902.

negative answer arrived Napoleon gave vent to his exasperation by breaking off the negotiations with England, so that Lauderdale at the beginning of October quitted Paris. The last police bulletin in which he is mentioned absurdly describes him as a spy, who had doubtless sent home information of military movements and of public feeling in Paris.

Both he and Yarmouth now disappear from the scene, but Lady Yarmouth remained in France, being allowed to pay occasional visits to England.[1] Lady Hester Stanhope alleges that she had a French lover. If this scandal has any foundation Yarmouth shared the fate of Lord Elgin, who, as we have seen, was liberated with him. His too was a hard case. Returning from the Constantinople Embassy, he had passports from French consuls in Italy, and though not reaching Paris till after Whitworth's departure had been assured by Talleyrand that he might safely remain, and he doubtless hoped French waters might relieve his chronic rheumatism. Lord Hawkesbury (afterwards Lord Liverpool), who, according to Trotter's *Life of Fox*, had in 1802 accepted a handsome Sèvres dinner-service from Napoleon, in his diplomatic circular of the 30th April 1804 made a pointed allusion to Elgin when he said :—

'They (the French Government) promised their protection to such of the subjects of England as were resident in France who might be desirous of remaining there after the recall of His Majesty's ambassador. They revoked this

---

[1] Her son, Lord Henry Seymour, born in 1805, is said to have never set foot in England.

promise without any previous notice, and condemned these very persons to be prisoners of war, and still retain as such in defiance of their own engagements and of the universal usage of all civilised nations. They applied this new and barbarous rule even to individuals who had the protection and authority of French ambassadors and ministers at foreign courts to return in safety through France to their own country.'

Talleyrand, in his annotations to this circular in the *Moniteur* of the 5th November 1804, and in his counter-circular, was significantly silent on this passage, which indeed was obviously unanswerable. Elgin, at first detained with sixty fellow-captives at Orleans, was allowed to go to Barèges and to send to England in October 1803 for Dr. William Scott, on whose report he was permitted to repair to Paris. Owing, however, to an unfounded rumour that General Boyer was incarcerated in Scotland, whereas he was really on parole at Chesterfield, Elgin was ordered back to the Pyrenees. His wife remained in Paris, and he was not allowed to go thither to her confinement, which took place on the 4th March 1804; but the infant expired on the 20th April. He arranged, however, for daily tidings of her. When Thiébault delivered a message from him to her she showed no sign of affection, and General Sebastiani was then lolling on her sofa as though quite at home. She had, however, already made the acquaintance of Robert Ferguson of Raith, son of William Ferguson, who in 1793 had succeeded to the property of his uncle Robert Ferguson, a rich China merchant. Being also one of the British captives, Ferguson was

frequently invited to the Elgins' Paris house. He was
released as an F.R.S. and a mineralogist in 1805. Lady
Elgin, who had joined her husband at Barèges in June
1804, went over to England in 1806 to try and get her
husband exchanged for General Boyer. Thence she
wrote affectionate letters, and Ferguson also wrote as
though interested in the exchange. But Elgin on his
release in 1807 discovered letters addressed to her by
Ferguson, which Garrow, Ferguson's counsel at the
crim. con. trial, described as 'a most ridiculous medley
of love and madness, or love run mad.' 'They would
disgrace,' he said, 'the worst novel of the last century.'
£10,000 damages were awarded. Ferguson married
the frail lady—Anne Nesbit was her maiden name[1]—
got into Parliament for Fife in 1806, and died in 1841.
He was cousin to the Miss Berrys, and had once been
engaged to Agnes. Before leaving Elgin, it should be
stated that Napoleon, styling him 'one of the greatest
enemies of the nation,' had rebuked General Olivier
for showing him attentions at Livourne. Napoleon
had a grudge against Elgin, who, he imagined, sent the
information which enabled Nelson to follow the French
fleet and destroy it at Aboukir. Elgin married again
in 1810, was the father of Dean Stanley's wife, and
died in Paris in 1841.

Lady Elgin was not the only faithless wife, for in
1808 Scott, formerly vice-consul at Naples, declined to
take back his wife, who had been arrested while
cohabiting with an Englishman at Saarlibre, and he

[1] Her father, Hamilton Nesbit, had in 1802 returned through Paris
from a visit to her at Constantinople.

recommended her being sent to England, as he had long disowned her and she was penniless.[1] Lady Webb, letting herself down from a window in Paris, is said, moreover, to have eloped with Fursy-Guesdon, a novelist, and grandson of the actor Préville.[2] She knew Madame Récamier and Chateaubriand.

Lord Beverley and Lord Lovaine, the eldest of his fourteen children, found more indulgence. Though not released, they were permitted in 1805 to reside at Moulins, which Lovaine liked so well that he remained with his young family after 1814, though no longer a captive. He was fond of hunting, lived in style, and was very charitable. At the age of eighty-seven he became Duke of Northumberland, but enjoyed the honour only two years. Just after the capitulation of Paris in 1814 he and two of his sons lunched with Josephine, who told him that the English were the only people generous enough to speak respectfully of the fallen Napoleon. In order to have done with peers, let me here note that Lord Duncannon must have been released before November 1805, when he married in England, and that the Duke of Newcastle, who came just within the age of Napoleon's terrible decree, was released with his mother in 1807. The mother had pleaded ill-health and family affairs, had offered a profusion of compliments to Napoleon, and had adduced her succour to French prisoners previously to the peace. She had been allowed in 1804 to go to the Pyrenees and in 1806 to settle at Tours.

Some scientists, scholars, and physicians owed their

[1] F. 7, 3716.   [2] *Revue Rétrospective*, vol. 14.

release to Banks and Jenner on the one hand, and Carnot, Cuvier, and French doctors on the other. Lord Shaftesbury appears to have been liberated as an F.R.S, but possibly as a friend of Fox. James Forbes, another F.R.S., who with his wife and daughter arrived in Paris from Brussels the very day after the decree was issued, was liberated in June 1804 through Carnot. He had previously been allowed to visit at Tours his brother Major Charles Forbes, with his wife and five children.[1] Pinkerton, the geographer, was likewise released in 1805. Dr. Carmichael Smyth, having in early life travelled in France and kept up a correspondence with French physicians, profited by their intervention.[2] Dr. Maclean urged that he had not been in England for ten years, and this plea availed him. Jenner sent a letter to Napoleon in behalf of William Thomas Williams, which Napoleon at first cast aside, but Josephine picking it up told him it was from Jenner. 'Ah,' he then exclaimed, 'I can refuse nothing to so great a man.' Williams, who on watching Napoleon for a full hour at the Paris Opera had noticed that he never once smiled, thought his countenance, on seeing him again at Nancy in 1805, mild, though haughty. Jenner, a correspondent of the Institute in 1808 and a foreign associate of it on the death of Maskelyne in 1811, also secured the release of Dr. Wickham,[3] and through Corvisart, the Emperor's physician, that of Nathaniel Garland and Valentine Goold. Corvisart

---

[1] Charles escaped in August 1810.
[2] *Notes and Queries*, February 3, 1900.
[3] Baron, *Life of Jenner*.

likewise intervened for Dr. Burrell Davis, who after graduating in medicine at Montpellier had been relegated to Verdun, and who published a striking pamphlet against premature burial. This he forwarded to Corvisart, along with a petition to Napoleon. Doctors indeed, as was but right, were less harshly treated. They were permitted to make journeys to English patients, and in 1810 nine were granted passports for England. Alexander Hamilton, though not yet an F.R.S., doubtless owed his release to having catalogued the Sanscrit manuscripts in the Paris Library. Colclough became a member of a literary society at Nîmes, in order to procure release as a scholar, but whether this availed him is doubtful, for we do not hear of him as a resident Irish landlord till after Napoleon's fall.

John Spencer Stanhope, of Cannon Hall, Yorkshire, treacherously delivered up in 1810 by a Gibraltar privateer, was liberated in March 1813, at the intercession of the Institute, in order to make an archæological visit to Greece: but literary or artistic accomplishments did not always secure release. Joseph Forsyth discovered this to his cost. An Elgin man, his father intimate with Isaac Watts, he had eagerly embraced the opportunity of visiting Italy. Starting as early as October 1801, he reached Nice on Christmas Day and spent seventeen months in Italy, but on reentering France in May 1803 he found himself a prisoner and was confined at Nîmes. Attempting in the winter to escape, he was relegated to Bitche, where for two years he was in close confinement. He was then allowed to go on parole to Verdun. There he prepared and published in London an account of his artistic tour, and had copies sent to France in the hope that it would serve him a good turn. But from want of interest, perhaps too on account of his unlucky attempt to escape, he could obtain no greater favour than permission to live in Paris, and even this after four months was revoked. He had to repair to Valenciennes and wait till 1814. He died in the following year. Curiously enough, he regretted the publication of his book, albeit it possessed considerable merit.

Monroe, author of the famous 'doctrine,' then American Ambassador at London, was applied to by prisoners' friends to solicit their liberty through his Paris colleague Livingston, whose dispatches to Washington were sent by flag of truce through Morlaix. Ferguson, Lady Elgin's paramour, seems to have been thus released, and a Colonel Johnston was thus allowed to go to France to see a kinsman named Oliphant.

But while release came to some after a few months, it did not come to others till after long years. Robson, ex-M.P., confined at Nîmes, must have had influential friends to obtain permission to embark at Emden as early as November 1803. Sir Thomas Hare and young Augustus Foster were apparently indebted to friends in high quarters for release. A wife's heroic efforts, which, however, are not particularised, also effected the liberation of General Sir Charles Shipley.

Chenevix, whose friendship with Berthollet stood

him in good stead, in July 1803 read a paper before the Institute on 'palladium,' the metal discovered in platinum ore by Wollaston, and sent articles to a French chemical journal. He was one of the original contributors to the *Edinburgh Review*, in which, according to Thomas Moore, who met him at Paris in 1821, he wrote against France. He was able without hindrance to visit Germany and Spain, as well as the Black Sea. In 1812 he married a French countess, and remained in France until his death in 1830.

One of the likeliest ways of obtaining release was to petition Napoleon or Josephine in person. Mrs. Tuthill managed to present her petition to the Emperor while out hunting, and he could not deny a lady, especially a great beauty. Mrs. Cockburn obtained an introduction to her fellow-Creole Josephine, whereupon Napoleon[1] in July 1803 wrote, 'Do what is proper for Coxburn' (*sic*). It was not, however, till 1805 that he obtained permission to go to England for twelve months, doubtless a euphemism for release. Cockburn, like Yarmouth, had been allowed to go out hunting at Verdun. John Maunde, an old Bluecoat scholar, was released in 1807, whereupon he went to Oxford to study for the Church, became curate of Kenilworth, and formed an intimacy with Lucien Bonaparte, in his turn a captive, whose poem he was translating into English when he died in 1813.

Sir Grenville Temple was allowed in 1804 to go to

---

[1] Who little imagined that Admiral Cockburn, a kinsman of the prisoner, would convey him in the *Northumberland* to St. Helena.

Switzerland, and in 1810 to embark for America with his rich Bostonian wife and their four children. Sampson Eardley was released in March 1806. Captain Walter Stirling was liberated in time to testify at the Elgin trial to the conjugal harmony which had previously existed. Colonel Molesworth in 1804 had permission to visit England, which probably meant release. John Parry, more fortunate than his brother James, was struck off the list of captives. He alleged that he had been expelled from England for writing in favour of peace, and he solicited and obtained permission in 1809 to go and see after his brother's property, intending to return and marry at Tours. Henry Seymour, the ex-M.P. and lover of Madame Dubarry, was allowed in 1809 to go to Switzerland. He had previously been permitted to reside at Melun and Paris. Richard Trench, who had been married at the British Embassy in March 1803 to Melesina, daughter of the Rev. Philip Chenevix and widow of Colonel St. George, was allowed in August 1803, on account of ill-health, to go to Orleans, his wife having managed through influence to save her husband from being sent to Verdun. From Orleans she made repeated visits to Paris to intercede for him. Her husband once in 1805 accompanied her, and in a secluded part of the Bois de Boulogne meeting the Emperor, told him which way the stag had gone. Napoleon, however, was angry at thus meeting alone a tall young Englishman who had come to Paris without leave, and after a night in prison Trench was ordered to Verdun. He was soon allowed to live in Paris, but it was not till 1807 that Mrs. Trench, by personally presenting her petition, secured her husband's release.[1] Meanwhile she had given birth to Francis, a theological writer whom I remember as rector of Islip, but Richard, the archbishop, was not born till 1808, after her return to Dublin.

There is no record in the police bulletins of the release of Thomas Manning, who hastened to Paris from Angers on hearing of the rupture. The family tradition is that he owed his deliverance to Carnot and Talleyrand. Let us hope that he got back in time to be one of the Diss volunteers who in October 1803 received notice to be in readiness to march to London on the first notification of a French invasion— an invasion, however, which, argued a letter in the *Times*, should be welcomed as ensuring a grand haul of prisoners. In 1817, on his way back from Tibet, he stopped at St. Helena and presented the captive Emperor —their positions had been almost reversed—with tea, coffee, tobacco, two silk pocket-handkerchiefs, and two feather fans.[2] He had been strictly charged to address Napoleon as 'general,' but when asked by whom his passport in 1803 had been signed, he replied, 'By yourself, by the Emperor.' Napoleon's face lit up at this recognition of his rank by an Englishman. Impey was released in July 1804, perhaps through Madame Talleyrand, whom he must have known at Calcutta. Sir James de Bathe is said to have procured the intercession of the Pope, to whom it was represented that his children in England might in his absence be made

[1] *Remains of Mrs. Trench.*
[2] Mr. E. B. Harris, *Athenæum*, February 24, 1900.

Protestants. His son and heir was then only a boy of ten. Sir James died in 1808. Greathead, the lifeboat inventor, was released in December 1804, quite cured of democracy, it was said, by his French treatment. Greatheed, with whom he must not be confused, was allowed with his son to go to Dresden and thence to Italy. The son died at Vicenza in 1804 at the age of twenty-three. Granby Sloper, who had settled at Paris in 1789 and had been imprisoned there in 1794, though struck off the list of captives in 1803 and allowed to live in Paris, had been arrested in 1806 as an accomplice of Wickham; but on proof that he had simply when at Berne asked the latter for a passport for England he was liberated.[1] William Stone, who, as already stated, had taken refuge in France after his acquittal of high treason in London in 1796, was unmolested, and became eventually steward to an Englishman named Parker at Villeneuve St. George.

One of the most singular cases of lenity is the permission given in 1808, on the recommendation of a Paris professor, to the two brothers Lambert to leave Givet and exhibit themselves all over France. For several generations their family had had a scaly or horny epidermis.[2]

There is a solitary case of refusal to accept release. Richard Oliver, ex-M.P. for the county of Limerick, though in ill-health and anxious to leave with his mother and sister, declined without consulting them on learning that the passport had been granted at the instance of Arthur O'Connor, whom he had formerly

[1] A. F. iv. 1496.   [2] A. F. iv. 1512.

known. He disdained to be under obligation to a conspirator.

It would have been strange if money as well as influence had not sometimes secured release. The Rev. W. H. Churchill, of Colliton, Devon, was on his way to Lyons in May 1803 when he was stopped and ordered to return to Paris. There he was dismayed to learn that all the English had been consigned to Verdun. He pleaded for leave to escort an invalid brother home, but was told by Junot that unless he repaired to Verdun he would be sent to the Temple prison. He nevertheless resolved to wait and see what would happen. A gendarme duly appeared with an order to take him to the Temple, but the name was misspelt, and the gendarme for a consideration withdrew, promising to say that he had not found the man. Churchill then feigned illness, and a French doctor prescribed for an ulcerated throat. In January 1804 Churchill, through bribery, as is believed, was permitted to escort his invalid brother.[1]

Next to freedom the greatest favour was leave to visit or reside where the prisoners chose. Ill-health was naturally one of the commonest grounds for such applications, and naturally these were viewed with some scepticism. Lawrence states that Dr. Madan at Verdun made money by giving certificates of indisposition for exemption from morning roll-call. Two ex-M.P.'s, Nicholl and Waller, obtained permission to repair respectively to Lyons and Nîmes. Nicholl's son was also allowed to go to a neighbouring town to marry a Miss

[1] *Journal of Mary Frampton.*

Mount.[1] He was ultimately released. The bookseller Payne was authorised to go to Plombières and Barèges. We thus see that watering-places profited, as well as Verdun, by the detentions.

Sir Thomas and Lady Webb were in 1809 allowed to go to Savoy. Lady Webb, a convert to Catholicism, adopted in 1813 a little English girl seemingly lost by her parents and found among a troop of jugglers at Lyons.[2] The waif, after being educated and apprenticed, became a nun. Macnab was permitted to study medicine at Montpellier. James Heath, the engraver, was allowed in 1810 two months at Paris to copy architectural designs. In that year also visits to the capital were permitted to two clergymen, Maude and Lancelot Lee, as well as to Lord Shaftesbury, Captain Lovelace, Colonel de Blaquiere, and the brothers Tichborne, Henry being in ill-health. In June 1810, however, all or nearly all permissions for Paris were revoked. But in 1813 Halpin was allowed to return to Paris to complete his art studies. Colonel Phillips, who had accompanied Cook round the world, was permitted to

[1] This was not the only marriage among the captives.

[2] This was not the only case of unaccountable desertion. Edmund Wilson, born in Italy, was left behind in France at the age of three years by his English parents—there was an Andrew Wilson, an artist, a visitor, but surely he was not the delinquent—and was adopted by the Comtesse d'Aumale. He became a prominent liberal Catholic, and from 1829 to 1831 contributed to the *Correspondant* till it was superseded by the more advanced *Avenir* of Lamennais. It was, however, revived in 1842 and still exists. For seventeen years 'le sage Wilson,' as he was called on account of his habitual circumspection, presided over Sunday gatherings of Parisian apprentices. He was unmarried, a sort of lay monk, was very charitable, and was never naturalised in France. He died in 1862.

visit England in the summer of 1804, and General
Scott was allowed to visit his family at Versailles;
but on refusing to name a man who had extorted
money from him by pretending to have obtained such
permission he was ordered back to Verdun.[1] Sir
Thomas Clavering, whose father had been one of
Warren Hastings' opponents at Calcutta, had married
a Frenchwoman, the daughter of an Angers dressmaker, and was consequently allowed to remain at
Orleans. There he drove his own carriage and had
fine English horses. He was friendly with his neighbour, the actress Raucourt, and once took young
Bonneval (afterwards Marquis and General) to her
house, where there was much card-playing and the
youth lost all his pocket-money. In 1808 he was
permitted to live at St. Germain. In 1810 he sent his
wife to England to try and effect an exchange. Meanwhile he was at Paris, living with a Vaudeville
actress, Arsène. She treacherously sent the police
an anonymous letter warning them that he talked
against Napoleon and intended to escape. Cuthbert
Sharpe, through Regnier, Minister of Justice, was in
1804 struck off the list of captives, allowed to live in
Paris, and ultimately liberated. Cramer, a man of a
good Irish Protestant family, though originally detained at Verdun, had leave, on its being known
that he was against the war, to travel freely about
France. Settling at Tours, he married a Mademoiselle
Fereau and made the acquaintance of Courier, the
future pamphleteer. He died at Florence in 1827.

[1] A. F. iv. 1498-1499.

Calais, was at once, in consideration of her age, sent back to England.

Sometimes women who had gone home on business did not find return an altogether easy matter. Thus Mrs. Clarke, who had obtained a passport for England *via* Holland in April 1807, was arrested by the English authorities on attempting to return, was sent in custody to London, and was interrogated on suspicion of being a spy in the French service. She easily cleared herself, but then waited to see her elder daughter Eleanor married to Frewen-Turner, M.P. for Athlone, and in 1808 she landed in France from Jersey. She was arrested, however, at St. Lô, and had to give an account of herself. She stated that in 1791 she visited Toulouse with her daughter and her mother, Mrs. Hay,[1] and that in 1801 she took her mother and a younger daughter Mary to Toulouse; that they removed to Paris two days before Whitworth's departure, that her visit to England had been purely on business, and that had she not got a passage from Jersey she should have tried going round by America. She was allowed, on her story being verified, to rejoin her mother and daughter.[2] The latter as Madame Mohl, ultimately famous for her receptions in Paris, coquettishly concealed her age, not liking to confess to seniority to her German husband. At her death in 1883 she was ninety years of age. Miss Lemprière, probably sister of the author of the *Classical Dictionary*, was permitted to return. Mary Masquerier,

[1] They then saw the royal family dining in public at the Tuileries.
[2] F. 7, 3716.

a governess, sister, doubtless, of the artist already named, was allowed in 1812 to embark at Morlaix for London. A Mrs. Cornuel in the same year obtained permission to go to England to fetch her two daughters, one of whom had for ten years been in the charge of an uncle in London, and all three returned on board a smuggling vessel.[1] A girl named Warren, eleven years of age, on board a vessel captured by a privateer in 1805, was restored to her father, quartermaster at Malta. Three children named Crane, aged from ten to sixteen, who had been sent to school in Paris in 1802, but whose father could no longer afford to pay for their education, were permitted in 1805 to embark at Rotterdam.[2] Mrs. Story and her four little children, also captured by a privateer, were liberated in December 1813, as likewise 'Madame Kirkpatrick' with her four children and two nieces, who had all been residing in Paris. We shall hear presently of her husband. Catherine Russell, a young woman captured in 1812 by a privateer and landed at Amsterdam, showed such despair at being parted from her friends that she was allowed to return to England.[3] Mrs. Mary Bishop in 1813 had leave with her four daughters to pay a visit to England, ostensibly to obtain possession of property, but really, so she alleged after the Restoration when appealing to Louis XVIII. for recompense, on a mission from royalists. Lady Boyle had like permission in July 1813, but her husband, the future Earl of Glasgow, could merely obtain leave to visit Paris. Occasionally

[1] F. 7, 3744.   [2] F. 7, 3750.   [3] F. 7, 3744.

the English authorities objected to the landing of such passengers. Thus a Mrs. Borel, wife of a London merchant, was refused permission to land at Dartmouth in 1813 for want of a formal permit; she took passage on another vessel for Portsmouth in the hope of there finding less difficulty.[1] The English Government apparently suspected that some of these arrivals might be spies in French pay.

Englishwomen, sometimes accompanied by little children, having obtained leave from both Governments, mostly in order to rejoin captive husbands, continued to land at Morlaix up to 1813. Thus Mrs. Dorothy Silburn, who had liberally befriended French *émigré* priests in England, was authorised in 1807 to settle at Roscoff, where she spent the remainder of her life, her tomb being still prominent in the old churchyard. The Countess Bruce, separated wife of Puschkin—he made in 1810 curious experiments in galvanism, as it was then called—went from Venice to Paris in 1811 to solicit the pardon of a negro servant who had been condemned to death for the murder of a female servant, whereas the two domestics had agreed to die together because they could not legally marry. He accordingly shot her, and wounded, but failed to kill, himself. Among the arrivals was also the notorious Lady Craven, Margravine of Anspach. This fair but frail lady, who had sat to Reynolds and Romney, had visited the Austrian and Russian Courts, had immediately on becoming a widow married the Margrave, a nephew of Frederick II., and had

[1] F. 7, 3779.

lived with him at Hammersmith, but had been cold-shouldered by London society and even by her own daughters. She had paid a short visit to Paris in 1802, and she went again in 1807 to take possession of her second husband's property. We hear little more of her till her death at Naples in 1828, where she had settled in 1805, being joined by one of her sons, Keppel Craven, of whom we have already heard.[1] Another restless woman, wife of Colonel Henry (brother of Viscount) Dillon, arrived in Paris in 1808, ostensibly to join her husband but really to bring over letters from royalist exiles, perhaps also to meet her lover, Latour du Pin. She was arrested, and her husband disowned her. In 1810 he notified the police that she had taken her children from Bordeaux and gone with them without his knowledge to England, where he feared she would divulge his offer to join the French army. Sir Robert Adair's French wife in 1808 obtained leave to remove from Vienna to Rheims, in order to bring up her daughters by her former marriage.

The celebrated Pamela, widow of Lord Edward Fitzgerald, was allowed in 1810 to come to Paris, Napoleon directing Fouché to 'pump' her on English and Irish affairs,[2] as also probably on Count Stahremberg, Austrian Ambassador at London, her reputed lover, for she had quitted her second husband Pitcairn,

---

[1] Keppel, author of books on Southern Italy, died at Naples in 1851. He had a natural son Augustus, a diplomatist, who married Mdlle. de la Ferronaye, the French authoress.

[2] A. F. iv. 1504.

American Consul at Hamburg. Her daughter by the latter, who survived till a few years ago, seems to have been left behind, either in Germany or in England.

Julia Sayers, who had been a visitor in 1802, was allowed in 1805 to come over and marry Pougens, the blind author,[1] natural son of the Prince de Conti, to whom she had been introduced in London in 1786. His fortune had disappeared in the Revolution, and he had turned bookseller. She was a niece of Admiral Boscawen and of the Duchess of Beaufort.

Wives were sometimes, however, refused permission to come over and join their captive husbands. Margaret Stuart, who in 1806 had married Hingston Tuckey, both having been captured at sea, on returning in 1810 from a visit to England was unceremoniously shipped back. Sir Thomas Lavie, stranded on the French coast in 1806, was refused his wife's company, whereupon England forbade the wives of French prisoners to land in England. This retaliation apparently brought the French to reason, for as late as January 1813—so little was Napoleon's fall foreseen—Englishwomen landed at Morlaix.[2]

Nor did women always escape imprisonment. A Mrs. Moore was arrested in 1810 on the charge of facilitating her husband's escape from Bitche. She was, however, soon released. Again in 1812 an Englishwoman named Taylor, living at Rouen, returning to Morlaix after a visit to England, met at the

[1] A. F. iv. 1493.
[2] A. F. iv. 1523. One of these was the wife of Montmorency Morris, with her four children and two female friends.

inn three sailors who had just been liberated from
British pontoons. 'Ah,' said she, 'you only come
from one prison to enter another. You will be forced
to serve in the French navy, and will be no better
off than in English prisons. You will never be better
off till Bonaparte'—here she made a gesture indicating
the guillotine. On being arrested for this imprudent
speech she at first denied everything, but on being
confronted with the sailors admitted all except the
remark on Bonaparte. She was ordered to be sent
back to England.[1]

The banker Coutts wrote in 1810 to Lafayette,
asking him to obtain passports for the south of
France for his invalid daughter, Lady Bute, her
husband[2] and two children, a doctor and two servants.
Lafayette, in endorsing the application, stated that
Coutts was banker (he should have said son-in-law)
to Burdett, who had rendered service to the French
prisoners. Lady Bute and her sister had been
educated in Paris previously to the Revolution by
Madame Daubenton. Lord Bute died at Geneva
in November 1814, and his remains were conveyed
to England. Coutts also obtained permission for
another son-in-law, Lord Guilford, to revisit France,
but Guilford died before being able to profit by it.
He had long suffered from injury to the spine,
occasioned by a fall from his horse in the act of
presenting a basket of fruit to his future wife. His

---

[1] A. F. iv. 1504.
[2] A. F. iv. 1504. Bute, son of George III.'s favourite, also wrote
himself to Talleyrand.

brother, who succeeded to the title, established himself at Corfu during the Greek struggle for independence, and was attired like a Greek professor.

J. Cleaver Bankes was allowed, on the recommendation of Benjamin Constant, to come and examine Sanscrit manuscripts at the National Library. In 1813 Sir Humphry Davy and his wife, with his secretary young Faraday, passed through Paris on their way to Italy. They visited the laboratory of Chevreul (not the future centenarian) at the Jardin des Plantes, and at Malmaison were shown by Josephine books and extracts relating to Cromwell, marked in pencil by Napoleon. The institute had in 1809 awarded Davy the £60,000 prize for electrical improvements.

Mrs. Bathurst and her brother, George Call, were allowed to pass through France in 1810, on their search for her husband. Call on his way back solicited an audience of Napoleon,[1] whose portrait adorned his snuff-box, a request which shows that he had not the slightest idea of accusing Napoleon. His belief, indeed, and that of the widow, was that Bathurst had been wrecked in the Baltic.[2] Colonel Macleod of Colbeck, uncle of Lord Moira, after being liberated, actually in 1810 asked leave to settle in France. He was described by the police bulletin as honest but weak-minded, and as having incurred unpleasantness in Scotland by his liking for France and his advocacy of peace.

Shirley, a Jamaica planter, was also allowed in 1806 to settle in the south, and Colonel Vesey, on the recommendation of the King of Prussia, was permitted to

[1] F. 7, 3768. [2] *Westminster Review*, 1890.

to pass the Rhine, he was given up by the German authorities at Lindau—entailed incarceration in filthy and stifling casemates, but in a third attempt in 1808 he reached the Austrian frontier and was able to resume service. He published a full account of his adventures,[1] which was reprinted in 1902. Another sailor, Miller, captured in 1804 in the man-of-war *Wolverine*, escaped in 1811, and published an anonymous narrative. Moir, a naval surgeon captured at sea, was joined by his wife, who in 1808 gave birth to a son, destined to become the 'father' of the Royal College of Physicians, and to reach the age of ninety-one. That son, John Moir, a prominent Free Churchman, remembered being taken in his mother's arms or by her hand when she waited on Napoleon to entreat her husband's liberation, but we are not told whether she was successful. Moir on regaining his liberty settled in Edinburgh. Francis Milman, brother of the future Dean, was captured in Spain, and detained at Verdun till January 1814,[2] when Jenner obtained his release. Edward Boyse, midshipman of the *Phœbe*, was captured in July 1803 in a boat off Toulon, and conducted first to Verdun and then to Valenciennes; but with two comrades he escaped from the latter fortress.[3]

Clandestine visitors were naturally suspected of being spies.[4] Thus the son of Dickinson, the artist,

[1] Some of these suggested incidents in *Peter Simple*.
[2] A. Milman, *Life of Dean Milman*.
[3] *Narrative of Captivity*.
[4] Napoleon judged the English Government by his own standard, for, not to speak of Mehée de la Touche, he sent over to England in 1808 Bourlac, who, pretending to be a royalist emissary, obtained interviews with Hawkesbury and Canning.

ex-secretary to the Ottoman Embassy in London, entered France under the name of Lambert in 1805, apparently in order to join his father in Paris; but he had given up painting and had been in the employ of the British Government. He proved that he had come to see a Madame Gourbillon, of whom he had been enamoured in London, but the authorities suspected that he might occupy his leisure in sending reports to England, and he was consequently despatched to Verdun,[1] albeit his sister was companion to Madame Talleyrand. But he must have been liberated, for we hear of another visit in 1810.

Thomas Graham, arrested at Pepignan in 1810, had entered France from Spain, but having a mission to General Clarke and Arthur O'Connor he was released. William Hayne, lace-maker of Nottingham, and having an extensive continental trade, was arrested in Paris in 1807, having a stock of lace in his possession. What was done with this venturesome trader is not stated. Nathaniel Parker Forth, a diplomatic emissary, the satellite of the Duke of Orleans who procured Pamela for Madame de Genlis, was reported to be in Paris in 1805, and was ordered to be watched;[2] but if such 'a consummate intriguer' had really been there he would certainly have been arrested and expelled. James Mathews, another diplomatic interloper, who had been arrested in Paris in 1793, landed at Havre without a passport in 1807 and vainly tried to pass for an American. The notorious swindler, Lisle Semple, was also reported to have been seen in Paris in 1805, yet

[1] A. F. iv. 1498. [2] A. F. iv. 1493.

this too is unconfirmed. He had been expelled as a spy in 1802.

There was even a report in Paris in 1805 that six English officers had come over to witness the coronation, but this seems highly improbable. Napoleon's long arm reached not only to Hamburg but to Italy. In 1806 all Englishmen found there were ordered to be arrested, and Graham, consequently apprehended at Venice, was sent to Valenciennes. Edward Dodwell, living at Rome, had to apply for leave to visit England in order to publish a work on Greece. John Wilson, a native of Liverpool, residing in Italy, was authorised in 1810, on account of his health, to live at Geneva. He afterwards asked permission to become partner in a firm at Bordeaux.[1] The Earl of Bristol, Bishop of Derry, would probably have been arrested, as he had been in 1798, had he not died at Albano on the 8th July 1803, before Napoleon had had time to look so far afield for his prey.

Sir George Rumbold, British Minister at Hamburg and son of Warren Hastings' opponent at Calcutta, was seized by order of Napoleon in 1804. It is believed by the Rumbold family that this was instigated by the famous Pamela, Lady Edward Fitzgerald, who was then at Hamburg and in league with the Irish exiles there, to whom Rumbold's vigilant observation was very irksome.[2] If so, she was guilty of treachery, for she had been very intimate with him.

Rumbold lived in a neighbouring village, going twice

[1] F. 7, 3116.
[2] Sir Horace Rumbold, *Recollections of a Diplomatist.*

a week into Hamburg on mail days. A hundred soldiers
under Major Maison landed at night on the coast, and
ten or twelve of them drove in two carriages to the
spot to surround the house and prevent any alarm.
A sentinel was placed in front of every door and window.
On the arrival of the rest of the detachment, a German
civilian knocked at the door and stated that he had
brought despatches. A servant bade him deliver them
at the window, but the door was forced open and Rumbold was arrested in his bed. He expected nothing
less than to be shot, as the Duc d'Enghien had been
six months before, but Maison assured him that his life
was safe. All his papers were seized, and these were
expected to implicate the British Government in plots
to assassinate Napoleon, an expectation, however, which
was not realised. The Prince Regent, moreover, according to a police bulletin of 1805, referring to such
plots, had said, 'Let us meet Bonaparte like men, not
like assassins.'[1] Rumbold, on being taken to Paris,
was induced on the promise of the restitution of his
papers to sign an engagement never to approach on
non-British territory within a hundred miles of any
post occupied by French troops. In Paris, if we may
credit a police report, his terror revived. He asked for
time to pray and to write to his family, adding that for
eighteen months he had been disgusted with politics,
and but for his children's interests would have thrown
up his appointment. He passed ten days in the Temple,
and here is the description given of him:—

'5 ft. 11 in. Hair brownish grey. Eyebrows dark grey.

[1] A. F. iv. 1494; F. 7, 3750.

Forehead ordinary. Eyes greyish brown. Nose short, slim above and rather thick below. Mouth medium. Lips thick. Chin round. Face oval and full. A small mark on the left cheek.'

The King of Prussia had remonstrated against such a violation of German territory, and had ordered his Ambassador to Paris to demand his passports unless Rumbold were released. Accordingly the preposterous intention of trying him for conspiracy, if ever entertained, was abandoned, and he was escorted to Cherbourg, where, not without renewed apprehensions of being shot, he was handed over to a British frigate. He had already repented of signing the engagement, an act of cowardice, he said, tantamount to resignation. The gendarme major told him he might keep the matter secret, but Rumbold replied that he should be bound to inform his Government. He also expressed regret at his family affairs being pried into in his papers.[1] Rumbold, if the French reports are to be trusted, certainly showed pusillanimity, but the recent fate of the Duc d'Enghien was in his mind. The promise of restoring his papers was not fulfilled, and being censured by the English Government for the engagement entered into by him, he offered to go back to France and revoke that engagement. This, of course, was not allowed. In the following spring he repaired to Berlin to thank the King of Prussia for his intervention, and he followed the royal family in their retreat to Memel. There, tended by Prince Augustus when attacked with fever, he expired in December 1807.

[1] Grasilier, *Enlèvement de Rumbold*, Paris, 1901.

His widow in 1810 married Sir Sidney Smith, who likewise had had experience of the Temple prison. Both she and Sir Sidney ended their days in Paris.

In 1876 Sir Horace Rumbold obtained permission to inspect his grandfather's confiscated papers in the French Archives, but found the family matters in them very meagre, while he suspected that the political portions had been withheld from him.[1]

Talleyrand, in a diplomatic circular justifying such high-handed acts, charged England with prostituting the functions of ambassadors by making them instigate the assassination of the Emperor; but Lord Hawkesbury in reply, while indignantly denying the charge, insisted that a belligerent was entitled to have dealings with malcontents, and he twitted France with incitement of Irish rebellions. Napoleon's evident maxim, however, was that all was fair on his own side, and it must be confessed that, whereas no Irishman proposed to assassinate George III., French malcontents looked for no success unless through Napoleon being kidnapped or murdered.

A Colonel Butler was also arrested at Hamburg in November 1806. In the French Dragoons until the Revolution, he had for eleven or twelve years, along with Dutheil, been an agent for the Bourbons and had paid secret visits to Paris. Two of his many children were there and were rich with their mother's property. What became of him is not stated. Possibly he escaped.

James Smithson, natural son of the Duke of

[1] *National Review*, August 1903.

Northumberland, born in France in 1765, and future
founder of the Smithsonian Institute at Washington,
was likewise arrested at Hamburg in 1809, but at the
solicitation of Banks received a passport for England.
He had visited Paris in 1791, when he wrote—'The
office of king is not yet abolished, but they daily feel
the inability or rather the great inconvenience of con-
tinuing it. May other nations at the time of their
reforms be wise enough to cast off at first the contemptible incumbrance!' Smithson, who must by this
time have been sadly disillusioned with the Revolution,
died at Genoa in 1829, having mostly spent his later
years in Paris.

George Sinclair, eldest son of Sir John, the great
agriculturist, in 1806, at the age of sixteen, was arrested
by the French as a spy, having been found between the
French and German lines just before the battle of Jena.
Sinclair, who became a general and lived till 1868,
published in 1826 in the *Representative* an interesting
account of his interview at Auma with Napoleon, before
whom he was taken, together with his companion, a
German named Rigel, by Count Frohberg. He found
Napoleon in a dressing-gown and white night-cap, and
he was required not only to show that he had been on
purely private business, but to trace all his movements on
a map and to answer questions as to the German troops
through which he had passed. 'All Napoleon's questions,' he says, 'were remarkable by their perfect clearness. He omitted nothing that was necessary; he asked
nothing superfluous.' 'What guarantee can I have,'
said Napoleon, 'of the truth of your story? Englishmen

do not usually travel on foot and without a servant and in such a dress.' Sinclair was wearing a coarse brown overcoat. 'It is true, sire,' he replied, 'that my conduct may seem a little odd, but imperative circumstances and the impossibility of procuring a horse forced me to do all that I have done.' He produced some family letters, which Napoleon asked Frohberg to skim, and one of them was from Sir John Sinclair, commending his study of Greek and Latin and exhorting him to master German and French. Thereupon Napoleon, softening his tone, said, 'So you have learned Latin and Greek. What authors have you read?' Surprised at such a question, Sinclair named Homer, Thucydides, Cicero, and Horace. It was well he could not or did not name Tacitus, the object of Napoleon's aversion. 'Very good, very good,' he rejoined, and turning to General Berthier, he said, 'I do not think this young man is a spy, but the other is probably less innocent, and they must be kept together to avoid suspicion.' A nod indicated that the interview was over, and Sinclair, bowing, withdrew. 'When taken before him,' he writes, 'I had the strongest prejudice against him. I considered him the enemy of my country and the oppressor of the rest of Europe. On quitting him, the grace and fascination of his smile and that superior intelligence which illumined his face had entirely sub-jugated me.' Napoleon directed Frohberg to tell the young man he was much pleased with the frankness of his answers. Rigel in like manner exonerated himself, and both, subjected to a few days' honourable detention, were liberated after the battle of Jena, a place which

Sinclair had passed on his route and had pointed out to Napoleon on the map.

Should we reckon among the British—she was at any rate among the notable—involuntary visitors the Countess of Albany, widow of the Young Pretender, quasi-widow of the poet Alfieri, and quasi-wife of Fabre of Montpellier ? She started from Florence for Paris in 1806, with the view of publishing Alfieri's works, but turned back at Turin on finding that François Xavier Fabre, as an *émigré*, would not be allowed to re-enter France. In the autumn of 1809, however, Napoleon required her to come to Paris to exculpate herself from a charge of intrigues with England. All that she had really done had been to refuse to receive Clarke when French Minister at Florence, and to apply to the English Government for an annuity to compensate the one lost by the death of her brother-in-law, Cardinal York, the titular Henry IX. She had accordingly been granted £1000 a year. She easily cleared herself, and Napoleon seems to have been a little ashamed of disturbing so inoffensive a woman. He jestingly told her that her influence on Florentine society hampered the fusion desired by him between Tuscans and French. This, he said, was why he had summoned her to live in Paris, where she would have more ample opportunity of gratifying her artistic tastes. The interview lasted only a quarter of an hour, Napoleon gave her his box at the theatre one night that she might see Talma. It was not till the end of 1810 that she was permitted to return to Florence.[1] A letter addressed to her in

[1] *Archives du Nord de la France*, iii. 449.

1814 piquantly contrasted her husband's expulsion
from France in 1748 with her own enforced residence
there, adding, ' You have left many regrets in the great
Babylon.'

Such of the English as were allowed to inhabit Paris,
the permits for which, however, were, as we have seen,
grudgingly granted and liable to be cancelled by whole-
sale, had the slender consolation of reflecting that
they were in the ' hub' of the universe, for Paris in
the height of Napoleon's rule was more the centre of
fashion and business than it has ever been since. It
swarmed with Jews—bankers, jewellers, and merchants
—to whom the war afforded many opportunities of
enriching themselves. It also swarmed with adventurers of all nationalities, so that in February 1803 the
regulations as to visitors, whether French or foreign,
were made almost as stringent as those issued during
the Revolution. A list of the inmates had not indeed,
as then, to be placarded outside every house, but every
householder was required to notify the police of the
arrival of any visitor or lodger and to send in the passport. This had to be applied for within three days by
such guest or lodger, to whom a permit to stay in or
quit Paris was then granted. A foreigner's permit was
conditional on the certificate of his ambassador, or, in
default of an ambassador, by a banker or two well-known
citizens.[1]

On the other hand there was no lack of celebrities
or of men who interest us on account of distinguished
descendants. Let us begin with Pius VII., the first

[1] *Moniteur*, February 14, 1803.

Pope who had touched French soil since the return to Rome from Avignon in 1408. Like the Doge of Genoa at Versailles, he must have thought himself the most surprising object in Paris. Manzoni, the Italian poet and novelist, Oersted, the Danish scientist, and Francis Arago, the future astronomer, whose family had sought at Perpignan a refuge from Spanish commotions, may next be noted. Spurzheim, the phrenologist, comes considerably lower down in eminence. The statesmen include Baron Hardenberg, destined to regenerate Prussia, and Count Nesselrode, the future author of the Holy Alliance and the Crimean War. The Poles include Prince Constantine Czartoryski, who, though a member of a great patriotic family, served in the Russian army, Count John Wielopolski, and Stanislas Wolowski, probably a collateral ancestor of the economist who sat in the French National Assembly of 1871. Marquis Emanuel del Campo, Spanish Minister of Foreign Affairs, ex-ambassador at London and in 1795 at Paris, was the natural son of a Spanish grandee, an envoy also to London, by an Englishwoman named Field, a name which he had turned into Campo. He commenced life in an orphanage. James and Julius Beccaria were probably kinsmen of the Milanese philosopher. Count Tolstoi, the Russian ambassador, and Andrew Tolstoi, apparently his son, may have been ancestors of the great novelist. Ferdinand de Hérédia was probably the father of the French Minister of Public Works in 1887, and grandfather of the academician and poet. Dias and Emanuel Oliveira, the former a merchant at Oporto, the latter a doctor, were probably ancestors of the Benjamin Oliveira who in the House of Commons anticipated Cobden by advocating reduced tariffs on foreign wines. Joseph Bamuda, a Barcelona merchant, was probably uncle of the great East London shipbuilder and M.P. Philip Gavazzi, an Italian merchant, may have been the father of the anti-papal ecclesiastic who joined Garibaldi in Naples and died in 1889.

Englishmen domiciled, if not naturalised, abroad were not subject to detention, which indeed was not prospective in the decree, but was limited to persons then on French soil. The Berlin decree of 1807 ordered, it is true, the capture of all British subjects irrespective of sex or age found in territories occupied by French or allied troops; but this does not seem to have been enforced. Hence the police registers[1] show visits to Paris between 1806 and 1813 by Englishmen settled on the Continent, but it is not always easy to distinguish these from men of English names, descendants of Jacobites or other emigrants, born abroad. In any case the registers are evidence that British subjects or men of British descent were sprinkled all over Europe, some as soldiers of fortune, others as manufacturers or artisans, and a few as landowners. Thus the register of Spaniards gives us Colonel Peter Aylmer, Patrick MacMahon, a merchant at San Sebastian, Thomas Moore, a landowner born in Spain, William Mulvey, a native of Cadiz, O'Farrill, Ambassador to Berlin, William Stirling, a merchant born at Barcelona, Charles Willcox, a landowner also

[1] F. 7, 2241-56.

R

born there, and Colonel Charles Augustus Joseph
Walsh de Serrant, one of whose family conveyed
the Young Pretender to Scotland in 1745. The
so-called Portuguese included Henry Gallwey and
Joseph O'Moran, latter a commercial traveller.

The Dutchmen comprise General O'Connor, a native
of Holland, Benjamin John Hopkinson, a domiciled
landowner, and Robert Twiss, a merchant, apparently
the father of Francis and Richard Twiss, and the
grandfather of Horace Twiss. The Belgians were
considered Frenchmen, or we should have heard of
William Cockerill, one of the three sons of the man
who founded the famous ironworks at Seraing. The
Prussians and Poles, who are classed together, comprise
William Flint and Augustus and John Simpson,
merchants, Catherine and Richard Fitzgerald, land-
owners, natives of Dublin, Samuel Turner, 'president
of canton,' whatever that may mean, also from Dublin,
and Baron Butler, a major captured in the field.
Among Danes are Edmund de Bourke, Ambassador
to Spain, and David Turnbull, a manufacturer at
Altona. The Russians include Baron John Richard
Bourke, Reuben Beasley, a merchant, Dr. William
Birt, and William Lind, surgeon, both natives of
St. Petersburg.

Among Swiss are John Archer and Walter and
David Johnston, two sons of a wine merchant at
Bordeaux who had not yet been naturalised in France,
but was unmolested and allowed in 1812 to visit Paris.
Last but not least is William Kirkpatrick, a son of
the Scottish (Closeburn) baronet, who was a wine-

merchant at Malaga, and had married Françoise de
Grévignée, daughter of a Walloon, also settled at
Malaga. Kirkpatrick, who had been appointed Consul
at Hamburg by the Grand Duke of Oldenburg, was
in Paris in 1808 and was anxious to return to Malaga,
but the French police suspected him of relations
with England and had arrested his partner Turnbull.
His daughter Maria Emanuele, born in 1796, was
destined to be the mother of the Empress Eugénie,
while her mother's sister, wife of Mathieu de
Lesseps, was destined to be the mother of Ferdinand
de Lesseps.

There were of course in eleven years deaths, and
even tragical deaths, among the captives. The Marquis
and Marchioness of Tweeddale were allowed to visit
Paris in November 1803, but were soon relegated to
Verdun, and the gendarme who escorted them thither
insisted, Lawrence tells us, on riding inside the
carriage and even on dining with them. Lady Tweeddale, sister of Lord Lauderdale, died at Verdun in
1804, and her husband, while awaiting permission
to have her buried in England, was also taken ill,
and died two months afterwards.[1] Napoleon's offer,
' as a mark of respect for Fox,' of twelve months'
leave, came too late. James Parry, ex-editor of the
Courier, had been imprisoned in 1799 for six months
for an article animadverting on the Tsar, whom the
British Government then wished to court; he had
sold his newspaper to Daniel Stuart, proprietor of
the *Morning Post*, and in 1802 had settled at Arles.

[1] Both bodies were conveyed to England.

Though for three years a paralytic he was mercilessly ordered to Verdun and died there. His young son was adopted by Ginguené, the eminent literary critic.

James Payne, the bookseller, died in Paris in 1809 at the age of forty-three, leaving a young widow who went back to England in 1811. She was escorted by the Widmers, nephews of the calico-printer Oberkampf, who thus returned the long compulsory stay with their uncle of Robert Hendry. Hendry was a Glasgow dyer, whom Napoleon on a visit to Oberkampf's calico-factory allowed to return home, nominally for a visit; but this was doubtless an euphemism for release. John Leatham, formerly of Madras, died at Nantes in 1811. Peter Colombine, of London, died in Paris in 1813. He was probably the brother of the Norwich alderman known to Mrs. Opie, who in 1802 was defrauded of his property and reduced to accepting an annuity of £100 from the Corporation of that city.

The Rev. J. Bentinck, an Oxonian who is said to have been promised a bishopric, died at Paris in June 1804. The Rev. John Dring, rector of Heathfield, Sussex, died at Orleans in 1806. Coulson Walhope, ex-M.P., was subjected to special surveillance, apparently on account of a report, doubtless calumnious, that he had visited France just after Napoleon's return from Egypt with the design of shooting him. Walhope likewise ended his days at Verdun in 1807, shortly after giving a dinner-party. A doctor captured at sea committed suicide in 1805, leaving a bottle inscribed, 'No more medicine after this.' A third clergyman, White of Lancaster, died at Verdun in 1806, and a fourth, Annesley, at Geneva in 1807, his widow being then allowed a passport for England. He was probably a kinsman of the colonel already mentioned, but I cannot trace him in the Annesley pedigree. Thomas Talbot, aged twenty-eight, suffocated himself by charcoal at Paris in 1806, leaving a letter to his mother with a list of his debts (probably at cards) which he begged her to discharge.[1] Dr. Walter Kirby also died at Paris. A man named Burgh or Burke, on account of gambling debts, shot himself at Paris in August 1813.

A considerable number of incurable prisoners had been sent back by England, and in 1810 there were negotiations for an exchange. Colin Alexander Mackenzie[2] was sent to Morlaix for that purpose, with William Dickinson as his secretary. He went on to Paris, to witness Napoleon's marriage festivities. France proposed an exchange *en masse*, with payment of a sum of money to cover the difference in numbers. On this being declined, she suggested an exchange, man for man, grade for grade, and offered to throw 20,000 Spaniards into the bargain. She wished 3000 Frenchmen to be exchanged for 1000 English and 2000 Spaniards. England offered to give 3000 French for 17,000 Hanoverians, but France insisted on 6000 of the former. As for the *détenus*, the British Government, reluctantly waiving the legality of their arrest, proposed that Lord Lovaine should be exchanged for a general, sons of peers or privy

---

[1] A. F. iv. 1498. 　　　　[2] General in 1814; died in 1815.

councillors for colonels or navy captains, baronets and knights for officers, untitled gentlemen for captains of the line or naval lieutenants, tradesmen for subalterns, servants and mechanics for privates or seamen. There was a difficulty, however, as to Hanoverians and Spaniards, and no agreement was arrived at. Mackenzie, who had arrived on the 24th April, accordingly left on the 6th November. During his stay at Morlaix his movements had been closely watched, and objection was taken to his wolf-hunting expeditions, as though these might screen confabulations with royalists or observations on privateers. There had been, however, and continued to be, individual liberations. England continued to send back prisoners incurably ill, and on the other hand a sailor who had become blind was released in 1809 by France. He took with him a book in which a number of Verdun captives had written messages to friends. Powell, vicar of Abergavenny, having shown much kindness to French prisoners there, Clarke recommended, let us hope successfully, the exchange of an English sailor in whom the vicar was interested.[1] Admiral Villeneuve in 1806 was exchanged at Morlaix, but unwilling to face Napoleon after his defeat, he committed suicide at Rennes on the way to Paris. There was also an offer to exchange Admiral Jurien de la Gravière for two colonels, but this was not accepted. The balance of prisoners was always largely against France, while the balance of escapes was—shall we say in favour?— of France. Thus in 1812 the British Government

[1] A. F. iv. 1158.

published a list of 270 escapes and 590 attempted escapes by French officers, whereupon the *Moniteur* gave a list of 355 English escapes, which it was urged was a much greater proportionate number. Sir James Craufurd figured at the head of the list. But the great majority of these English fugitives were officers or sailors of merchant vessels captured at sea after the resumption of hostilities. Some of the French escapes were effected through a noted English smuggler named Robinson; we do not hear of his assisting any of his own countrymen, as this would obviously have stopped his favourable reception in France.

Applications for release or for permission to visit England latterly became numerous. Release was besought in many instances on the plea of age and infirmity (and we may suppose that doctors were complaisant in granting such certificates) or for having rescued French citizens from fire or shipwreck. Two sailors who in a rescue from the waves had actually been captured had irresistible claims not so much to clemency as to gratitude. Poor Colonel Cope's botanical studies, moreover, had not apparently warded off insanity, on which ground his sister in 1813 petitioned for his release. William Story, the chemist, had reached the age of sixty-three, and Napoleon's decree had fixed sixty as the limit of detention. He applied for six months' leave of absence to take possession of property bequeathed to him. Viscountess Kirkwall urged that unless her brother, whose father's death had made him Lord De Blaquiere, was allowed to settle affairs in person, the family would be ruined. Lord Lovaine, with his sons Algernon and Percy, born in France, likewise petitioned for a business visit.[1] Sir Michael Cromie in 1811, pleading that he had been a friend of Fox, and had purchased property in France, asked leave to go to England to his daughter's wedding.[2] Samuel Hayes, who in 1802 had come over with his children that they might learn French, was allowed in 1813, having become nearly blind, to return home. As late as the 18th March 1814, sixteen released prisoners embarked at Morlaix.

Curiously enough, an escaped prisoner was sent back by the English Government on the very eve of the termination of the war. It is the only case on record. A Lieutenant Sheehy, aged twenty-seven, of the 89th Infantry, had escaped from Verdun in October 1813, but the Prince Regent and the Commander-in-Chief, rebuking him for breach of parole, despatched him by flag of truce to Morlaix, where he arrived on the 5th March 1814. The Morlaix commissary reported that he denounced the Prince Regent as a sot, and that if he had talked like this in England it might account for his being returned, but that such talk might be a blind for some secret mission. Pending instructions from Paris, Sheehy was kept in custody, and we hear no more of him.[3]

The failure of the Mackenzie negotiations must have been a terrible disappointment for captives who had already waited nine years and a half. As late as 1812 there was so little prospect of deliverance that a

[1] A. F. iv. 1158.   [2] A. F. iv. 1158.   [3] F. 7, 3882.

prisoner at Briançon amused himself by scratching a
sun-dial on a slate, appending to the motto 'Rule
Britannia' imprecations against Napoleon.[1] In April
1813, twenty-five chests of Bibles and Testaments had
been sent by a flag of truce, apparently by the Bible
Society, to Morlaix for distribution among the captives.
They were detained at the custom-house pending a
decision, and we do not hear the result,[2] but in any case
the books could scarcely have reached their intended
recipients.

Yet although nobody foresaw the end of the war,
Napoleon seems to have shown a little more leniency,
while England in 1813 sent back 8000 invalided
prisoners, and agreed, moreover, to occasional exchanges
even of soldiers for civilians. Thus in 1812 she offered
to exchange a French captain for the banker Boyd, but
this offer must have been declined, for in 1814 Boyd
pleaded the loss of the sight of one eye as ground for
repeating it.[3] Release must soon have ensued without
the necessity of an exchange. In December 1813,
fourteen English doctors were exchanged for French
prisoners, and we may hope that these included Moir,
Armstrong, Watt, Campbell, Hogarth, and Jones, whose
volunteer services to the French wounded had been
notified to Napoleon by General Clarke, as a hint for
their release.[4]

The allies having entered France on the north-east
and Wellington on the south, the Verdun, Arras, and
other captives were removed further inland. Napoleon,

[1] *Intermédiaire*, February 10, 1902.
[2] A. F. iv. 1527.   [3] A. F. iv. 1158.   [4] *Ibid.*

writing on the 11th January 1814 to Clarke, said, 'I
suppose you have removed the English from Verdun';
but it was not till the following day that the first
detachment started for Blois. Prisoners with means
provided their own vehicles or horses, but others,
mostly captains and officers of merchantmen, seem to
have been marched on foot. Most of them, Lord
Blayney[1] says, were accompanied by French mistresses
who had acquired a surprising mastery of English
sailors' oaths. A second detachment set out next day.
This sudden removal had caused consternation, for
though many had been captured during the war, many
others had been at Verdun ever since 1803, and had got
to feel at home there. Those, moreover, just under
sixty when originally detained, were getting into years
and disinclined to stir. Logically, of course, they
should have been released on reaching that age, but
logic was not to be looked for from Napoleon. Tradesmen and house-owners, moreover, had given numerous
prisoners credit, yet the latter, if out of funds, had
perforce to leave their creditors in the lurch. They
could not wait for remittances, the order for departure
in three days being imperative. Some, indeed, borrowed
money of friends, but when the Verdun shopkeepers
collected at the gate to make a last demand for their
dues, some of the prisoners who could have paid coolly
showed their purses to their creditors and then returned them to their pockets, sarcastically remarking

---

[1] He stopped a night at Nohant on his way to Blois, and again on
repairing to Paris. Did he notice there a tomboy ten years old
destined to be famous as George Sand?

that the Cossacks would discharge the debt. Five Arras captives made their way to the coast in lieu of going south, but finding no boat gave themselves up. Two others succeeded in their purpose. On the way to Blois, the younger child of Tuckey fell ill and died. On reaching their supposed destination, the prisoners were ordered on to Guéret. That town on the 11th of March 1814 had no less than 1064 English prisoners. Tidings of Wellington's advance naturally created restlessness among them. Sixty-four escaped from the convent at Périgueux, to which they had been consigned, although the officers had some days before, lest they should head a rising, been transferred to Cahors. A hundred and one escaped in a body from Angoulême, and as many more, under a negro named Louis, conspired to follow suit, but were detected in time. The gendarmerie captain recommended their removal to spots more out of reach of the English army.[1] There had, moreover, been escapes on the way south. In February seven men, ordered from Arras to Tours, gave their convoy the slip, but were arrested in a barn near St. Valéry. Five other fugitives were apprehended near Montreuil. A Frenchman at Dunkirk was arrested for offering to facilitate escapes.

News soon arrived of Napoleon's abdication. The Bitche prisoners, who had been sent to Chatellerault, would but for that event have been sent on to Rennes. A few of the English in Paris had obtained permission to remain, and were there witnesses of the short siege and the entrance of the allies. One of these

[1] F. 7, 3782.

was James Richard Underwood, for whom the
dethroned Josephine had interceded. He published
in the *London Magazine* an account of the siege and
capitulation.

Article 3 of the treaty of peace of 1814 stipulated
'that the respective prisoners of war shall be bound to
pay before their departure from the place of their
detention any private debts which they may have
contracted there, or at least to give satisfactory
security.' This doubtless took effect in England, where
prisoners could not leave without the knowledge or
sanction of the authorities, but in France, occupied
by foreign armies, there were obviously no means of
enforcing it. Hence it is not surprising to find that
at Verdun there were indignant creditors. We do not
hear of complaints in any other town, but at Bitche
and other fortresses the captives were lodged and
victualled by the French Government, and though
clothes must have worn out, the shopkeepers were
probably chary of giving credit, while the captives on
parole in Paris, Orleans, and other towns were men of
means and doubtless of a high sense of honour. The
eight or eleven hundred prisoners at Verdun, on the
other hand, were of all sorts and conditions. Some
could not, others would not, pay. When, therefore,
Verdun learned that the sixty millions paid by France
to England to satisfy claims for compensation for
confiscation had left a balance of nine millions, it
perceived an opportunity for sending in its bill. What
could be more legitimately paid out of this balance
than the three and a half million debts of the

prisoners? Negotiations were carried on from 1837, and in October 1839, doubtless by the advice of the French Government, Routhier, a barrister, empowered to represent the creditors, went over to London. On a second visit he was accompanied by four townsmen, themselves apparently creditors. The memorial drawn up by them said :—

'During twelve years' residence in a town in which they were debarred the opportunity of procuring aid from their families and their country,[1] the English prisoners could not but contract debts and obligations, and they will doubtless acknowledge that the kindness and generosity of the inhabitants may have helped them to forget the disasters and misfortunes of war. . . . At the moment of the invasion the majority of the prisoners waited neither for official orders to depart nor for the conclusion of treaties. They quitted the country with all the facilities which circumstances naturally afforded. By depriving the creditors of their pledge, by sending the general officers, some to India, others to China, in the service of His Britannic Majesty, and thus rendering it impossible for the inhabitants of Verdun to sue their debtors, the English Government made itself responsible for the payment of the debts. The inhabitants put forward their claim from the outset, and from the outset notes on the subject were exchanged between the different Ministers. . . . If in that list there should prove to be a single usurious debt, one that cannot be verified by proper vouchers, let it be immediately rejected. . . . The number of prisoners always exceeded 1200, and frequently amounted to 2000.'[2]

The memorial asked for an instalment of 5000

[1] This, as we have seen, is not quite accurate.
[2] *Réclamation de Verdun.* The number never exceeded 1100.

francs 'to relieve the most urgent cases of distress'
pending examination of the claims by a mixed commission.

The *Times* of October 18, 1839, says :—

'A deputation from the inhabitants of Verdun in France
has just arrived in London to claim the payment of
£140,000, the amount of private debts incurred by English
prisoners detained in that city during the war. The
deputation, composed of MM. Routhier, Quentin, Leorat,
Massé, and Trebout has, we are assured, been most kindly
received by Lord Palmerston, who seems to have impressed
the members of the deputation with the belief that no time
will be lost in submitting the demand of the inhabitants of
Verdun to a mixed commission charged with the liquidation
of the debts. Marshal Soult,[1] we understand, has written
personally to Lord Palmerston to suggest that a part of the
nine million francs (the unappropriated balance of a sum of
sixty millions paid by France in 1815 in liquidation of the
claims of British subjects) ought to be applied in payment to
the inhabitants of Verdun.'

But nothing came of this mission, and we hear of
no further attempt by Verdun to obtain satisfaction.
Thus ends the history of these involuntary guests.

[1] Then Ambassador at London.

V

TWO RESTORATIONS

The Restoration—Aristocrats and Commoners—Unwelcome Guests—Wellington in Danger—Misgivings—Napoleonic Emblems—Spectacles—Visits to Elba—Egerton's Siege—St. Helena—Eyewitnesses and Survivors.

WHILE the fall of Napoleon thus enabled numbers of Englishmen to return home, it allowed and tempted a smaller but yet considerable number to make or renew acquaintance with France. According to Wansey, there were four or five hundred of these,[1] scarcely any, however, staying more than a fortnight or three weeks. The through fare from London was now £5. The visitors had the interesting spectacle of the restoration of the Bourbons, while the very few who made a more lengthened stay witnessed also the Hundred Days' reign of Napoleon, and his second and final fall. Never surely in Europe in modern times were more startling vicissitudes crowded into so brief a period. Even Spain with its *pronunciamientos* was not destined to present such a kaleidoscope. For a parallel we must go forward to the Central American republics or backward to the time when the pretorians made and unmade Roman emperors.

---

[1] A Paris paper absurdly estimated them in October 1814 at 12,000.

These visitors, like those who hurried over in
1802, included all sorts and conditions of men.   There
were statesmen like Castlereagh, anxious to weigh
the chances of stability of the reinstated dynasty.
He paid two visits, the first in August 1814 on his
way to the Vienna Congress, the second in February
1815.   It was probably on the first visit that Ney,
dining with him and with officers of the allied armies,
had the bad taste or want of tact to argue that an
invasion of England, which he said he had strenuously
urged on Napoleon, would certainly have succeeded.
There were subordinate officials like Wellesley Pole,
Master of the Mint and brother to Wellington, and
Croker who, as we learn from the police bulletins,
preferred a complaint that American privateers were
still being sheltered at Bordeaux.   It was not at
this visit but at a subsequent one in July 1815 that
Croker inspected the memorable scenes of the Revolution, discovered in the possession of Marat's old
printer Colin a large collection of pamphlets, and
was introduced by him to Marat's sister, whom he
found as repulsive-looking as her brother.   'Colin,'
said Croker, 'had in some small dark rooms up two
or three flights of stairs an immense quantity of
brochures of the earlier days of the Revolution.   What
he had least of were the works of Marat, even those
which he himself printed, which he accounted for
naturally enough by saying that there were times
in which it might be somewhat hazardous to possess
them.'   Croker induced the British Museum in 1817
to purchase the collection, and he afterwards formed

a collection of his own which ultimately had the same destination. There were politicians like Grey, F. J. Robinson, Fazakerley, Grattan, Whitbread, and Brougham. Brougham attended the sittings of the Institute, of which he was afterwards to be an associate, saw Laplace, and had a long conversation with Carnot. This was his first visit to France, for his step-grandson Sir Edward Malet is mistaken in stating that he once heard Mirabeau speak. 'I never,' says Brougham, 'spent any time by half so delightful. My fortnight passed like a day.' Are we to attribute to this visit the birth of an infant afterwards known as Madame Blaze de Bury, who died in 1894 at the age of eighty, and who in spite of her alleged birth as a Stewart in Scotland was believed to be Brougham's daughter by a French mother? She strongly resembled him both physically and mentally. Her husband had an English mother named Bury; her daughter, like herself a writer, died in December 1902.

There was Thelwall, the acquitted Radical of 1794, who had temporarily renounced politics and taken to the cure of stammering. There was Arthur Thistlewood, who, it is said, had visited Paris in 1794, and who soon entered into conspiracies, the last of which, named from Cato Street, resulted in his conviction and execution in 1820. He was decidedly an exception among the visitors, yet the Paris air may have helped to lead him astray, for it was an atmosphere of conspiracy.

There were philosophers and historians such as Sir James Mackintosh, who was anxious to explore

s

the French archives, taking ten copyists with him ; but these formidable preparations not unnaturally occasioned obstruction from a suspicious curator, Hauterive,[1] so that Wellington had to urge that no mischief could result from the disclosure of political secrets half a century old.   Mackintosh's son-in-law, Claudius James Rich, the traveller, accompanied him, and the transcripts then made are now in the British Museum. They are limited to the times of the Stuarts.

Archibald Alison, the future historian, accompanied by a fellow Scot and fellow historian, Patrick Fraser Tytler, also went in May 1814, returning by Flanders. It is not clear from their joint narrative whether both or Tytler alone went in the autumn to Aix, staying till the eve of Napoleon's return.

There were three poets, Rogers, Moore, and Campbell, the last stopping at Rouen to see his brother Daniel, from whom he had parted at Hamburg in 1800. Mrs. Siddons took over her daughter Cecily, who did not continue her mother's fame, but married a Scottish lawyer, George Combe.   Kemble escorted her, with Mrs. Twiss, whose brother-in-law Richard had seen Paris in 1792.   There was Mrs. Damer, the artist, of whom we have already heard and shall hear again. There was the more eminent sculptor Chantrey, who made the acquaintance of Canova.   There was Curran, who had just resigned his judgeship, and Serjeant Best, not yet a judge.   The Duke of Sussex had given Curran an introduction to the future Charles x. Everything he heard intensified his hatred of Napoleon.[2]

---

[1] Artaud, *Vie de Hauterive.*   [2] *Life of Curran.*

There were military men like General Ramsay, Bruce, destined to assist in the escape of Lavalette, and Lord Cathcart, who had taken part in the expedition to Copenhagen and was subsequently Ambassador to St. Petersburg. Madame Junot, in whose house Cathcart was quartered, and who speaks highly of his courtesy, had also to receive Lord and Lady Cole, who sent for Eliza Bathurst. She was the handsome daughter of the diplomatist who so mysteriously disappeared. Another military visitor was Colonel William Carmichael Smyth, who had accompanied his father in 1802; but Count Nugent, though born in Ireland, was an Austrian officer. The Navy was represented by Sir Sidney Smith, who was bound for the Congress of Vienna to plead for the reinstatement of Gustavus IV. on the throne of Sweden. He also advocated an international expedition against the piratical Dey of Algiers, of which he would himself have taken the command. Nothing came of either scheme, but he got up a subscription dinner, attended by royal and other celebrities, the proceeds of which were devoted to the redemption of prisoners in Algiers. Science was represented by a Scottish professor, John (afterwards Sir John) Leslie, an Edinburgh Reviewer and eminent mathematician, who formed the habit of paying yearly visits to the Continent. There were philanthropists like Clarkson, who, as on his visit in 1789, was eager to obtain the consent of the new French Government to the abolition of the slave-trade, while Wilberforce and Zachary Macaulay, the historian's father,

were interesting themselves at home in the same
cause, the latter sending over, or taking advantage
of the presence of, his brother General Macaulay.
Clarkson found sympathy from Lafayette, Bishop
Grégoire, and Madame de Staël. The antiquary and
connoisseur, James Millingen, passed through Paris
on his way to or from Florence, as also William
Stewart Rose, translator of Ariosto, friend of Ugo
Foscolo, Walter Scott, and the Countess of Albany.
He was destined to find a wife at Venice. There were
painters like Stothard, Wilkie, and Haydon, to the
last of whom we are indebted for the liveliest account
of Paris, though this, like the rest of his journal, was
not published till after his tragical death. He represents Wilkie as constantly exclaiming, 'What a fool
Napoleon was to lose such a country! dear, dear!'
Both Wilkie and Haydon sang 'God save the King'
in the streets of Rouen, to the amazement or amusement of the townsmen, one of whom said they were
English milords. In Paris Wilkie tried to sell his
prints, and had frequent disputes at restaurants
about change. Another note-taker was Thomas Raikes,
brother of the founder of Sunday-schools, but unfortunately his diary does not begin till 1832. A third
diarist was Henry Crabb Robinson, to whom street
urchins at Dieppe shouted 'Be off!' and who in a
Rouen theatre heard a line against England applauded.
He spent five weeks in Paris without a moment's *ennui*,
yet left it without a moment's regret, travelling to
Boulogne in company with Copleston, 'a very sensible,
well-informed clergyman,' just elected Provost of Oriel

at Oxford, and destined to be Bishop of Llandaff.
Stephen Weston and William Shepherd went doubtless
with the intention of again reporting their adventures.
William D. Fellowes found material for one of his
books, and on another visit in 1817 he visited the
old monastery of La Trappe. There were agriculturists
like Morris Birkbeck of Wanborough. There were
doctors like Hume, chief physician to the army, and
Williams the oculist.

Among the aristocratic visitors were Viscount Pon-
sonby, afterwards Ambassador to Constantinople and
Vienna, and the Duke and Duchess of Rutland, parents
of the present Duke of Rutland, the Duke publishing
his fortnight's journal and receiving many attentions
from Count Dillon. There were also the Earl of
Charlemont, the Earl of Bradford, Lord Forbes, Lord
Lucan, the Earl of Oxford, Lord Kinnaird, Lady
Aldborough (who remained till after Waterloo),
the Marquis and Marchioness of Lansdowne, the
Marquis of Downshire, Lord Ilchester, Lord Hill, the
Marquis and Marchioness of Bath, the Earl and
Countess of Hardwicke, Lord and Lady Coventry,
the Duke and Duchess of Richmond, Lord Binning
(afterwards Earl of Haddington), Lord Compton, the
Marquis of Exeter, Lord and Lady Ranelagh, the
Duke of Portland, Lord Gosford, Lord Trimleston,
the Earl and Countess Darnley, the Duke of Devon-
shire, his step-mother, Lord and Lady Morpeth, Lord
Geo. Leveson-Gower, Sir John Sebright, M.P. for Hert-
fordshire, Lord Sunderland, grandson of the Duke of
Marlborough, Sir John and Lady Stepney, Lady Augusta

Cotton, Lord and Lady Holland, the Earl of Clare, Lord Carington, Lord Brownlow, Lady Bentinck, the notorious Lady Hamilton, the aged Duchess of Melfort with her son, the Marquis of Aylesbury, Lord Miltown, who, paralysed in his legs from childhood, went about in a chair, William Henry (afterwards Lord) Lyttelton, Lord Burghersh (as Earl of Westmorland he became a diplomatist), Lord Apsley, son and heir of Earl Bathurst, the Earl of Essex,[1] Sir John and Lady Knatchbull, Sir W. Clayton, Bagot (afterwards Sir Charles), and the Marquis of Clanricarde, who married Canning's daughter, was famous for gymnastic feats, and was afterwards Ambassador to Russia, Postmaster-General, and Lord Privy Seal. Edward John Littleton, M.P. for Staffordshire, a classical scholar, was accompanied by his handsome wife, Hyacinth Mary, natural daughter of the Marquis Wellesley, but recognised by the Wellesley family. Lady Priscilla Wellesley, daughter of the Earl of Mornington, another but legitimate niece of Wellington, just of age and destined to be Lady Burghersh and Countess of Westmorland, was in time to see d'Artois enter Paris. She survived till 1879.[2] Lord Fitzroy Somerset, son of the Duke of Beaufort, in 1852 became Lord Raglan and was destined to die before Sebastapol. He married in August 1814 Wellington's other favourite niece, Lady Emily Wellesley. The Earl of Harrowby was accompanied by Wellesley Pole and Gerald Wellesley, son

[1] An octogenarian, who in 1838, three months a widower, married Catherine Stevens, the vocalist, whose age was forty-four.
[2] *Letters of Lady Burghersh.*

of Sir Henry and afterwards Prebendary of Durham.
Lord Aberdeen, Ambassador at Vienna, who had
accompanied the Austrian army in its march into
France, was one of the English diplomatists who
signed the Treaty of Paris of May 1814. John William
Ward, afterwards Viscount and Earl of Dudley, a
contributor to the *Quarterly* and M.P. for Ilchester,
was also in Paris on his way to Italy. He rated
Napoleon above Alexander and Cæsar. Ward's travelling companion from Calais was General Montagu
Mathew, M.P. for Tipperary, brother of the Earl of
Landaff and a strenuous advocate of Catholic Emancipation. Thompson, M.P. for Midhurst—it is not clear
whether he was the ex-M.P. for Evesham, a captive
in 1803—was second on the 9th February 1815 in a
bloodless duel between Colonels Quentin and Palmer,
the latter firing in the air after his antagonist had
fired and missed.

We should not omit among the visitors Anne
Perry, the wife of James Perry of the *Morning
Chronicle*. Perry himself had spent a year in Paris
in 1792, sending of course letters to his paper, and
he may be regarded as the earliest of Paris correspondents. He had, moreover, for the previous twelve
months obtained the services of a French barrister
named Sanchamau, the translator of several English
works. Sanchamau at first found a seat on suffer-
ance in the Assembly, in the gallery allotted to the
suppléants, that is to say, the men destined to fill up
vacancies from death or other causes; but he applied
on the 22nd January 1792 for a permanent seat in

the new journalists' gallery.[1] To return to Perry's
wife, she was captured by Algerian pirates on her
way home from Lisbon, and although soon released,
captivity and seventeen weeks of a boisterous sea
aggravated her already precarious health. She expired
at Bordeaux in February 1815, at the age of thirty-
eight. We do not hear whether her husband attended
her deathbed.

Even London shopkeepers went over for a week.
John Scott, editor of the *Champion*, encountered one
full of anti-French prejudices, ignorant of the language,
unprovided even with a passport, and equipped only
with Bank of England notes.[2]

To accommodate the visitors, an Anglican service
was held in a chapel of the Protestant Oratoire, probably the upper room which was hired from about
1860 to 1885 by the Church of Scotland, and *Galignani's Messenger* was started, an edition of which, after
Waterloo and during the stay of the British garrison,
was published at Cambrai.

' The English at that time,' says Madame de Chastenay,
' almost did us the honours of Paris '; that is to say,
they seemed hosts rather than guests, and after the
first ball both sexes discarded their eccentric costumes.
Yet they did not find themselves altogether welcome.
The middle classes feared an English monopoly of
trade, returned prisoners told stories of ill-treatment
in England, and the populace resented the arrogance
of conquerors. Miss Anne Carter must have been

[1] National Archives, Paris, A. A. 40.
[2] *A Visit to Paris in* 1814. Scott went again after Waterloo.

strangely mistaken in writing to her sister, 'It is impossible to describe the enthusiasm with which we are everywhere received as English.'[1] Thomas Campbell, on the other hand, had been hooted at Dieppe, which he found incensed against the English, yet he does not speak of any incivility in Paris, where he danced attendance for nearly two months on Mrs. Siddons.[2]

A confidential police bulletin of the 17th October 1814 says:—

' The attention of the police has been called to the multitude of English who inundate Paris, and whose obscure station occasions uneasiness as to their destination and intentions. It is remembered on this point that after the Treaty of Amiens the French Government made an official complaint that the London police had vomited (sic) six or seven hundred persons, the scum of England, who secretly influenced trade, public opinion, and police. We see collected here a number of disreputable people who appear to be without means of subsistence, and whose arrival from England seems an enigma.'

Again on the 4th November :—

' It is positively stated that on Saturday last Lord Wellington complained to the King of the mortification and ill-treatment which various Englishmen have experienced and are daily experiencing in Paris, as well as of the lack of supervision shown by the French authorities in putting an end to these dangerous aggressions. It is a fact that at the Café Tortoni, the Opera, the restaurants, and in other public places, Englishmen are constantly affronted. These disorders are attributed

---

[1] Letters from a Lady to her Sister.
[2] Beattie, Life of Campbell.

to a troop of half-pay officers or to some turbulent men
discharged from the Guard of Honour. It seems certain,
moreover, that Lord Wellington has expressly enjoined the
English who are in Paris to behave very circumspectly, and
not to notice provocations which might disturb the harmony
necessary between the two nations.'

And on 19th December :—

'Every day there are fresh occasions of remarking the
hatred of the Parisians for the English. Yesterday at the
Salon the most violent language was used respecting them,
and that to their faces.'

In flat contradiction, however, to the police bulletins,
Wansey describes the Parisians as glad to see English
visitors once more amongst them.[1] The British milord
was good-naturedly burlesqued, as Weston tells us, in a
farce called *La Route de Paris*. A provincial innkeeper
welcomes milord and miladi. His bad French and her
veil excite amusement. The lord asks for beefsteak
for dinner. The lady is enchanted with everything.
The lord cries 'God dem, vive la paix,' while the lady
remarks that French and English have always been
near enough to shake hands. The landlord rejoices
that the lily after twenty years' preservation in an
English conservatory is as flourishing as ever. Birk-
beck, moreover, testifies to the welcome given to
Englishmen at Montpellier, which he attributed to
the kindness shown to French prisoners in England.
Yet Haydon relates that on the performance of Ducis'
Hamlet at the Comédie Française, the whole pit rose

[1] F. 7, 3784.

and applauded a line against England, shouting 'Bravo,
à bas les Anglais,' and pointing to the English present.

If the French authorities looked askance on English
visitors, it is but fair to say that some of the latter
sympathised with Napoleon. Lord and Lady Holland
were doubtless among them, for Lord Holland subsequently protested against the transportation to St.
Helena, and Lady Holland, as already stated, forwarded books thither to the captive. They were not
likely, when in Paris, to parade their anti-Bourbon
sentiments, but Hervey Montmorency Morris was less
scrupulous. He, on the 19th April 1814, presented
his newly born infant at the mairie of the tenth
arrondissement, and gave its name as Napoleon.[1]
A young Irishman named Charles Honoré Lyster,
describing himself as a student, a few months later
landed at Toulon from Elba, and the authorities very
naturally ordered him to be watched. Lord Oxford's
papers, moreover, were seized, and Wellington acknowledged that this was justified by his conduct and conversation, and by the Bonapartist correspondence of
which he had taken charge.

I have spoken of Wellington, but it should be stated
that the Embassy was at first filled by Sir Charles
Stuart, afterwards Lord Stuart de Rothesay. He presented his credentials to Louis XVIII. on the 22nd June,
but was soon transferred to The Hague. Wellington
arrived with his troops from Spain on the 7th May,
but went back to Madrid to see the Spanish dynasty
restored, returned to England to take his seat in the

[1] F. 7, 3785.

Lords as Duke, and was then appointed ambassador. He presented his credentials on the 24th August, but with much greater pomp than Stuart. Three royal carriages, each drawn by eight horses, escorted from the Embassy his three carriages, each drawn by six horses. He was accompanied by Major Fremantle and Major Percy. On reaching the foot of the throne he made a profound reverence, whereupon the King rose, then sat down again, putting on his hat and motioning to Wellington and the princes of the blood to cover also. The crowd murmured at these honours, though they were also accorded to all the other ambassadors, while the ultra-royalists professed indignation at the Duke's fixing a ball in honour of Queen Charlotte's birthday for the 18th January 1814, as being a date too close to the 21st, the anniversary of Louis XVI.'s execution. They were also suspicious of his intimacy with the Duke of Orleans. He paid a visit to the Abbé Sicard's deaf and dumb boys, who were not, however, dumb, for they articulated 'Vive notre bon roi Louis XVIII.!' The Duchess of Wellington was presented by the King with a Sèvres dinner-service. The British Government was very uneasy lest Wellington should be 'kidnapped'—an euphemism for being murdered—in some military rising. Anxious, therefore, for him to leave, its first idea was to send him to America to command in the short war with the United States. He himself, however, wished to remain in Paris, thinking that his departure would weaken Louis XVIII. A mission to the Vienna Congress he considered a poor pretext, but the Government persisted, though allowing him to choose his own time for departure. General Macaulay meanwhile went back to London with alarming reports. Wellington, writing to Lord Liverpool on the 23rd October, said :—

'It appears to me that Macaulay considers the danger of a revolt more certain and more likely to occur than I do, that is to say, he believes it certainly will occur within a very short period of time. I think it may occur any night, but I know of no fact to induce me to believe it is near, excepting the general one of great discontent and almost desperation among a very daring class of men.'

Macaulay feared that the royal family would be massacred and Wellington 'detained.' Wellington stayed, however, till the 22nd January. Meanwhile he was besieged with all sorts of applications. Hervey Montmorency Morris asked permission to return to Ireland, promising to be a loyal subject. Wellington demurred, suggesting that in spite of his good intentions he would fall back into the company of his old associates through the disinclination of loyalists to associate with him. Morris accordingly remained in the French army, was naturalised in November 1816, and remained in France till his death in 1839.

A man designating himself representative of De Beaune, who in 1790 negotiated a loan for the three English royal dukes, also called on Wellington. He stated that the bondholders were pressing him for payment of the principal and of the twenty years' arrears of interest. Wellington forwarded his documents to London, but nothing more is heard of the affair. Impey was there again on the same errand as in 1802, and Long, ex-president of the Irish College, went over to seek restitution; but these claims all stood over till after the Hundred Days. The Scottish College, however, was restored to its owners, and on the 13th December Robertson, bishop-coadjutor of Dublin and inventor of a process of embossing books for the blind, solemnised a *Te Deum* there in the presence of numerous British ecclesiastics. Quintin Craufurd likewise sent in a statement of British claims to compensation, and he obtained the restitution of eighty pictures, engravings, and sculptures confiscated in 1792.

Wellington received directions to prevent Princess Caroline from repairing from Strasburg to Paris, though his own opinion was that she might safely have been permitted to amuse herself. Louis XVIII., out of consideration for the Prince Regent, had resolved not to receive her. She nevertheless in October paid an incognito visit.

But few of the English visitors could have been in time to see the Tsar, with his sons Constantine and Nicholas, the Emperor of Austria, and the King of Prussia, with his two sons, one of them the future William I., destined to re-enter Paris as a conqueror in 1871, for their stay was very short. The Russian and Prussian sovereigns went on to England in June, while the Austrian Emperor pleaded Italian affairs as preventing him from also going. The brilliant uniforms of their officers, however, continued to enliven the streets of the capital. Louis had pressed the Prince Regent to come over, telling him that the three monarchs seconded the invitation, but the

Prince, 'fat, fair, and forty,' or rather, as Leigh Hunt had been imprisoned for describing him, 'an Adonis of fifty,' probably shrank from the fatigue of the journey, or possibly he was not too confident of the stability of the restored dynasty. He made the excuse that a Regency Act would be necessary if he left his realm, yet his ancestors had paid visits to Hanover. His subjects were of course eager to be presented at Court. Shepherd speaks of Louis as 'uncomfortably corpulent and seemed very infirm in his feet, but his countenance is extremely pleasing, and if any reliance is to be placed on physiognomy, he is a man of a very benevolent disposition.'[1] Shepherd went in clerical costume, fancying that this would be sufficient, but Stuart telling him the contrary, he had to hurry off to a tailor to get properly equipped.

Dr. Williams presented the King with portraits of George III. and the Prince Regent, 'two princes to whom,' Louis said, ' he had vowed the most faithful remembrance.' Sir Herbert Croft presented to him verses addressed to the Duchess of Angoulême. Galignani, who, though an Italian ex-priest, may be considered an Englishman by marriage and adoption, presented thirty volumes of his English reprints, his *Paris Guide,* and his *Modern Spectator.* Street, editor and part proprietor of the *Courier,* also had an audience, and was complimented on his journal's ten years' advocacy of the cause of the Bourbons.[2]

---

[1] *Paris in* 1802 *and* 1814.
[2] Retiring in 1822, he lived till 1846. His co-proprietor, Daniel Stuart, died in 1847.

Those visitors who were not presented at Court had an opportunity of seeing the King on his way to chapel. Haydon, who describes him as ' keen, fat, and eagle-eyed,' joined in shouting ' Vive le roi!' He remarked that Napoleon's initials still dotted the vestibule of the chapel. The Duke of Rutland also remarked that the draperies of the Tuileries were dotted with bees, and that ' N' or an eagle was visible on all the furniture. This was a perpetual reminder to the Bourbons of the dethroned ruler. But few of these emblems appear to have been at first effaced in Paris, lest this should provoke counter-demonstrations, though provincial authorities displayed more zeal and less tact. Yet Stephen Weston speaks of thousands of workmen being employed in removing them, and Birk-beck observed men busily effacing Napoleon's name and eagles from public buildings, which he thought very pitiful, while Scott noticed ingenious attempts to turn ' N ' into ' L ' or ' H ' in honour of Louis xviii. or Henri iv. He also speaks of a sign ' Café de l'Empereur ' being converted into 'Café des Empereurs' in honour of the Russian and Austrian monarchs.

On the 21st January, the anniversary of Louis xvi.'s execution, there was an imposing procession on the transfer of his and his Queen's remains to St. Denis, and requiem masses were celebrated all over France, the Protestant pastors Monod and Marron also holding services, albeit the latter had flattered Napoleon. These masses were ordered to be annual, but were never repeated. There were other spectacles. There was the proclamation of peace by a herald on the

1st June with all the revived formalities of the old
Monarchy. The spoils of Italian art, including the
Venetian horses, still embellished Paris, though
destined to removal as a punishment for the Hundred
Days. Sunday and festival observance was enforced
on shops and factories, by a decree of the Prefect
of Police on the 7th June. The host, for the first
time since the Revolution, was carried through the
streets on Corpus Christi day, all houses on the route
having to be draped, and bystanders being expected,
if not required, to uncover as it passed. The streets,
says Haydon, were hung with tapestries, and altars
were erected at various points. It was the first
Sunday since the Revolution that shops had been
shut, yet the gaming-tables were open as usual.
Parisians did not fail to remark that these measures
were decreed by a notorious sceptic, Beugnot. When
Corpus Christi day came round again on the 25th May
1815, Napoleon was once more on the throne. On
the 29th August the King paid a State visit to the
Hotel de Ville, in honour of which Paris illuminated.
The fountains in the Champs Elysées poured forth
wine for all comers, and comestibles were also
gratuitous.[1]

The London newspapers expressed distrust in the
stability of the new government, and doubtless on
that account were prohibited admission to France.
English officials seem to have shared this sentiment,
for in July 1814 Admiral Mackenzie, who had brought
over the Duc de Berri, suddenly renounced his

[1] F. 7, 3783.

T

intended wintering in the south and recrossed the
Channel.   Crabb Robinson remarked that when the
King reviewed the National Guard the cheers were
very faint, and that there were some cries of 'Vive
l'Empereur!'   Even the Rev. R. W. Wake, curate
of Maidstone, who, having only a week's holiday,
went no further than Calais and Boulogne, was
struck by the regret with which Napoleon's fall
was spoken of.[1]   Yet some of the visitors descried
no troubles ahead.   Wansey, who was in Paris in
June, going thither by Dieppe and returning by
Boulogne, says :—

'That there are many dissatisfied with the new order
of things, particularly among the military, there is no doubt,
and we may expect to hear of partial insurrections and
commotions among the men returned from the wars. . . .
But a Government that employs men of such talents as
those I have mentioned (Talleyrand, Fouché, Louis, and
Montesquiou) will not be easily overturned, particularly as
the leaders of the army are with the Court; and as to
the return of Napoleon, he ran the full length of his tether.
You will hear no more of his rule in France.'[2]

John Scott, however, in the diligence between
Dieppe and Paris, heard an officer with Napoleon's
portrait on his snuff-box say, in reply to English
expressions of satisfaction at the peace, 'All very
well, this tranquillity of Europe is a fine thing, but
will it not keep me always a captain?'   Another officer,
though originally forced away from the study of

[1] *Mon Journal de Huit Jours.*
[2] *Visit to Paris in June* 1814.

little realm, General Spallannchi reported from
Florence that some Englishmen had gone out of
curiosity to Elba but had returned in ill-humour,
the fallen monarch having barely allowed them to
see him and that only in his garden. It seems from
the statement of Vice-Consul Innes that the party
numbered seven, including one lady, and that after
being kept a long time waiting for an answer the
garden interview was assigned them for the next
day. A Warwickshire man who had passed through
Paris and whose letter, intercepted by the Leghorn
police, was signed ' Richard,' evidently his Christian
name, sailed from Leghorn with his sister on the
24th November, but was told that Napoleon refused
to receive curiosity-mongers. Not easily to be foiled,
however, he made a second voyage and on alighting
at an hotel at Porto Ferrajo on the 2nd December
found covers laid for thirty Corsican functionaries
in honour of the anniversary of Napoleon's coronation
in 1804. Such a celebration did not argue renuncia-
tion of empire. On the following day he was allowed
an audience, but nothing having been said about
his sister he had to leave her outside. Napoleon,
whom he found standing in a small room, advanced
with an affable air and asked, ' Where do you come
from ? '

' Warwickshire.'

' I do not remember the name.'

' It is in the very centre of England.'

' What is your occupation ? '

' General commerce, but chiefly manufactures.'

'Do you find much custom in Italy?'

'Tolerable.'

'None in France, eh?'

'None at present, for want of a commercial treaty.'

'A commercial treaty would suit you?'

'Certainly, but I do not think we shall get it.'

'I did your commerce much mischief.'

'Not so much as was supposed. Our trade found outlets out of Europe which were very profitable.'

'The troubles in Spain will open up their colonies to you?'

'Yes, but at first they will be jealously closed.'

'Your licence system was bad. It was semi-robbery.'

'This kind of conversation' (says Richard), 'lasted about an hour, and then turned on France. . . . He asked me whether I was in Paris during the Peace of Amiens. "Yes." "You found it now much altered?" "Yes, much larger than in 1802." "It is a fine city," he added. . . . I took the opportunity of reminding him of my sister, but he took no notice. He then conversed for a few minutes, making altogether half an hour. On getting up to leave he asked me to introduce my sister, whom he received with the greatest affability, keeping up a conversation with her till a carriage was heard coming, when he bowed and we retired. . . . He frequently put his fingers into a small snuff-box, but did not seem to take much notice of its contents. He asked me whether I thought the Bourbons were really popular in France. He told me he had found the heat more trying in Russia in the month of August than in any other part of Europe, and he explained the reason. I remarked evident signs of interest and inquisitiveness when speaking of the Bourbons. He twice asked me whether they were popular in France and what was said of them, and was not satisfied with a vague reply.'[1]

Frederick Douglas, M.P., son of Lord Glenbervie, on his way home from Athens had a courteous reception, which did not however prevent him from speaking and voting in 1815 for the renewal of the war.

'Why have you come?' asked Napoleon.

'To see a great man.'

'Rather to see a wild beast,' rejoined Napoleon, who inquired whether Douglas had seen Murat or the Pope. The latter, said Napoleon, 'is an obstinately resigned old man. I did not treat him properly. I did not go the right way to work with him.' As to the state of France, Douglas reported that there was much enthusiasm for the Bourbons, though there were a few malcontents. 'Yes,' remarked Napoleon, 'people who belong to whatever party pays them and make much stir in order to get money.' Napoleon went on to complain of the treachery of his officers, of the pamphleteers who styled him a usurper, of his brothers for not having seconded him, and of the sovereigns who had abandoned him. Douglas reported that he could no longer mount a horse, and that he had fallen into profound apathy. Perhaps Napoleon intentionally gave him this erroneous impression, knowing that he was on his way to Paris, which he reached in January 1815.[2]

Lord William Bentinck, afterwards Viceroy of India, with a friend were sumptuously regaled, but we have

---

[1] Livi, *Napoleon a Elba*, 1888; *Siècle*, August 23, 1887.

[2] *Quotidienne*, February 6, 1815.

no record of the conversation, and an English lady 'of angelical beauty,' whom Pons does not name, but who may have been Lady Jersey, for he says she showed the Emperor continued sympathy during the St. Helena captivity, was received with marked favour. When, on her return to London, she saw the Russian and Prussian sovereigns pass by, she said to the fashionable gathering round her, 'Those men cannot seem imposing to persons who like me have had a close view of the Emperor Napoleon.' Another visitor in September 1814 was John Barber Scott, of Bungay, Suffolk, ultimately a Fellow of Emmanuel College, Cambridge, but then a graduate twenty-two years of age, who was accompanied by Major (Patrick?) Maxwell, R.A., Colonel (afterwards General) John Lemoine, R.A., Captain Smith, and Colonel Niel Douglas.

They encountered Napoleon as he was out riding, and on their saluting him he stopped for a few minutes to question them. They thought he looked more like a crafty priest than a hero. On being told that Scott was a Cantab he said, 'What, Cambridge, Cambridge? Oh yes, you are a young man; you will be a lawyer. Eh, eh, you will be Lord Chancellor?' Being told by Douglas that he belonged to a Highland regiment, Napoleon asked whether they did not wear kilts (*jupes*). On Douglas replying in the affirmative, Napoleon asked whether he had brought his kilt with him, as he should like to see it, but Douglas was unable to gratify his curiosity.[1]

Equally short, or even shorter, had been the interview of Sir Gilbert Starling and a Mr. Campbell.[2]

[1] *Temple Bar*, October 1903.   [2] *Ibid.*

One visitor said he was as pleased to have spent nine days at Elba as if he had won £30,000. Napoleon, however, refused audiences to Englishmen whom he suspected of simple curiosity or of exultation at his fall.[1] When he went to Longone, the second town in the island, there were numerous English visitors, and it was remarked to him that they followed him wherever he went. He replied, 'I am an object of curiosity; let them satisfy themselves. They will go home and amuse the gentlemans (*sic*) by describing my acts and gestures.' He added in a sad tone, 'They have won the game; they hold the dice.'

Yet so far from showing him disrespect, Pons states that these sixty visitors of all classes vied in extolling him. Pons also acknowledges that Colonel Campbell, though deputed by his Government to watch Napoleon, veiled his supervision so carefully that only the closest observation could detect it.[2]

But the principal visitor, and the only one invited to dinner, was Lord Ebrington, afterwards Earl of Fortescue and in 1839-1841 Viceroy of Ireland. He first waited on the Emperor at 8 P.M. on the 6th December, and for three hours walked up and down the room with him. 'You come from France; tell me frankly,' said Napoleon, 'whether the French are satisfied.' 'Only so-so,' replied Ebrington. 'It cannot be otherwise,' rejoined Napoleon; 'they have been too much humiliated by the peace. The appointment of the Duke of Wellington as Ambassador must have seemed

[1] *Nuova Antologia*, January 1887.
[2] Pons de l'Hérault, *Souvenirs d'Elbe*, edited by Pelissier, 1897.

an insult to the army, as also the special attentions
shown him by the King. If Lord Wellington had
come to Paris as a visitor, I should have had pleasure
in showing him the attentions due to his great ability,
but I should not have liked his being sent to me as
Ambassador.'

The justice of this remark is obvious. Napoleon
extolled the House of Lords as the bulwark of the
English constitution. He denounced the duplicity of
the Emperor Alexander, expressed esteem for the
Austrian Emperor, and spoke slightingly of the King
of Prussia. 'How should I be treated,' he asked
Ebrington, 'if I went to England? Should I be
stoned?' Ebrington replied that he would run no risk,
and that the irritation formerly existing against him
was daily dying out. 'I think, however,' rejoined
Napoleon, 'that there would be some danger from
your mob'—he used the English word—'at London.'

'The grace of his smile and the simplicity of his
manner,' says Ebrington, 'had put me quite at my ease.
He himself appeared to wish me to question him. He
replied without the least hesitation, with a promptitude
and clearness which I have never seen equalled in any
other man.'

Next day, just as Ebrington was preparing to sail,
came an invitation to dinner, and this second interview
lasted from seven till eleven. Napoleon inquired for
the Duke and Duchess of Bedford, Whitworth, Erskine,
and Holland, and spoke especially of Fox. Informed
that Fox felt much flattered at his reception in 1802,
Napoleon said, 'He had reason to be so. He was

everywhere received like a divinity because he was known to be in favour of peace.' 'Tell Lord Grenville,' added Napoleon, 'to come and see me. I wager that you in England thought me a devil, but now that you have seen me and France also you must be somewhat disabused.' He justified the detentions of 1803. Ebrington, however, maintained that the embargo on French shipping in British ports prior to the formal declaration of war was in accordance with precedent, on which Napoleon replied, 'Yes, you considered it right because it was to your advantage; other nations who lost by it thought it wrong. I am sure that at heart you in England approved me for showing force of character. Do you not see that I am a bit of a pirate like yourselves?'

Napoleon half in earnest advocated polygamy, especially in the colonies, where a planter might have a wife of each colour, so that the two families might grow up together harmoniously. He inquired for 'my good friend Ussher'—Captain, afterwards Sir Thomas Ussher —who had conveyed him to Elba.

On surprise being expressed by Ebrington at his calm endurance of adversity, Napoleon said, 'It is because everybody was more surprised at it than myself. I have not too good an opinion of mankind, and have always distrusted fortune. Moreover, I had little enjoyment. My brothers were much more kings than I was. They tasted the sweets of royalty, while I had only the worries and cares.' [1]

[1] Ebrington's *Memorandum of Two Conversations*, published in 1823 as a pamphlet of thirty-one pages and never reprinted.

Lord John Russell, the future statesman, then twenty-three years of age, being taken by his father to Florence in the autumn of 1814, embraced the opportunity of visiting Elba. 'When I saw Napoleon,' he says, ' he was in evident anxiety respecting the state of France and his chances of again seizing the crown which he had worn for ten years. I was so struck with his restless inquiry that I expressed in a letter to my brother in England my conviction that he would make some fresh attempts to disturb France and govern Europe.' [1]

But by far the most curious incident of Napoleon's reign at Elba was his presence at an entertainment in honour of George III.'s birthday, given on the 4th June 1814 by Captain Tower on board the frigate *Undaunted*. Napoleon, on reaching Fréjus after his abdication in April, had embarked in the *Undaunted* in preference to a French vessel assigned for his passage to Elba, and had taken a fancy to the captain, Ussher. The *Undaunted* went to and from Elba and Leghorn, and it might have celebrated the royal birthday at the latter port. Napoleon afterwards thought that Colonel (ultimately Sir Neil) Campbell purposely planned the celebration at Elba. When, however, Towers invited him to come on board, and sent round invitations to the principal inhabitants of Porto Ferrajo, he readily accepted the invitation, and directed his courtiers, if such a phrase can be used, to do likewise. One of these, Pons de l'Hérault, to whom we are indebted for the fullest account of the festival

---

[1] Earl Russell, *Recollections*. See Appendix C.

—not published, however, till 1897 [1]—was inclined indeed to regard the invitation as an insult and the festival as a bravado; but his master told him that it was the duty of British sailors to observe their sovereign's birthday wherever they might happen to be. A 'throne,' says Pons, had been prepared for the Emperor on the bridge; and he continues:—

'The Emperor arrived, and the ship's officers received him at the top of the ladder. Guns could not be fired, as they were not mounted, but the crew, clustered on the rigging, gave him three hearty cheers, and the Emperor looking up at them raised his hat. He then passed to the quarter-deck. There all were ranged in a circle, and the Emperor, as though quite at home, his left hand as usual in his fob, put the trivial questions which he nearly always employed on such occasions, for he did not bother himself with finding remarks appropriate to each particular individual. It was not his moment for parade. When the circle had broken up the Emperor asked for an interpreter and went to talk to the sailors, especially to a mate with whom he had several times conversed during his passage from Fréjus to the isle of Elba. The entire crew seemed eager to see him again. The countenances of these good fellows expressed the very contrary of the perversity of their Government. Captain Tower sincerely admired the Emperor, and watched all his movements with a gaze full of respect and interest. He had one of those open countenances which inspire confidence. The Emperor said to me . . . "The English Government will never forgive me for having been the most determined Frenchman in breaking down its supremacy. Not that hatred actuated me, it was duty, it was love of country. [2]

[1] *Souvenirs de l'île d'Elbe.*
[2] We know how Napoleon as a youth detested France, regarding

302 NAPOLEON'S BRITISH VISITORS

All well-bred Englishmen consequently honour me. If I went to England the English Government would be afraid of my popularity and would pack me off." . . . The same cheers accompanied the Emperor on his departure, and he responded with the same salute.'[1]

Pons, with his wife and children and the other guests, remained to the dinner and ball. Unfortunately, two of the ship's officers drank a little too much, and so misbehaved themselves as to oblige several of the ladies to withdraw. It is pathetic to think that Napoleon's next and last acquaintance with British tars was when, thirteen months later, he gave himself up to the *Bellerophon*, and was conveyed as a captive in the *Northumberland* to St. Helena.

One Englishman at least was a spectator of Napoleon's departure from Elba. A Mr. Grattan (probably the father of Thomas Colley Grattan, the traveller and novelist) had landed on the island on the 24th February. On the evening of the 26th he noticed unusual bustle, as though something was about to happen, and at 9 P.M. he saw Napoleon, escorted by General Bertrand, come out in his sister Pauline's four-horse carriage, enter a boat, and go on board the brig *Inconstant*. Thereupon the whole flotilla got under way, the soldiers shouting 'Vive l'Empereur!' Scarcely believing his eyes, Grattan hired a boat to go alongside the brig, and thence he saw Napoleon in his grey overcoat and round

Corsica alone as his country, but he doubtless got to consider himself a real Frenchman.

[1] According to an English account Napoleon, on the band striking up the National Anthem, hummed the tune. (*Temple Bar*, October 1903.)

hat pacing the quarter-deck. One of the boatmen, however, cried out that there was an Englishman on board, upon which an officer on the poop of the *Inconstant* demanded who he was and what he wanted. Grattan had to explain that he had merely come to have a look at the Emperor, whereupon he was told to be off, and he complied with alacrity, expecting every instant to be fired at or arrested.[1]

Up to the 20th March the *Moniteur* had continued publishing loyal addresses to Louis XVIII., but on the 21st it announced, 'The King and the Princes left last night. His Majesty the Emperor arrived this evening at eight o'clock in his palace of the Tuileries.' One of Napoleon's first inquiries to a lady of his court was whether there were many English in Paris. On being told that nearly all had left he exclaimed, ' Ah, they recollect what I did before, but those times are past. You do not repeat yourself.' John Cam Hobhouse, Byron's friend, afterwards Lord Broughton, tells us this, and he adds that the detentions of 1802 were against French feeling and could not have been repeated in 1815 in defiance of such a feeling. Napoleon, moreover, may have thought there was a chance of his recognition by the allies,[2] and the detention of foreigners would have been a virtual declaration of war. Yet

[1] Sir Neil Campbell, *Napoleon at Fontainebleau and Elba*, 1869.

[2] As it was, the Marquis Wellesley (Wellington's brother), the Duke of Sussex (the Prince Regent's brother), Lords Lansdowne, Grey, Byron, Lauderdale, Guilford, Bessborough, and three other peers voted in his favour, as also Mackintosh, Romilly, Whitbread, Tierney, Lord Morpeth, Sir Timothy Shelley (the poet's grandfather), Lord Stanley (father of the ' Rupert of Debate '), Lord Duncannon, and twenty-nine other members of the Lower House.

the stampede was obviously prudent, and the principal
Englishman who remained did not escape molestation.
Francis Henry Egerton, as we have seen, had come
over to Paris in 1802, and he had apparently continued
to reside uninterruptedly, for he published several
works there, both in English and French, between
1812 and 1826. He had hired a house till 1814, but
on the restoration of the Bourbons he purchased the
mansion of the Noailles family in the rue St. Honoré,
and to show his sympathy with the new Government
he paid up at once, on the 2nd March 1815, in lieu
of by instalments, the stamp duty of 30,000 francs.
This seems to have marked him out for Napoleon's
resentment.   The house with its contents was requi-
sitioned to serve for a Government office.   Egerton
resisted, stood a kind of siege, and appealed to the
tribunals. He could not, it is obvious, have permanently withstood Napoleon, but he seems to have held
his ground until Waterloo arrived and put an end to
the affair. He lost no time in securing legal domicile
and civic rights, for in default of the latter one alien
could not bequeath property to another, such property
being forfeit to the French Crown.   His support of
the Bourbons should have shielded him from further
annoyance, but in 1818 he had an unpleasant episode.
Workmen who were placing flower-pots on the pillars
of the Tuileries gardens found it convenient to fasten
ropes to the wall of his back garden in the rue de
Rivoli.   Egerton drove out in his carriage and required
them to desist.   An altercation ensued, there were cries
of 'Down with the Englishman!' and he was dragged

out of his carriage to the guardhouse.   Though promptly
released, he was very punctilious in exacting an apology
for this indignity, threatening otherwise to quit France.
He was very eccentric in his latter years, if we are to
believe that cats and dogs dressed up as human beings
sat at his dinner-table, and that he kept rabbits and
partridges in his garden in order to have shooting on
his own premises.   He died as Duke of Bridgewater
in 1829, aged seventy-nine, and left £8000 for eight
prize treatises which were named after him.   The Hôtel
St. James, into which his house has been converted,
contains the original staircase and other relics of the
mansion in which Marie Antoinette welcomed Lafayette
and Noailles on their return from America.

Englishmen who, like Egerton, remained or arrived
during the Hundred Days witnessed curious scenes.
Hobhouse in his passport of 1814 had seen the word
empire erased and *royaume* substituted.   He now
found a contrary change made.   He saw Napoleon
review the National Guard on the 16th April, and attend
the Comédie Française on the 21st, on both which
occasions his reception was enthusiastic.   He also witnessed the ceremony on the Champ de Mars, when
Napoleon closely scrutinised the crowd with his eye-
glass during the mass on which he had resolved in
order to show that the Empire was not anti-catholic.
Hobhouse, though strenuously opposed to the renewal of
the war by the allies, acknowledges that Napoleon was
not popular in Paris except with the military, and that
the cheers were very faint.   Yet he courted popularity by
visiting public institutions and by walking about almost

unattended and conversing with people of all classes. He removed on the 17th April from the Tuileries, where, however, he still held his councils, to the Elysée, close to the Borghese palace which Wellington had purchased for the British Embassy. The latter was of course vacant, for all the ambassadors had followed Louis XVIII. to Ghent, Fitzroy Somerset assuring him previously to his flight that England would stand by him. In the absence of ambassadors foreigners could not of course be formally presented, but Mrs. Damer obtained an interview to give Napoleon the bust of Fox, which she had promised him in 1802. The jewelled snuff-box bearing his own portrait which he gave her in return is now in the British Museum. Up to the 4th May, if not later, the Calais and Dover mail-packets continued to run, and took many French passengers. When Corpus Christi festival arrived the processions, as from the Revolution till 1813 and as ever since, were confined in Paris to the churches or their enclosures.

Napoleon affected liberal views, not only by summoning Benjamin Constant to his councils, but by inviting to return to Paris his friend Madame de Staël, who had not joined in the exultation at his fall, and indeed had sent him warning to Elba, through his brother Joseph, of a plot against his life. She did not accept the invitation, but wrote to Quintin Craufurd a letter intended for transmission to the English Government, in which she affirmed the sincerity of his liberal professions. Yet she might justly have distrusted these.

Among the Frenchmen who fled to England was one whose Irish extraction entitles him to mention.

Jean Baptiste Lynch, whose Jacobite ancestors had settled at Bordeaux, was imprisoned during the Revolution. In 1808 Napoleon made him Mayor of Bordeaux, and in 1810 created him a Count. Lynch was lavish in his professions of fidelity to the Empire, but in 1813 he had secret dealings with a royalist emissary, and in 1814, on the approach of Wellington's army, he proclaimed Louis XVIII. at Bordeaux. He was the first man in France to do this, and he also sent a deputation to Louis in England. On hearing of Napoleon's return from Elba and unopposed march on Paris, he despatched the Duchess of Angoulême to England to be out of his reach, and he himself followed her. He was at Newcastle on a visit to a relative when news of Waterloo arrived, and he was cheered by the populace.[1] Louis, who in 1814 had awarded him the grand cross of the Legion of Honour, thus giving him a Napoleonic decoration for deserting Napoleon, made him a peer. In a letter written to a Bordeaux editor in 1816 Lynch urged the justice of Catholic emancipation, but deprecated Irish independence, and expressed a wish to go and deliver loyalist speeches in Ireland, that he might render service to his ancestral as he had done to his native country.

No foreigners applied during the Hundred Days for domicile or naturalisation, whereas previously Philip Dormer Stanhope had obtained domicile,[2] as also James

---

[1] Mackenzie, *History of Newcastle*, 1827.

[2] Philip Dormer Stanhope had settled in France or Belgium about 1790, and during the war procured remittances from England through the Paris bankers Perregaux and Laffitte. Was he a son of Lord

George Hartley, a law student, and naturalisation had
been accorded to two Irish officers in the French service
—Julius Terence O'Reilly and William Corbett.

On the 12th June Napoleon left for the frontier,
and a period of suspense followed. Hobhouse started
on the following day for Geneva, but found he could
not pass through the armies, and accordingly returned
to Paris on the 28th. 'I cannot help wishing,' he says
in his letters to Byron, which the *Quarterly* character-
ised as 'infamous libels on the English name and
character,' 'that the French may meet with as much
success as will not compromise the military character
of my own countrymen; but as an Englishman I
cannot be witness of their triumph; as a lover of
liberty I would not be a spectator of their reverses.'
This was an utterance published after the event. Perhaps Hobhouse at the time, like Byron, was nevertheless sorry to hear of Waterloo. He seems to have
quitted Paris before the re-entry of Louis XVIII., but
British residents like Helen Williams, Croft, Craufurd,
and Egerton, witnessing the first fall of Napoleon, the
accession of Louis, his flight, the arrival of Napoleon,
his return from Waterloo, and the re-accession of Louis,
beheld in the short space of fourteen months a series of
vicissitudes unexampled in human annals.

No Englishman who saw Napoleon in Paris after
Waterloo, if any such there were, has left any record

Chesterfield's illegitimate son? If so, the latter was a father at the
age of nineteen, for he was born in 1732, and this Philip Dormer
Stanhope gave his age in September 1814 on applying for domicile in
France as sixty-three. Possibly, however, this last figure is a misprint
in the *Bulletin des Lois*.

of it. It is obvious, indeed, that the few Englishmen then in Paris would shun observation during those days of suspense. An Englishwoman, daughter of one of the officers detained in 1803 and herself born in captivity, may, however, have then seen him. In any case her husband, Legouvé, the Academician who died in March 1903, at the age of ninety-four, was in all probability the last survivor of those who had seen Napoleon in Paris, for he was six years of age in 1815. The last survivor who had mixed in his society at St. Helena was Madame Hortense Eugénie Thayer, daughter of General Bertrand by Henrietta, daughter of General Arthur Dillon. This was one of Napoleon's compulsory marriages, but Bertrand succeeded in gaining his unwilling bride's affection. Hortense, born at Paris in 1810, was presented by Napoleon at St. Helena with a pair of earrings, and he witnessed the boring of her ears for this purpose, complimenting her on her composure during the operation. She married Amédée Thayer, a French Senator under the Second Empire, of American extraction. Dying in 1890, she bequeathed to Prince Victor Bonaparte a red damask coat presented to her by Napoleon for a spencer to be made out of it, but preserved intact, together with other relics. We do not hear what became of the earrings. Her mother gave Napoleon lessons in English at St. Helena, and I subjoin a short article on this subject published by me in the *Atlantic Monthly*, November 1895:—

A recent exhibition of Napoleonic relics in Paris comprised, among numerous specimens of handwriting—one of them the draft abdication of Fontainebleau, another the draft 'Themistocles' letter to the Prince Regent—a lesson in translating French into English. Pitying Napoleon as we must, though conscious that captivity alone secured France and Europe against another Hundred Days, his attempt to learn English is irresistibly pathetic. We are reminded of Ovid learning to speak, and even to versify, in Dacian, but Napoleon does not seem to have mastered English sufficiently to be able to write in prose without numerous mistakes. He had been acquainted from his youth, by translations, with several English authors. He was fond of Ossian, and a collection of thirty-four books, given him by his sister Pauline to take with him to Egypt, included Bacon's Essays, in which he marked in pencil two passages : one in the chapter Of Great Place, from the third sentence, 'It is a strange desire to seek power and to lose liberty,' to the sentence preceding the lines from Seneca; the other in the chapter Of Kingdoms and Estates, from ' triumph amongst the Romans ' to the end. Patronised by the younger Robespierre and by Barras, he had already exemplified the saying, 'By indignities men come to dignities'; and he was destined also, like Bacon himself, to find that 'the standing is slipping, and the regression is either a downfall or at least an eclipse.' He never, apparently, saw acted even an adaptation of Shakespeare, yet on the eve of the rupture of the Treaty of Amiens he surprised his Council of State by diverging from a coinage question into a tirade against both Shakespeare and Milton. Too busy, even if inclined, to study English, he would, had he invaded England in 1803 and commissioned Sir Francis Burdett to organise a republic, have taken with him one hundred and seventeen interpreter guides, in red coats and white trousers—a corps which he expected to recruit from Irish and other refugees. One of these refugees, the notorious Lewis Goldsmith, read the London newspapers for him. But Napoleon was not fated to get nearer to English soil than William III.'s landing-place, Torbay.

Captivity afforded him the requisite leisure and also a strong inducement, for he was anxious, not to acquaint himself with English literature, but to see what was said of himself in the English press. Accordingly, on the six weeks' voyage to St. Helena, he took two lessons from Las Cases, who, when himself an exile, had taught French and learned English in London. It seems likely that he had acquired just a smattering before Waterloo, if not before Elba; for while waiting at Balcombe House till Longwood was ready for him, he occasionally spoke English (desiring her to correct his mistakes) to the lively Betsy Balcombe, that *enfant terrible* who coolly questioned him not only as to his supposed atheism, but as to the 'happy dispatch' of the wounded French at Jaffa and as to the execution of the Duc d'Enghien. He sent, moreover, for some English books, one of them an edition of Æsop, and, pointing to the picture of the ass kicking the sick lion, he remarked in English, ' It is me (*sic*) and your governor ' (Sir Hudson Lowe). His accent then, and probably to the last, was very peculiar, and he usually talked and joked with Betsy in French, though her French was not of the best. He got her to translate to him Dr. Warden's account of the voyage of the *Northumberland*. Though addicted to teasing, he had so won her affection that she shed many tears on quitting the island, where, according to a recent French visitor, the recollections of Napoleon have been effaced by a wild-beast show, a visitor quite as rare as an imperial captive. When settled at Longwood, Napoleon resolved on seriously renewing the study. Las Cases gave him a daily lesson; sometimes finding him a diligent scholar, at other times so inattentive that Napoleon would himself laughingly ask his teacher whether he did not deserve the rod, regarded by him as an essential adjunct

to education. He even wrote several letters in English to
Las Cases, but the irregular verbs overtaxed his patience.
He managed, however, to read after a fashion, and, according
to Las Cases, might at a push have made himself understood
in writing; but it does not appear that the lessons went on
more than a few weeks. They had probably ceased long
before December 1816, when Las Cases had to quit the
island. A scrap of paper, presented by him to a friend, and
also included in the exhibition, is the only trace of these
lessons. We read on it, in his pupil's handwriting: 'Gone
out, *aller dehors, sortir*. Opened, *ouvert*. To see, *voire* (*sic*),
regarder.'

Napoleon's next professor, after how long an interval we
cannot tell, was Countess Bertrand, daughter of General
Arthur Dillon by Anne Laure Girardin, cousin to the
Empress Josephine. She had never even visited England,
but her father, guillotined when she was eight years of age,
had probably taught her his native tongue. Napoleon, dis-
posing of rich heiresses with Oriental despotism, had required
her to marry Bertrand, one of his generals; and though the
poor girl was at first in despair and refused to see her suitor,
she speedily became attached to him, and they lived happily
ever after. One of their children, named Arthur, not, as
one of the St. Helena narratives states, after the Duke of
Wellington, but after the grandfather—was born on the
island in January 1817, and archly introduced by the
mother to Napoleon as 'the first Frenchman who had entered
Longwood without a pass from Sir Hudson Lowe.' She was
extremely fond of society, and though, with her husband,
she had accompanied the Emperor to Elba, she was so averse
to St. Helena that she stormed at Napoleon for involving
Bertrand and his family in his banishment, and even tried
to throw herself overboard. This, unlike some of her other
antipathies, she never overcame, and at the time of Napoleon's
death she was arranging for a return to France, on the plea

of getting her children educated. One of those children,
whose ears were bored in Napoleon's presence that he might
present her with earrings, survived, as Madame Thayer,
widow of one of Napoleon III.'s senators, till 1890. Madame
Bertrand, apparently, gave a specimen of Napoleon's lessons
to Madame Junot, whose grand-daughter, Madame de la
Ferrière, lent it to the recent exhibition. A sheet of letter
paper, yellow with age, contains alternate lines of French
and English; but it will be more convenient to give first
the theme, and then the translation, which has never yet
been published. The italics in brackets indicate the erasures.

' Quand serez-vous sage ?

' Quand je ne serai plus dans cette île. Mais je le de-
viendrai après avoir passé la ligne.

' Lorsque je débarquerai en france, je serai très content.
Ma femme viendra près de moi, mon fils sera grand et fort,
il pourra boire sa bouteille de vin à dîner, je trinquerai avec
lui. Ma mère sera vieille, mes sœurs seront laides, ce qui ne
leur sera pas agréable, elles seront *toujours* coquettes, car les
femmes se croient toujours jolies.'

' When will you be wise ?

' Never [*then that*] as long as I [*should*] could be in this
isle, but I shall become vise after [*have*] having passed the
line. When I shall [*landed*] land in france I shall be very
content. Mi [*wive*] wife shall come [*after, bef-*] near me.
Mi son shall be great and [*fort*] strong. He [*shall get*] will
be able to take his bottle of wine at dinner. I shall trink
with him. Mi mother shall be olde, mi sisters shall . . .
for the women believe they . . .'

The pronoun *I* is uniformly written *j*. The corrections
are mostly inserted above the line, but some are a continuation of the line, showing that the translation was written in
Madame Bertrand's presence. The first sentence, it is
evident, had been playfully uttered by her on account of
Napoleon's teasing her for being boisterously gay; for it is

the question addressed to obstreperous or fretful children, and Napoleon himself used to say to Betsy Balcombe, ' Quand seras-tu sage ? ' *Sage* does not here mean wise, but good or well behaved. Madame Bertrand passed over this and some other obvious blunders, either because her own English was defective, or because she would not discourage her pupil by too many corrections. At one corner of the sheet is a rude drawing of a ship, the imaginary ship in which Napoleon was to return to France, and in another corner is a sketch apparently meant for a line of muskets extended for firing. There are also the words, ' Qui vous a apporté cette lettre ? (Who has brought you this letter ?) The writing is small and cramped, but fairly legible ; much more so than other specimens at the exhibition, such as the audit of Napoleon's accounts. The allegation that he wrote a scrawl to conceal his bad spelling seems far-fetched. Like many people, he had a hasty scrawl for drafts, which he was sometimes himself unable to decipher, and a plainer hand for his correspondents.

To quote from Manzoni's famous ode :—

> ' He vanished, in a narrow isle
> His vacant days to keep,
> Object of boundless envy once,
> Now of compassion deep,
> Of inextinguishable ire
> And of unconquered love.'

There still survive two English witnesses of Napoleon's funeral, for *Public Opinion* of the 28th March 1903 contained a letter from Mr. G. B. Bennett of Cape Town, who states that he was born at St. Helena on the 30th November 1816, that he attended the funeral, and that his sister, three and a half months old, was also present in her nurse's arms.

The daughter of Sir Hudson Lowe, born at St. Helena in 1818, is also still living, unmarried, at Balham, near London.   Considering, however, the strained relations between her father and Napoleon, she is scarcely likely, in her nurse's arms, to have seen the caged lion.

PS.—Miss Clara Lowe died at Tooting on the 7th May 1904.

APPENDIX

A (see p. 34)

MEMBERS OF PARLIAMENT

Asterisks indicate members not re-elected in 1802, and italics new members.

Acheson, Arch., Armagh.
Adair, Robert, Camelford.
Barclay, Sir Robert, Newton, Hants.
Baring, Sir F., Chipping Wycombe.
*Benfield, Paul, Shaftesbury.
Best, Wm. Draper, Petersfield.
*Bird, Wm. Wilberforce, Coventry.
*Boyd, Walter, Shaftesbury.
Brodrick, Wm., Whitchurch.
Burdett, Sir F., Middlesex.
Cavendish, Lord G. A. H., Derbyshire.
*Chambers, (Sir) Geo., Honiton.
*Clarke, Edward, Wootton Basset.
*Clifden, Viscount, Heytesbury.
Cockerell, (Sir) Chas., Tregony.
Combe, Alderman H., London.
Cowper, Edward Spencer, Hertford.
Cust, John, Clitheroe.
Dalkeith, Lord, Ludgershall.

*Dallas, Sir Geo., Newport, I.W.
Dillon, Augustus, Mayo.
Douglas, Marquis of, Lancaster.
Egerton, Wm., Cheshire.
Ellis, Chas. Rose, Seaford.
Erskine, Thos., Portsmouth.
Fitzgerald, Lord Rt., Kildare.
Fitzpatrick, General, Tavistock.
Foster, Jno. Leslie, Louth.
Fox, Chas. Jas., Westminster.
Francis, (Sir) Philip, Appleby.
Frankland, Wm., Thirsk.
Garland, George, Poole.
Gower, Lord Granville Leveson, Staffordshire.
Graham, Sir Jas., Ripon.
Graham, Jas., Cockermouth.
Green, Wm., Dungarvan.
Hamilton, Lord Arch., Lanark.
*Hare, James, Knaresborough.
Hinchingbrook, Lord, Hunts.
Huntingfield, Lord, Dunwich.
Jekyll, Joseph, Calne.
Johnstone, Geo., Heydon.
Kinnaird, Chas., Leominster.

216

Knox, Hon. Geo., Dungannon.

Lascelles, Edward, Northaller-
ton.

Loftus, Earl, Wexford.

Long, Charles, Wendover.

Lovaine, Lord, Beeralston.

Mackenzie-Fraser, Gen. Alex.,
Cromarty.

*Macpherson, Sir John, Horsham.

Mathew, Viscount, Tipperary.

Montagu, Lord Fred., Hunts.

Morgan, Sir Chas., Brecon.

Morpeth, Viscount, Morpeth.

*Morshead, Sir John, Bodmin.

*Nicholl, John, Tregony.

Paget, Hon. Edw., Carnarvon.

*Parnell, Henry, Maryborough.

Pelham, Hon. Chas., Grimsby.

Petty, Lord Henry, Calne.

*Pollen, Col. G. A., Leominster.

*Pringle, Mark, Selkirk.

*Robson, Richard B., Oke-
hampton.

St. John, St. Andrew, Beds.

Scott, Hon. Jno., Borough-
bridge.

Smith, John Spencer, Dover.

Smith, William, Norwich.

Spencer, Lord Robert, Tavistock.

*Sturt, Charles, Bridport.

Thellusson, Chas., Evesham.

Thellusson, Peter Isaac, Castle
Rising.

*Thompson, Thos., Evesham.

Tierney, George, Southwark.

*Tufton, Henry, Rochester.

*Turner, Sir Gregory, Thirsk.

Tyrwhitt, Thos., Portarlington.

Villiers, Jno. Chas., Dartmouth.

*Walhope, Hon. Coulson, And-
over.

*Wallace, (Sir) Thomas, Penrhyn.

*Waller, John, Limerick.

*Wyndham, Chas., Shoreham.

Yarmouth, Earl of, Lisburn.

B (see p. 51)

PEERS

An asterisk indicates that the wife accompanied her husband.

Dukes—Bedford, Cumberland (Duchess), Gordon (Duchess), Newcastle (and Dowager-Duchess), *Somerset.

Marquises—Bute,[1] *Donegal, *Tweeddale.

Earls—Aberdeen, *Bessborough, *Beverley, Buckinghamshire,
Cadogan (see p. 54), Caledon, Camelford, *Carhampton, Cavan,
*Cholmondeley, Clarendon, *Conyngham, Cowper, Dysart (Countess),
Egremont, *Elgin, *Fife, Fitzwilliam, Granard (Countess), *Guil-
ford, *Kenmare, Kingston (Countess), Lanesborough (Countess),

---

[1] He seems to be the visitor who registered himself as Lord John
Stuart.

Lauderdale, Longford, Mexborough (Countess), Minto, Mount Cashell, *Mount Edgecumbe, *Oxford, Pembroke, Pomfret, Sefton, Shaftesbury, *Shrewsbury, Winchilsea, Yarborough.

Viscounts—Annesley (Viscountess), Barrington, Castlemaine, Falkland, Gosford, Maynard (Viscountess), Monck, Strangford.

Barons—Blayney, Boringdon, *Bradford, *Cahir, Carington (Baroness), Cloncurry, Coleraine, Crofton (Baroness), Grantham, *Holland, Hutchinson, Longford, *Montfort, Northwick, *Say and Sele, Stawell, *Whitworth.

Eldest sons or other successors of Peers—General George Abercromby (son of Baroness Abercromby), William Annesley (Earl of Annesley), Archibald Acheson (Viscount Gosford), Viscount Althorp (Earl Spencer), Lord Charles Beaulieu (Earl of Beaulieu), Viscount Boyle (Earl of Glasgow), Viscount Brooke (Earl of Warwick), Lord John Campbell (Duke of Argyll), John Somers Cocks (Lord Somers), Earl of Dalkeith (Duke of Buccleuch), John De Blaquiere (Lord De Blaquiere), Augustus Dillon (Viscount Dillon), Marquis of Douglas (Duke of Hamilton), Lord Duncannon (Earl of Bessborough), Sampson Eardley (Lord Eardley), Francis Henry Egerton (Earl of Bridgewater), Viscount Fincastle (Earl of Dunmore), Admiral Garlies (Earl of Galloway), Lord Gustavus Hamilton (Viscount Boyne), Viscount Hinchingbrook (Earl of Sandwich), John Hely Hutchinson (Earl of Donoughmore), Charles Kinnaird (Lord Kinnaird), Edward Lascelles (predeceased the Earl of Harewood), Viscount Loftus (Marquis of Ely), Lord Lovaine (Earl of Beverley), Viscount Maitland (Earl of Lauderdale), Viscount Mathew (Earl of Landaff), Colonel W. J. Molesworth (Viscount Molesworth), Viscount Morpeth (Earl of Carlisle), Viscount Ossulston (Earl of Tankerville), Charles Pelham (Lord Yarborough), Viscount Petersham[1] (Earl of Harrington), Lord Henry Petty (Marquis of Lansdowne), Dudley Ryder (Viscount Sandon, afterwards Earl of Harrowby), St. Andrew St. John (Lord St. John), John Scott (predeceased the Earl of Eldon), Admiral Tollemache (Countess of Dysart), John Hampden Trevor (Viscount Hampden), Charles Tufton (Earl of Thanet), Colonel John Vesey (Viscount de Vesci), John Charles Villiers (Earl of Clarendon) and Earl of Yarmouth (Marquis of Hertford). Several of these have been mentioned among actual or prospective M.P.'s. There was also Lady Ancrum, daughter-in-law of the Marquis of Lothian.

---

[1] A dandy famous for his collection of snuff-boxes, said to number 365.

C (see p. 300)

LORD JOHN RUSSELL AT ELBA

I have been favoured by the Hon. Rollo Russell with a copy, and permission to publish it, of the letter addressed in 1868 by his father, Earl Russell, to the eminent Belgian statesman, M. Van de Weyer. A few copies were then printed for private distribution.

PEMBROKE LODGE : *Nov.* 28, 1868.

MY DEAR VAN DE WEYER,

You wish to have some account of my visit to the First Napoleon at Elba.

It is long since I paid that visit, and I can give you only glimmering recollections.

I was at Florence in December 1814, with my father and his family.

I wished very much to see Napoleon; some of my friends had been to Elba; a cousin of mine by marriage, Mr. Whitmore, was going there.

I was told that the season was bad, and that I should do well to put off my journey till the spring. But I determined to go then.

Colonel Campbell, the Commissioner of the British Government, was usually resident at Florence; he was then returning to Elba, and a brig-of-war had been placed at his disposal. I was glad to take advantage of the opportunity. He told us on the way that Napoleon had sate up late at night, revising the list of the Municipal Council of Porto Ferrajo for the ensuing year. Colonel Campbell seemed to consider this circumstance a proof that the deposed Emperor could be as busy upon a trifling affair as on the destinies of Europe. But no doubt Napoleon wished to have a municipality on whom he could rely in case of need.

The first person Whitmore and I saw at Porto Ferrajo was General Bertrand, and he introduced us to his wife, a Dillon by birth.

In conversation with General Bertrand, he asked us the meaning of a paragraph in the *Courier* newspaper, sent him by Colonel Campbell, to the effect that the Congress of Vienna had it in contemplation to send the Emperor to St. Helena. We had not seen the paragraph, and could not account for it. I have never referred to the *Courier* newspaper of that period to ascertain its wording, or guess at its origin. But it had evidently made a great impression on General Bertrand.

In the evening of that day, about eight o'clock, I went to the house at the top of the town where Napoleon resided. He received me in his drawing-room. He was dressed in uniform—a green coat, single-breasted, white breeches, and silk stockings. I was much struck with his countenance—eyes of a muddy colour and cunning expression; the fine features which we all know in his bust and on his coins; and, lastly, a most agreeable and winning smile. He was very courteous in his manner. I was with him for a long time—I think an hour and a half. He stood the whole time, only sometimes leaning on the chimney-piece.

What struck me most in his conversation was a certain uneasiness about his position—a suspicion that something serious was about to happen to him, and he seemed to have a desire to entrap me into giving him information which I was neither able nor willing to afford. With this view, as I supposed, he asked me a number of questions of little interest to him—such as, whether I was in the House of Commons or the House of Lords, whether my father had kept up much state as Lord-Lieutenant of Ireland, and whether the Lady-Lieutenant had any *dame d'honneur* in her suite? When I replied that she had only a young lady, who was her cousin, in the house with her, he remarked, '*C'était une dame de compagnie, pas une dame d'honneur.*' These questions he would intersperse with eager enquiries respecting the state of France; and when I replied that I had not come through France, but by sea from Portugal, he would not let me off, but asked me what Lord Holland, whom I had seen at Florence, thought of French opinion— enquiring, with much emphasis, '*L'armée est-elle contente?*'

He spoke also of Italy; and when I said that Italy had no union, and therefore would probably remain quiet, he said, '*C'est vrai.*' I told him that I had heard everywhere, that during his reign the robberies and pillage, which had been so common before, had almost ceased; he said quickly, '*C'était la gendarmerie.*'

He seemed alarmed regarding his own safety, asking me, more than once, whether our Minister at Florence was a man to be trusted; whether fearing that he might be carried off by force, or wishing to obtain some assurance of safety and protection from Lord Burghersh, the British Minister, I cannot tell. I told him that Lord Burghersh had been attached, as a military officer, to one of the allied armies which had invaded France; but of this he seemed to know nothing.

It was evident to me that the paragraph in the *Courier*, which had been mentioned to me by General Bertrand, had been shown to Napoleon, and had produced a great impression upon him. He seemed to me to be meditating some enterprise, and yet very doubtful whether he should undertake it. When we

X

heard afterwards of his expedition from Elba, the
Count de Mosbourg, a minister of Murat, was asked
what could have induced Napoleon to run so great
a hazard; '*Un peu d'espoir et beaucoup de déses-
poir*,' was his reply. Such appeared to me to be,
when I saw him, the state of his mind; and when I
got to Rome, I wrote to my brother, Lord Tavistock,
that I was sure Napoleon was thinking of some fresh
attempt.

Napoleon seemed very curious on the subject of
the Duke of Wellington. He said it was a great
mistake in the English Government to send him
Ambassador to Paris. '*On n'aime pas voir un homme
par qui on a été battu*.' He had never sent as
Ambassador to Vienna a man who had entered Vienna
as an officer of the French invading army. (Count
Lebzeltern, the Austrian Ambassador at Rome, denied
the truth of this assertion.) As I had seen a good
deal of the Duke of Wellington in Spain, Napoleon
asked me what were likely to be his occupations. I
answered that during his campaigns the Duke had
been so much absorbed by his attention to the war
that I did not well understand how he could give his
mind to other subjects. He remarked, rather sharply,
as if he thought I was inclined to think lightly of
military talents, '*Eh bien, c'est un grand jeu, belle
occupation!*' He spoke at some length of his plans
respecting Spain. He would have divided the large
landed properties in the hands of the grandees, of the
monasteries, and of the clergy. He would have introduced into Spain the enlightened principles of religious
toleration and facilitated commercial intercourse in the
interior, etc.

I said that I thought Spain was not ready for such
changes, and that the Spanish people would resist

them. *'Ils succomberaient,'* he said, and then the subject dropped.

He asked me whether I knew anything of what was passing at the Congress of Vienna. I said, 'Nothing.' He said he expected that each Power would have confirmed to it by treaty the territories which its forces occupied. In respect to the three great military Powers, Austria, Russia, and Prussia, this prediction was nearly verified. Mr. Pitt, however, had intended, in 1805, to give Belgium to Prussia; Lord Castlereagh gave it to the Netherlands.

Napoleon spoke of Lord Ebrington, whom he had recently seen, and said he was *'un homme fort instruit; du moins, il m'a paru un homme fort instruit.'* It struck me afterwards that while he had spoken to Lord Ebrington of great events of his past life—of Jaffa, of the execution of the Duc d'Enghien, and other acts on which the world had passed its judgment—he spoke to me almost entirely of the existing aspect of affairs. His past history had ceased to be his main object, and his mind was busy with the present and the future. He said, 'You must be very well satisfied, you English, to have finished the war so successfully.' I answered, 'Yes, Sire, especially as at one time we thought ourselves in great danger.'

He burst out laughing, *'Ha! ha! ha! C'était le système continental, eh?'*

I said, ' Yes, Sire; but as that system did not ruin us, it did us a great deal of good. For men are much governed by their physical wants.'

The interview ended soon after this. The next morning I was told that a horse from the Emperor's stable was at my disposal, and I rode to a villa which he was constructing for his summer occupation.

The day after I embarked, in the gun-brig in which
I had come, for Civita Vecchia.

I remain, my dear Van de Weyer,

> Yours truly,
>
> RUSSELL.

Lord J. Russell in his diary, wrote of Napoleon :—

' His manner is very good-natured, and seems studied to put one
at one's ease by its familiarity ; his smile and laugh are very agreeable ; he asks a number of questions without object, and often
repeats them, a habit which he has no doubt acquired during fifteen
years of supreme command.   To this I should also attribute the
ignorance he seems to show at times of the most common facts.   When
anything that he likes is said, he puts his head forward and listens
with great pleasure . . . but when he does not like what he hears,
he turns away as if unconcerned, and changes the subject.   From
this one might conclude that he was open to flattery and violent
in his temper.'

Sir Spencer Walpole in his *Life of Lord J. Russell*, adds :—

Lord John was with him [Napoleon] an hour and a half, conversing on many subjects—the Russell family, Lord John's own allowance from the Duke, the state of Spain and Italy, the character of the
Duke of Wellington, and the arrangements likely to be made at
Vienna for the pacification of Europe.   He used to say in his old
age, that as the Emperor became interested in his conversation, he
fell into the singular habit which he had acquired, and pulled him
by the ear.

INDEX OF NAMES

(Members of a family are mostly indexed together).

325

INDEX OF NAMES 327

Browning, Oscar, 10, 175.
Brownlow, Lord, 57, 83, 278.
Bruce, Countess, 239.
—— Lieutenant Michael, 275.
Bryant, George, 92.
Buckingham, Duke, 42.
Buckinghamshire, Lord, 317.
Bulow, T. H., 159.
Buonarotti, M., 6.
Burdett, Sir F., 36, 64, 66, 133, 242, 310, 316.
Burgess, Rev. J., 168.
Burgh or Burke, 261.
Burghersh, Lord, 278, 321.
Burke, Edmund, 34, 50.
—— General F., 66.
Burlington, Lord, 36, 121.
Burney, Fanny, 4, 123.
Burrell, Sir C., 48, 179.
Burton, Sir F., 64.
Bute, Lord, 242, 317.
Butler, Baron, 258.
—— Colonel, 251.
Butterfield, 212.
Byrne, Miles, 187.
Byron, Lord, 22, 54, 170, 303, 308.

CABARRUS. See Tallien.
Cadogan, Lady, 54, 178, 317.
Cadoudal. See Georges.
Cahir, Lord, 59, 318.
Caledon, Lord, 317.
Call, Sir W., 179, 196, 200, 243.
Callender, General J., 66, 213.
Calonne, C. de, 124, 134.
Cambacérès, J. J., 31.
Cambridge, Duke, 37.
Camelford, Lord, 14, 54, 146, 317.
Cameron, Doctor, 209.
Campbell, 296.
—— Sir A., 67.
—— Doctor (Edward?), 265.
—— Lord, 79.
—— Lord J., 51, 179, 318.
—— Sir Neil, 303, 319, 320.
—— Thomas, 274, 281.
Campe, J. H., 156, 164.
Candler, Captain T., 244.
Canning, George, 16, 33, 118, 278.
Canova, A., 274.
Cantillon, André N., 39.
Caraccioli, L. A., 161.
Caradoc. See Cradock.
Carducci, Barth., 97.
Carhampton, Lord, 46, 317.
Carington, Lord, 59, 278, 318.
Carlisle, Lord, 16, 40, 277, 303, 317, 318.

Carnot, Lazare, 85, 90, 128, 152, 225, 273.
Caroline, Queen, 286.
Carr, Sir J., 101, 125, 128, 142.
Carter, Anne, 240.
Carysfort, Lord, 17.
Casimir Périer, 109.
Casti, J. B., 161.
Castlemaine, Lord, 318.
Castlereagh, Lord, 272.
Cathcart, Lord, 275.
Caulfeild, St. G., 168.
Cavan, Lord, 56, 68, 317.
Cavendish, Lord G., 61, 316.
—— See Burlington.
Cazalès, J. A., 125.
Cerutti, J. A. J., 6.
Chalmers, 190.
Chambers, Sir R., 79, 168, 316.
Champagny, J. B., 220.
Champernowne, A. H., 48.
Chantrey, Sir F., 274.
Chaptal, J. A., 31.
Charlemont, Lord, 277.
Charles x., 2, 67, 274, 278.
—— xiv. See Bernadotte.
—— Edward, Prince, 177.
—— J. A. C., 128.
Charlotte, Princess, 7, 155.
—— Queen, 284.
Chastenay, Mme. de, 280.
Chateaubriand, F. R. de, 71, 90, 116, 143, 224.
Chatham, Lord, 32.
Chatterton, Thomas, 115.
Chenevix, R., 13, 85, 227, 229.
Chénier, André, 91.
Cherubini, L. C., 129.
Chevreul, 243.
Chichester, Sir A., 49.
—— Sir J., 64.
Childers, Hugh C. E., 61, 200.
Cholmondeley, Lord, 56, 138, 161, 164, 317.
Christie, J. H., 214.
—— Thomas, 6.
Churchill, Rev. W. H., 232.
Clanricarde, Lord, 278.
Clare, Lord, 277.
Clarendon. See Villiers.
Clarke, C. J., 23.
—— General, 18, 188, 198, 203, 235, 245, 247, 254, 262, 265, 266.
—— Mrs., 237.
—— Sir Simon, 64.
—— Dr. T., 208.
Clarkson, Thomas, 275.
Clavering, Sir T., 64, 234.

Jay, John, 155.
Jefferson, Thomas, 13, 139.
Jekyll, Joseph, 39, 45, 316.
Jenner, Dr. E., 80, 225, 246.
Jerningham, C., 65, 122, 138, 142, 235.
Jersey, Lady, 296.
Jervis, John, 73, 235.
Jessopp, J. S., 119, 138.
Joan of Arc, 182.
Jodrell, F. and T., 64, 210.
Johnson, Dr., 79, 115, 149.
Johnston, Colonel, 227.
—— Dr., 81.
—— W. and D., 258.
Johnstone, George, 39, 316.
Jomini, Baron Henri, 7.
Jones, Dr., 265.
—— Paul, 6, 70.
—— Rev., 292.
Jordan, Rev., 197.
Josephine, Empress, 91, 100, 117,
    175, 224, 225, 228, 243, 312.
Joubert, Joseph, 116.
Junot, Marshal, 32, 131, 178, 194,
    232, 275, 313.
Jurien de la Gravière, Admiral, 262.

KAUNITZ, Prince, 6.
Kemble, J. P., 93, 140.
Kenmare, Lord, 56, 317.
Kennedy, W. B., 100.
Kent, Duke, 117, 180.
Ker, Walter, 14, 35.
Kilmorey, Lord, 68.
King, Frances, 109, 161.
—— John, 30, 100, 150, 166.
—— Rufus, 155.
Kingston, Countess, 56, 317.
Kinnaird, Lord, 39, 277, 316, 318.
Kirby, Dr. Walter, 261.
Kirkpatrick, Mme., 238.
—— William, 258.
Kirkwall, Lady, 263.
Kirwan, W. B., 27.
Klenke, Helmine, 159.
Klopstock, F. T., 157.
Knatchbull, Sir J., 278.
Knight, 144.
—— Cornelia, 143.
Knox, General John, 16.
—— George, 61, 317.
—— Waring, 197.
—— 210.
Kock, J. G. de, 6.
Kosciusko, Thaddeus, 59, 85, 105,
    130, 141, 156.
Kreutzer, Rod., 130.
Krudener, Mme. de, 156.

Krumholz, Mme., 43.
Kyd, Stewart, 79, 216.

LAFAYETTE, Marquis, 32, 38, 60, 70,
    85, 244, 276.
Laharpe, J. F., 90.
Lalande, J. J. L., 128.
Lale, 189.
Lally Tollendal, Gérard, 5, 124.
Lamartine, A., 128, 182.
Lamb, Charles, 129.
Lambert, 231.
La Métherie, Jean, 133.
Lammenais, F. de, 233.
Lamoignon, C. F. de, 143.
La Motte, Mme., 124.
Lancaster, Frances, 142.
—— Rev. T., 159.
Landaff, Lord, 279, 318.
Landor, W. S., 112.
Lanesborough, Lady, 57, 89, 102-104
    317.
Langdale, Lord, 117.
Langton, Roger, 245.
Lansdowne, Lord, 40, 277, 303, 317
    318.
Laplace, P. S., 129, 273.
Larochefoucauld, Duc, 153.
La Reveillière Lepeaux, 36.
Las Cases, G. P. B., 311, 312.
Lascelles, Edward, 317, 318.
Latouche, Elizabeth, 102.
Lattin, P., 154.
Lauderdale, Lord, 50, 51, 54, 57, 220,
    259, 303, 318.
Lauriston, Marquis, 18, 123.
Lauzun, Duc, 15.
Lavalette, A. M. C., 275.
Lavie, Sir T., 64, 241, 245.
Law, William, 158.
Lawless. See Burton, Dunsany, and
    Whaley.
Lawrence, J. H., 11, 209, 232, 259.
Leake. See Martin-Leake.
Leatham, John, 260.
Lebrun, Consul C. F., 31, 111, 114.
Lebzeltern, Count, 322.
Lechevalier, J. B., 36, 133.
Lee, Rev. Launcelot, 233.
Legouvé, Ernest, 309.
Lemaistre, J. G., 51, 101.
Lemoine, General John, 296.
Lempriere, Miss, 237.
Leopold, King, 7, 155.
Leorat, 270.
Leslie, Sir J., 275.
Leveson-Gower. See Granville and
    Sutherland.

OTHER VISITORS AND CAPTIVES.[1]

1801-1813

ABERNETHY, James. Adams, John. Addison, Dr., escaped. Ainsley. Ainsworth, Jas. Wroth. Aitken, David, surgeon, Glasgow. Aitken, Robert. Aitken, Thomas, banker. Allen, Major Alex. Allen, Major John. Allen, Luke. Allsop, Barleton. Anderson, Lieut. Thomas. Andrews, Alex. Andrews, Henry. Annesley, Gilbert. Anstey, Capt. Anstruther, Col. David. Arbuthnot, Major Thos. Arcedeckne, Jas. Archdall, Edward. Argle, Capt. Geo. Arthur, Daniel, secretary to Portuguese Embassy. Ashford, Wm. Ashton, Jno. Ashworth, escaped. Atkinson, Jno. Atkinson, Wm. Aubrey, Major. Austin, Jno. Austin, Thos.

Balfour, Jno. Balgrove. Ballantyne, Jas. Banks, Jos. Barber, Capt. Barretti, Jas. Barry, Edwd. Bateman, Wm. Battley, Geo. Bazalgette, Louis. Beamish, Chas. Beaumont, Chas. Beckwith, Samuel. Benson, Capt. Richd., escaped. Bentham, Wm. Bermingham, Lieut. Bernard, Geo. Berry, Jno. Best, Louis. Betts, Charles. Betts, Geo. Bevington, Geo. Bingham. Birch, Capt. Jno. Birch, Major Thos. Blackmore, Robt. Blair, Capt. Hunter. Blake, Arthur. Blake, Benj. Blake, Col. Wm. Blanckney. Bode, Jno., escaped. Bold, Peter. Bold, Lieut. Thos. Bonham, Jno., barrister. Boothby, Capt. (afterwards Rev.) Charles. Bord, Jno. Botwright, Wm. Bourne, Samuel. Bouverie, Capt. Bowles, Lieut. Humphrey. Bradby, Jas., barrister. Bradford, Lieut.-Col. Brandrum, Thos. Brenton, Sir J. Brettell, Jno. Brewer, Capt., escaped. Brewer, Edward. Bridge, Wm. Briggins, Dr. Brine, escaped. Brodie, Capt. Brown, Capt., escaped. Brown, Lieut. Bruce, Alex. Buchanan, Jas. Bunbury, Thos. Burke, Major Fras. Burns, Major. Burrows, Dr. Geo. M. Burton, Jas. Byrne, Jas.

Campbell, R. Campbell of Jamaica. Carleton, Jno. Carey, Capt. Carey, Peter. Carron. Casenove. Cavendish, Geo. and

[1] Subject to orthographic errors in French records.

340

Louis. Channing, Jno. and Thos. Chetham, Col. Christie, Fras. Clarke, Dr. Jas. Clifton, Capt. Colvert, Gen. Colville, Geo. Combe, Capt. Congreve, Capt. Conolly. Cooper, Rev. Sir Wm. Cope, Lieut.-Col. Corbett, Jas. Cotterell. Courtenay, Wm. Courvoisier, Peter. Cox, Col. Craufurd, Lieut. Jno. Hy. Craufurd, Rev. Jno. Creswick, Fred. Croke, Jno. Cussans, Thos. Cusy. Cuthbert, Jno. Ramsay. Cutler.

Dacre. Dale, Jos., escaped. Dalrymple, Capt. Dalyell, Wm. Daniell, Wm. Darby, escaped. Dare. David, Dr. Davies. Deane, Capt. De Boyne, Gen. Devonshire, Col. Fras. D'Ivernois, Col. Dobson, Geo. Douglas, Mrs. Dowse, Major. Duff, Col. Dukinfield, Sir N. Dupré, Wm. Dyson, Geo.

Elrington. Elwin. Este. Eustace, Major. Evans.

Fagin. Falkenham. Fane, Capt., released. Fiott. Fitzgerald, Richd. Fletcher, Edward. Floyd, Gen. Sir Jno. Forsyth. Foster, Peter Le Neve, father of the scientist. Fox, Dr., escaped. Fraser, escaped. Fulk.

Garland, Jno. Watt. Garland, Peter. Garnier. Gellibrand, Wm. George, Lieut. Gerrard, Alex., liberated. Gerrard, Capt. Jno. Giffard, Jno. Goodman. Gordon, Col. Green, Jos. Grey, Sir Thomas. Grosvenor, Mary.

Halifax. Hankey, Jno. Peter. Hare. Harvey, Col. Hawey, Col. Heathcote. Henderson. Hendley, Capt. Hewitson, Dr. Hibberd. Hill, Samuel. Hill, Thos. Hodgson, Thos. Carlisle. Hollond, Thos. Honywood, Courtenay. Hooke, Chas. Howard, Capt. Humphreys, Wm. Hunter, Orby. Hutchins.

Jackson, Edward. Jackson, John. Jackson, Mills, escaped. Jackson, Richmond. Jackson, Wm., liberated. Jenner, Wm. Johnston, Major. Jones, Lieut.

Kennedy. Kensington, Charles. Kensington, J. B. King, Geo. Kingston, Major Strickland. Kinnersley.

Later. Laurens, Dr. Geo. Lee, Wm. Leigh, Philip, escaped. Le Mesurier, Fras. Le Soulf, Hauteville. Leveson-Gower, Capt. Wm. Light. Little, escaped. Livie, Alex. Lloyd, Dr. Wm. Lorimer. Lynch, Gen.

Macdonnell, Jas. Macdonnell, Jos. Macfarlane. Mackay, Capt. Mackenzie, Major, escaped. Macnamara, Col. Macnamara, Geo. MacTaggart, Sir Jno. Madan. Mandeville, Robt. Massingberd, C. Burrell. Masterson. Maude, Jno. Baptist. May, Dr. Mercer, Jos., died at Bitche. Merivale, Robert. Montgomerie, Thos. and Geo., liberated. Moore, Anthony. Moore, Col. Moore, Jno. liberated. Mountney. Muriel. Murray, Col.

Nasmyth, Capt. Jas. Marshall. Newman, Henry. Newland, Gideon. Nicholson, Col., escaped.

O'Byrne. Oliphant, Edward. Olive. O'Reardon. Otto. Ouvrard. Palmer, Gen. Thos. Palmer, Mrs. Parsons. Pater, Capt. Paterson, Dr. Jas. Philipps, Jno. Burton and Nathaniel. Pigott, Gillery. Pigott, Jno., Hy., and Edwd. Pilling, Jno. Plunket, Oliver and Peter. Popham, Major. Potter, Ralph. Power, Capt. Power, Jno. Prescott, Lieut. Pridham, Lieut.

Raikes, Capt. Rennell, Capt. Richardson, Col. Ridman. Roberts. Roupell Sir (?) Wm. Ruddock, Col. Rumsey, Major. Russell, Wm. Thos.

St. Leger, Harewood (son of Viscount Doneraile ?). Scott, Col. Scott-Moncrieff. Shuttleworth, Jos. Sibbald. Smith, Rev. Dr. Spalding, Col. Spencer, Col. (qy. Gen. Wm.). Stack, Jno., mineralogist. Stacpoole, Capt. Stanhope, Capt. Chas. and Hy., midshipman (sons of Lord Chesterfield); Henry, escaped. Strachey, Capt., R.N. Sutton, Capt., escaped. Swayne, Col. Hy.

Taylor, Edward. Tindall, Lieut.-Col. Travers. Trevelyan. Truelock, Wm. Tupper, naturalised. Turton, Thos., bishop of Ely.

Walker, Capt., escaped. Walpole, Jno., Robt., Edwd. Wardrop, Cunningham, Glasgow, aged 17. Warburton, Willis. Warwick. Wayland. Wetherdown. Whitaker, Capt., escaped. White, Rev. Wm., vicar of Lancaster, escaped. Willis, Richd. and Thos. of Scarborough, died at Bitche. Windham, Frances. Wingfield, Col. Wolfe, Rev. Robt. Woodford, Jno. Alex. Worth, son of admiral. Wright, Jno. Masey, artist   Wyndham, Col.

1814-1815.

Ainslie, Miss. Bennett, Wm., bishop of Cloyne. Black, Capt. Clive. Colnaghi, jun., printseller. Du Cane. Heneage. James, Sir Walter. Leman. Lutwyche. Planta, Edwd. Robertson. Rotch, Benj. Seymour, Hy. Swinburne. Twining, Richd. Vyner, Miss. Whalley, Thos. Sedgwick, D.D. Wyburn.

Printed by T. and A. Constable, Printers to His Majesty
at the Edinburgh University Press